To:

From:

Message:

The Pocket Bible Devotional for Women

NORMA ROSSOUW

CHRISTIAN ART
PUBLISHERS

The Pocket Bible Devotional for Women

Published by Christian Art Publishers
PO Box 1599, Vereeniging, 1930, RSA

© 2017
First edition 2017
Second edition 2023

Cover designed by Christian Art Publishers

Images used under license from Shutterstock.com

Set by Christian Art Publishers

Printed in China

ISBN 978-0-638-00113-6

23 24 25 26 27 28 29 30 31 32 — 10 9 8 7 6 5 4 3 2 1

Introduction

God formed you and knitted you together in a wonderful way. He shaped your heart to love with compassion, to give without bounds, and to care for others with a cheerful heart.

Your value is beyond priceless jewels, daughter of the almighty King. He smiled, because what He made was very good. God made you in His likeness, and He knew that great and wonderful things awaited you. God knows your dreams and the desires of your heart. There are numerous promises and treasures locked up in His Word for you to discover as you read through its pages every day.

As the manna in the desert was new every morning, God's Word will be like fresh manna for your soul each new day. Pick it up and live by every word that comes from His mouth. Through your relationship with Him, you will discover His dreams for you as you get to know His kind, fatherly heart. Therefore, it is very important to read the Bible every day and keep it in your heart, treasuring it throughout your day. By reading the Word and spending time with God every day, you will surely get to know Him better.

We face many challenges these days and this Pocket Bible Devotional provides guidance on a number of issues and grounds its advice in Scripture. Mary chose to sit at Jesus' feet and learn from Him, while her sister Martha was busy with the preparations to serve Him. Jesus said that Mary had chosen what was better, and that it would not be taken from her.

May you choose to take some time every day to rest at Jesus' feet so that you can experience refreshment and blessings in Him. This Pocket Bible Devotional will be your companion in times of loneliness, comfort in times of sadness, and hope in times of uncertainty. On busy days—while you wait in the car for the children at school, before your next appointment, or even while waiting in line at the bank—you can reach for this Pocket Bible Devotional and indulge in wisdom from God's Word. His Word is a lamp that will show you the way, and in this light you can move forward boldly.

Each day of the year has a topic which is discussed in a short devotional thought and complemented by ample Scripture verses.

May each of these Scripture verses come to life as they shine through in your actions and words. The world around you will be richer for it. It is your love and care that will make the world a better place. Through your unique womanhood you have been handpicked to be salt and light in this world. This Pocket Bible Devotional is sure to help and support you on your faith journey. Be a woman of significance as you grow in faith.

~ *Norma Rossouw*

January

SHE
speaks
WITH
WISDOM
& faithful
INSTRUCTION
IS ON HER TONGUE.

Proverbs 31:26

God Will Not Forsake You

Even if my father and mother abandon me, the LORD will hold me close.

Psalm 27:10 NLT

"Never will I leave you; never will I forsake you."

Hebrews 13:5 NIV

"I will not abandon you as orphans—I will come to you."

John 14:18 NLT

O my God, lean down and listen to me. Open Your eyes and see our despair…We make this plea, not because we deserve help, but because of Your mercy.

Daniel 9:18 NLT

The LORD is near to the broken-hearted and saves the crushed in spirit.

Psalm 34:18 ESV

We are hard pressed on every side, but not crushed; perplexed, but not in despair; persecuted, but not abandoned; struck down, but not destroyed.

2 Corinthians 4:8-9 NIV

The LORD Himself goes before you and will be with you; He will never leave you nor forsake you. Do not be afraid; do not be discouraged.

Deuteronomy 31:8 NIV

For three hours it became dark as God's beloved Son called out, "My God, why have You forsaken Me?" For the first time, Jesus and the Father were not in fellowship. The Father turned His face away from the sin resting on the shoulders of His Son. Jesus tore the temple curtain so that we can have access to God and never feel abandoned again. When you trust in Jesus, the wall of your sin that separates you from God is removed; God is near.

Draw Closer to God

"Remain in Me, as I also remain in you. No branch can bear fruit by itself; it must remain in the vine. Neither can you bear fruit unless you remain in Me. I am the Vine; you are the branches. If you remain in Me and I in you, you will bear much fruit."
John 15:4-5 NIV

Everyone who goes on ahead and does not abide in the teaching of Christ, does not have God. Whoever abides in the teaching has both the Father and the Son.
2 John 1:9 ESV

"If you abide in My word, you are truly My disciples."
John 8:31 ESV

Remain in fellowship with Christ so that when He returns, you will be full of courage and not shrink back from Him in shame.
1 John 2:28 NLT

"I pray that they will all be one, just as You and I are one—as You are in Me, Father, and I am in You. And may they be in Us so that the world will believe You sent Me. I have given them the glory You gave Me, so they may be one as We are one. I am in them and You are in Me. May they experience such perfect unity that the world will know that You sent Me and that You love them as much as You love Me."
John 17:21-23 NLT

In order to have a full, satisfying life and to grow spiritually, we need to be in Christ. God is the Father who is intimately involved in every second of our lives. Jesus is the vine, and we are the branches that bear the fruit of love and joy. When we are in Him, He is our anchor when the storms of life rage around us. God comforts us in our sadness, and He is our advisor in uncertain times.

Your Unique Abilities

God has given each of you a gift from His great variety of spiritual gifts. Use them well to serve one another.
1 Peter 4:10 NLT

Now there are varieties of gifts, but the same Spirit; and there are varieties of service, but the same Lord; and there are varieties of activities, but it is the same God who empowers them all in everyone.
1 Corinthians 12:4-6 ESV

Every good and perfect gift is from above, coming down from the Father of the heavenly lights, who does not change like shifting shadows.
James 1:17 NIV

Stir up the gift of God which is in you...For God has not given us a spirit of fear, but of power and of love and of a sound mind.
2 Timothy 1:6-7 NKJV

Having then gifts differing according to the grace that is given to us, let us use them: if prophecy, let us prophesy in proportion to our faith; or ministry, let us use it in our ministering; he who teaches, in teaching; he who exhorts, in exhortation; he who gives, with liberality; he who leads, with diligence; he who shows mercy, with cheerfulness.
Romans 12:6-8 NKJV

God created you with unique abilities so that you can make a difference. You cannot do everything and be everything, but you can serve others with your God-given abilities. You won't be successful in your own strength, but God gives those He has called the ability to improve the lives of others. To share your abilities is to allow others to experience the gift the Holy Spirit has given you—you will be amazed at the great treasure you find.

Enjoying His Abundant Blessings

You prepare a table before me in the presence of my enemies. You anoint my head with oil; my cup overflows.
Psalm 23:5 NIV

"The thief does not come except to steal, and to kill, and to destroy. I have come that they may have life, and that they may have it more abundantly."
John 10:10 NKJV

How precious is Your unfailing love, O God! All humanity finds shelter in the shadow of Your wings. You feed them from the abundance of Your own house, letting them drink from Your river of delights.
Psalm 36:7-8 NLT

You crown the year with Your goodness, and Your paths drip with abundance.
Psalm 65:11 NKJV

God is able to bless you abundantly, so that in all things at all times, having all that you need, you will abound in every good work.
2 Corinthians 9:8 NIV

Now to Him who is able to do far more abundantly than all that we ask or think, according to the power at work within us, to Him be glory in the church and in Christ Jesus throughout all generations, forever and ever.
Ephesians 3:20-21 ESV

Go big or go home! We like to have things in abundance, especially financially and materially. If you woke up this morning and realized what you have today is what you thanked God for yesterday, would you still have abundance? Sometimes abundance fits in the smallest packages: a hug from your child, a thank you from a friend, a handshake from a stranger, a quiet moment with God, comfort after a funeral, peace after a storm, and an overflowing cup, because God's fullness is there.

Accept Yourself

"All that the Father gives Me will come to Me, and whoever comes to Me I will never cast out."
John 6:37 ESV

Since everything God created is good, we should not reject any of it but receive it with thanks.
1 Timothy 4:4 NLT

"Anyone who welcomes you welcomes Me, and anyone who welcomes Me welcomes the one who sent Me."
Matthew 10:40 NIV

Accept other believers who are weak in faith, and don't argue with them about what they think is right or wrong.
Romans 14:1 NLT

Accept one another, then, just as Christ accepted you, in order to bring praise to God.
Romans 15:7 NIV

Your beauty should not come from outward adornment, such as elaborate hairstyles and the wearing of gold jewelry or fine clothes. Rather, it should be that of your inner self, the unfading beauty of a gentle and quiet spirit, which is of great worth in God's sight.
1 Peter 3:3-4 NIV

"The LORD does not look at the things people look at. People look at the outward appearance, but the LORD looks at the heart."
1 Samuel 16:7 NIV

Acceptance is one of our most basic emotional needs. That feeling of belonging, that you fit in, and that you're loved despite your flaws. Start today with self-acceptance. You will not receive the acceptance of others or loved ones until you accept yourself. You can be sure that God accepts you through Jesus just the way you are, with all your baggage, because in Jesus you are washed perfectly clean.

You Are Accountable

For the Scriptures say, "'As surely as I live,' says the LORD, 'every knee will bend to Me, and every tongue will declare allegiance to God.'" Yes, each of us will give a personal account to God.
Romans 14:11-12 NLT

Nothing in all creation is hidden from God's sight. Everything is uncovered and laid bare before the eyes of Him to whom we must give account.
Hebrews 4:13 NIV

"I say to you that for every idle word men may speak, they will give account of it in the day of judgment."
Matthew 12:36 NKJV

"For by your words you will be acquitted, and by your words you will be condemned."
Matthew 12:37 NIV

They will have to give account to Him who is ready to judge the living and the dead. For this is the reason the gospel was preached even to those who are now dead, so that they might be judged according to human standards in regard to the body, but live according to God in regard to the spirit.
1 Peter 4:5-6 NIV

To whom are you accountable? Is there anyone loving enough who is willing to ask you tough questions without judging you? God holds you accountable for every thought and deed, which is why the Word motivates you to attend the gathering of the faithful in order to be part of a community where we stand in relation to one another and to God. Find a friend in faith with whom you can be transparent, whom you can trust, and who prays with you so that your accountability can lead to spiritual growth.

Maximum Achievement

I can do all things through Christ who strengthens me.
Philippians 4:13 NKJV

It is not that we think we are qualified to do anything on our own. Our qualification comes from God.
2 Corinthians 3:5 NLT

"Most assuredly, I say to you, he who believes in Me, the works that I do he will do also; and greater works than these he will do, because I go to My Father. And whatever you ask in My name, that I will do, that the Father may be glorified in the Son. If you ask anything in My name, I will do it."
John 14:12-14 NKJV

Remember the LORD your God. He is the one who gives you power to be successful, in order to fulfill the covenant He confirmed to your ancestors with an oath.
Deuteronomy 8:18 NLT

The LORD God is a sun and shield; the LORD bestows favor and honor. No good thing does He withhold from those who walk uprightly.
Psalm 84:11 ESV

"Those who remain in Me, and I in them, will produce much fruit. For apart from Me you can do nothing."
John 15:5 NLT

Overachieving has become the norm. On the sports field, at work, in your marriage, in your home, and even in your religious life, you must perform. Maybe you wonder about your spiritual performance, because God expects a perfect record. You cannot achieve this on your own, but Jesus already did and He came to write down your name next to His success rate. You are worth much more than medals on a wall or badges on a jacket. You were bought by Jesus' costly sacrifice on the cross.

Overcome Addiction

Don't copy the behavior and customs of this world, but let God transform you into a new person by changing the way you think. Then you will learn to know God's will for you, which is good and pleasing and perfect.
Romans 12:2 NLT

For whatever is born of God overcomes the world. And this is the victory that has overcome the world—our faith. Who is he who overcomes the world, but he who believes that Jesus is the Son of God?
1 John 5:4-5 NKJV

You, dear children, are from God and have overcome them, because the one who is in you is greater than the one who is in the world.
1 John 4:4 NIV

Don't be drunk with wine, because that will ruin your life. Instead, be filled with the Holy Spirit, singing psalms and hymns and spiritual songs among yourselves, and making music to the Lord in your hearts. And give thanks for everything to God the Father in the name of our Lord Jesus Christ.
Ephesians 5:18-20 NLT

Addiction is much more than alcohol and drugs—it can be fizzy drinks, TV, eating, shopping, Facebook, pornography, etc. Addiction is when you're no longer in charge and something takes control of you. Don't try to conquer the flesh on your own; this war can only be won through the Spirit. Most of your victories will start small, but don't despair, keep going. Jesus called out on the cross, "Tetelestai"—it is finished! With His help you can overcome your addiction.

Adopted by God

God decided in advance to adopt us into His own family by bringing us to Himself through Jesus Christ. This is what He wanted to do, and it gave Him great pleasure.
Ephesians 1:5 NLT

Though my father and mother forsake me, the LORD will receive me.
Psalm 27:10 NIV

As many as received Him, to them He gave the right to become children of God, to those who believe in His name.
John 1:12 NKJV

You are all children of God through faith in Christ Jesus.
Galatians 3:26 NLT

When the set time had fully come, God sent His Son, born of a woman, born under the law, to redeem those under the law, that we might receive adoption to sonship.
Galatians 4:4-5 NIV

See how very much our Father loves us, for He calls us His children, and that is what we are!
1 John 3:1 NLT

We believers...wait with eager hope for the day when God will give us our full rights as His adopted children, including the new bodies He has promised us.
Romans 8:23 NLT

Adoptive parents have an expectation, a longing for the arrival of a new child in their home. Everything is ready for that moment: The first time they will hold a child who will call them mom and dad, and maybe even the first time a child will be loved no matter what they have to offer. God desired to adopt you through Christ, regardless of your history, and through Christ He did. All the privileges of the Kingdom are yours. Accept this in faith and live your life as a child of God.

Dealing with Adversity

The righteous person faces many troubles, but the LORD comes to the rescue each time.
Psalm 34:19 NLT

We are hard pressed on every side, but not crushed; perplexed, but not in despair; persecuted, but not abandoned; struck down, but not destroyed.
2 Corinthians 4:8-9 NIV

"When you go through deep waters, I will be with you. When you go through rivers of difficulty, you will not drown. When you walk through the fire of oppression, you will not be burned up; the flames will not consume you."
Isaiah 43:2 NLT

"For I know the plans I have for you," says the LORD. "They are plans for good and not for disaster, to give you a future and a hope."
Jeremiah 29:11 NLT

The LORD is a stronghold for the oppressed, a stronghold in times of trouble. And those who know Your name put their trust in You, for You, O LORD, have not forsaken those who seek You.
Psalm 9:9-10 ESV

"Don't let your hearts be troubled. Trust in God, and trust also in Me."
John 14:1 NLT

Adversity is inevitable. Just ask Joseph who was sold as a slave; or Job who lost everything; or David who had to flee from the king; or Paul who was thrown in prison. All of these people learned that God's promises of care, rescue, and His presence are true, which is why they chose to face adversity through God's power. You can choose whether adversity will make you better because you have grown and learned from it or whether it will leave you bitter because you feel you were a victim.

Embracing Free Advice

The way of fools seems right to them, but the wise listen to advice.
Proverbs 12:15 NIV

Pride leads to conflict; those who take advice are wise.
Proverbs 13:10 NLT

Don't go to war without wise guidance; victory depends on having many advisers.
Proverbs 24:6 NLT

Perfume and incense bring joy to the heart, and the pleasantness of a friend springs from their heartfelt advice.
Proverbs 27:9 NIV

For lack of guidance a nation falls, but victory is won through many advisers.
Proverbs 11:14 NIV

It is better to be a poor but wise youth than an old and foolish king who refuses all advice.
Ecclesiastes 4:13 NLT

Listen to advice and accept discipline, and at the end you will be counted among the wise.
Proverbs 19:20 NIV

The fear of the LORD is the beginning of knowledge, but fools despise wisdom and instruction.
Proverbs 1:7 NKJV

Women easily receive gifts of clothing, recipes, food, and decor, but usually they are very skeptical to embrace the gift of free advice. Choose your advisors carefully and consult them often so you can make better and wiser decisions. Remember that people can give bad advice despite their good intentions, like Job's friends. Every bit of advice must be weighed and tested against the Word, so you can make the best informed decision. Even after all counsel has been given, the decision remains yours, and you are responsible for it.

Is Age Just a Number?

Gray hair is a crown of glory; it is gained by living a godly life.
Proverbs 16:31 NLT

Those who are planted in the house of the LORD shall flourish in the courts of our God. They shall still bear fruit in old age; they shall be fresh and flourishing, to declare that the LORD is upright; He is my rock, and there is no unrighteousness in Him.
Psalm 92:13-15 NKJV

Wisdom belongs to the aged, and understanding to the old.
Job 12:12 NLT

"Age should speak, and multitude of years should teach wisdom."
Job 32:7 NKJV

The glory of the young is their strength; the gray hair of experience is the splendor of the old.
Proverbs 20:29 NLT

"I will be your God throughout your lifetime—until your hair is white with age. I made you, and I will care for you. I will carry you along and save you."
Isaiah 46:4 NLT

Grandchildren are the crown of the aged, and the glory of children is their fathers.
Proverbs 17:6 ESV

Stand up in the presence of the aged, show respect for the elderly and revere your God.
Leviticus 19:32 NIV

For most women, age is more than just a number. It has become the barometer of what can be achieved. You are never too young or too old to succeed. Wolfgang Amadeus Mozart had already composed music at the age of five, and at age six he was highly skilled in sight-reading. Nelson Mandela became president of South Africa at age seventy-five. Ans Botha was seventy-three years old when she coached Wayde van Niekerk, 400m World Champion. Discover your destiny and live it in spite of your age.

The Power of Ambition

We urge you, brothers and sisters, to make it your ambition to lead a quiet life: You should mind your own business and work with your hands, just as we told you, so that your daily life may win the respect of outsiders and so that you will not be dependent on anybody.
1 Thessalonians 4:10-12 NIV

Do we all have the gift of healing? Do we all have the ability to speak in unknown languages? Do we all have the ability to interpret unknown languages? Of course not! So you should earnestly desire the most helpful gifts.
1 Corinthians 12:30-31 NLT

Whoever pursues righteousness and love finds life, prosperity and honor.
Proverbs 21:21 NIV

My ambition has always been to preach the Good News where the name of Christ has never been heard, rather than where a church has already been started by someone else.
Romans 15:20 NLT

Let nothing be done through selfish ambition or conceit, but in lowliness of mind let each esteem others better than himself. Let each of you look out not only for his own interests, but also for the interests of others.
Philippians 2:3-4 NKJV

What is your ambition? Are you allowed to live an ambitious life? Ambition is good if it drives you to live in humility with God's purpose for your life. Let your greatest ambition be to serve with the gifts and talents you have received. Ambition becomes negative when you drive it in a self-centered way and at the expense of other people for your own glory and achievement. Be careful that your ambition doesn't hurt people along the way, but rather serves them.

Angels under God's Command

For He will command His angels concerning you to guard you in all your ways.

Psalm 91:11 ESV

The angel of the LORD encamps around those who fear Him, and He delivers them.

Psalm 34:7 NIV

Daniel answered, "My God sent His angel, and He shut the mouths of the lions. They have not hurt me, because I was found innocent in His sight."

Daniel 6:21-22 NIV

"He will send His angels, and gather together His elect from the four winds, from the farthest part of earth to the farthest part of heaven."

Mark 13:27 NKJV

"The sign that the Son of Man is coming will appear in the heavens, and there will be deep mourning among all the peoples of the earth. And they will see the Son of Man coming on the clouds of heaven with power and great glory. And He will send out His angels with the mighty blast of a trumpet, and they will gather His chosen ones from all over the world—from the farthest ends of the earth and heaven."

Matthew 24:30-31 NLT

"Behold, I send an angel before you to guard you on the way and to bring you to the place that I have prepared."

Exodus 23:20 ESV

Angels were created by God to serve Him and to be under His control. The word "angel" means messenger of God. You don't honor and worship them, because they are creatures. God has equipped them with tremendous power and made them His army, ready to exercise His will. Michael is the main administrator, and Gabriel is responsible for bringing God's special word to people. You cannot tell them what to do, because they are in the service of God and respond to His command only.

Control Your Anger

"Don't sin by letting anger control you." Don't let the sun go down while you are still angry.
Ephesians 4:26 NLT

A gentle answer turns away wrath, but a harsh word stirs up anger.
Proverbs 15:1 NIV

Control your temper, for anger labels you a fool.
Ecclesiastes 7:9 NLT

Sensible people control their temper; they earn respect by overlooking wrongs.
Proverbs 19:11 NLT

A man without self-control is like a city broken into and left without walls.
Proverbs 25:28 ESV

So then, my beloved brethren, let every man be swift to hear, slow to speak, slow to wrath.
James 1:19 NKJV

People with understanding control their anger; a hot temper shows great foolishness.
Proverbs 14:29 NLT

"If anyone slaps you on one cheek, turn to them the other also. If someone takes your coat, do not withhold your shirt from them."
Luke 6:29 NIV

Many people think anger is due to stress and high expectations, but it is actually a character problem. Anger shows a lack of self-control and respect for others. Maybe you think your tantrums will hurt others, but it is just the opposite. It destroys you physically and spiritually. Learn how to control your anger by not responding immediately. Recognize your emotions and allow yourself some time out. Look up, take a deep breath, and pray to God for guidance.

God's Answer to Prayer

Jesus replied, "Truly I tell you, if you have faith and do not doubt, not only can you do what was done to the fig tree, but also you can say to this mountain, 'Go, throw yourself into the sea,' and it will be done. If you believe, you will receive whatever you ask for in prayer."
Matthew 21:21-22 NIV

"If My people who are called by My name will humble themselves, and pray and seek My face, and turn from their wicked ways, then I will hear from heaven, and will forgive their sin and heal their land."
2 Chronicles 7:14 NKJV

In my distress I called upon the LORD, and cried out to my God; He heard my voice from His temple, and my cry came before Him, even to His ears.
Psalm 18:6 NKJV

We will receive from Him whatever we ask because we obey Him and do the things that please Him.
1 John 3:22 NLT

"Truly, truly, I say to you, whatever you ask of the Father in My name, He will give it to you. Until now you have asked nothing in My name. Ask, and you will receive, that your joy may be full."
John 16:23-24 ESV

God's answer to your prayer doesn't mean He must provide everything according to your "shopping list." God hears every prayer and answers it in His own time and in a way He thinks is best for you. Although He knows what you need, He awaits your prayer, because a relationship with you is very important to Him. Sometimes the answer to prayer is "yes," other times "no," and often it is "wait a little while." At times, when we don't hear the answer clearly, we can sense a quiet contentment and peace because we can rest assured that He knows best.

Managing Your Anxiety

"So do not fear, for I am with you; do not be dismayed, for I am your God."
Isaiah 41:10 NIV

There is no fear in love, but perfect love casts out fear. For fear has to do with punishment, and whoever fears has not been perfected in love.
1 John 4:18 ESV

Do not be anxious about anything, but in every situation, by prayer and petition, with thanksgiving, present your requests to God. And the peace of God, which transcends all understanding, will guard your hearts and your minds in Christ Jesus.
Philippians 4:6-7 NIV

I have set the LORD always before me; because He is at my right hand I shall not be moved.
Psalm 16:8 NKJV

Anxiety weighs down the heart, but a kind word cheers it up.
Proverbs 12:25 NIV

Cast all your anxiety on Him because He cares for you.
1 Peter 5:7 NIV

"Therefore do not be anxious about tomorrow, for tomorrow will be anxious for itself. Sufficient for the day is its own trouble."
Matthew 6:34 ESV

Do you know the feeling of anxiety, fear, and worry? These feelings are very common among women and often lead to feelings of guilt. Some people say that when God's people are anxious, they are of little faith! A statement that makes women even more anxious. In Jesus' greatest crisis, He was not without anxiety. In the Garden of Gethsemane, His sweat became like drops of blood, and the next day on the cross, He experienced increased anxiety as His Father left Him. But Jesus overcame His fear through love. May perfect love also conquer your fears.

Looks Can Be Deceiving

Your beauty should not come from outward adornment, such as elaborate hairstyles and the wearing of gold jewelry or fine clothes. Rather, it should be that of your inner self, the unfading beauty of a gentle and quiet spirit, which is of great worth in God's sight.
1 Peter 3:3-4 NIV

"Blessed are the pure in heart, for they shall see God."
Matthew 5:8 ESV

"The LORD does not look at the things people look at. People look at the outward appearance, but the LORD looks at the heart."
1 Samuel 16:7 NIV

God is working in you, giving you the desire and the power to do what pleases Him.
Philippians 2:13 NLT

"Physical training is good, but training for godliness is much better, promising benefits in this life and in the life to come."
1 Timothy 4:8 NLT

Charm is deceptive, and beauty is fleeting; but a woman who fears the LORD is to be praised.
Proverbs 31:30 NIV

I praise You because I am fearfully and wonderfully made.
Psalm 139:14 NIV

What do you look like? Do you work out for hours in a gym or take a pill every morning and put on wrinkle cream? Do you wear designer clothing? While everyone around you envies you for your appearance, what do you look like in heaven? If God and His angels were to look at you, would they see the effects of spiritual discipline on your soul? Rather than designer clothes, bear spiritual fruit as your clothing, and know that you are beautiful to Him.

Seeking People's Approval

Am I now trying to win the approval of human beings, or of God? Or am I trying to please people? If I were still trying to please people, I would not be a servant of Christ.
Galatians 1:10 NIV

Do your best to present yourself to God as one approved, a worker who has no need to be ashamed, rightly handling the word of truth.
2 Timothy 2:15 ESV

Our purpose is to please God, not people. He alone examines the motives of our hearts.
1 Thessalonians 2:4 NLT

We make it our aim, whether present or absent, to be well pleasing to Him.
2 Corinthians 5:9 NKJV

"Let the one who boasts boast in the Lord." For it is not the one who commends himself who is approved, but the one whom the Lord commends.
2 Corinthians 10:17-18 NIV

For the kingdom of God is not a matter of eating and drinking but of righteousness and peace and joy in the Holy Spirit. Whoever thus serves Christ is acceptable to God and approved by men.
Romans 14:17-18 ESV

"Seek the Kingdom of God above all else, and live righteously, and He will give you everything you need."
Matthew 6:33 NLT

Do you have a full calendar? Do you try to meet the absurd expectations of people? Are you too afraid to take a stand because you are seeking people's approval? The fear of rejection and the search for acceptance can make that women become the best actors in an attempt to meet people's expectations. In the process they lose their true selves. Jesus gave Himself in order for you to be acceptable to God without any mask. Be yourself and live your life to the full without pretense.

God's Pleasant Aroma

We are the aroma of Christ to God among those who are being saved and among those who are perishing, to one a fragrance from death to death, to the other a fragrance from life to life.

2 Corinthians 2:15-16 ESV

Live a life filled with love, following the example of Christ. He loved us and offered Himself as a sacrifice for us, a pleasing aroma to God.

Ephesians 5:2 NLT

I urge you, brothers and sisters, in view of God's mercy, to offer your bodies as a living sacrifice, holy and pleasing to God—this is your true and proper worship.

Romans 12:1 NIV

Do not neglect to do good and to share what you have, for such sacrifices are pleasing to God.

Hebrews 13:16 ESV

"As a pleasing aroma I will accept you, when I bring you out from the peoples and gather you out of the countries where you have been scattered. And I will manifest My holiness among you in the sight of the nations."

Ezekiel 20:41 ESV

Let us offer through Jesus a continual sacrifice of praise to God, proclaiming our allegiance to His name.

Hebrews 13:15 NLT

Women love to find perfume that reflects their personality. What is your favorite perfume? There's nothing like the smell of perfume hanging in a room or that of pancakes and cinnamon. In contrast, nothing is as bad as the smell of rotten meat in a freezer or a rat that died in a room. What is the scent you leave behind after you lose your temper, next to the field where your child is playing sports, on the road, or behind your computer? Leave a pleasant aroma of life and love.

Human Arrogance

Do not think of yourself more highly than you ought, but rather think of yourself with sober judgment, in accordance with the faith God has distributed to each of you.
Romans 12:3 NIV

Talk no more so very proudly, let not arrogance come from your mouth; for the LORD is a God of knowledge, and by Him actions are weighed.
1 Samuel 2:3 ESV

The proud and arrogant person—"Mocker" is his name—behaves with insolent fury.
Proverbs 21:24 NIV

Whoever slanders his neighbor secretly I will destroy. Whoever has a haughty look and an arrogant heart I will not endure.
Psalm 101:5 ESV

You are not a God who is pleased with wickedness; with You, evil people are not welcome. The arrogant cannot stand in Your presence.
Psalm 5:4-5 NIV

Let someone else praise you, and not your own mouth; an outsider, and not your own lips.
Proverbs 27:2 NIV

To be humble is not easy. We live in a world where performance and keeping up with the Joneses is the standard. People love fame and honor. If you're not careful, however, your humility can soon give in to arrogance and pride. God doesn't share His glory. He despises arrogant people. The applause is owed to Him. Nobody claps for the instruments—the violin, piano, or flute individually—but indeed for the maestro, God.

Access to the Throne Room

Jesus led them to Bethany, and lifting His hands to heaven, He blessed them. While He was blessing them, He left them and was taken up to heaven.
Luke 24:50-51 NLT

"Very truly I tell you, it is for your good that I am going away. Unless I go away, the Advocate will not come to you; but if I go, I will send Him to you."
John 16:7 NIV

"You have heard Me say to you, 'I am going away and coming back to you.' If you loved Me, you would rejoice because I said, 'I am going to the Father,' for My Father is greater than I."
John 14:28 NKJV

While they looked steadfastly toward heaven as He went up, behold, two men stood by them in white apparel, who also said, "Men of Galilee, why do you stand gazing up into heaven? This same Jesus, who was taken up from you into heaven, will so come in like manner as you saw Him go into heaven."
Acts 1:10-11 NKJV

To each one of us grace has been given as Christ apportioned it. This is why it says: "When He ascended on high, He took many captives and gave gifts to His people."
Ephesians 4:7-8 NIV

When Jesus felt forsaken at Calvary, it sent shock waves through the world. Forty days after His resurrection, the clouds were assembling, not to give rain or to bring a storm, but to proclaim that the Father and Son will never be separated again. Jesus ascended into heaven and now sits at the right hand of the Father, the King of all kings. From there He whispers your name and your needs into the Father's ear. Christ's ascension guarantees your prayers will echo in heaven.

A Positive Outlook on Life

Do everything without grumbling or arguing, so that you may become blameless and pure, "children of God without fault in a warped and crooked generation."
Philippians 2:14-15 NIV

A cheerful heart is good medicine, but a broken spirit saps a person's strength.
Proverbs 17:22 NLT

Whatever you do, in word or deed, do everything in the name of the Lord Jesus, giving thanks to God the Father through Him.
Colossians 3:17 ESV

You must have the same attitude that Christ Jesus had.
Philippians 2:5 NLT

Do nothing out of selfish ambition or vain conceit. Rather, in humility value others above yourselves, not looking to your own interests but each of you to the interests of the others.
Philippians 2:3-4 NIV

Whatever is true, whatever is noble, whatever is right, whatever is pure, whatever is lovely, whatever is admirable—if anything is excellent or praiseworthy—think about such things. Whatever you have learned or received or heard from me, or seen in me—put it into practice. And the God of peace will be with you.
Philippians 4:8-9 NIV

The trick to finding quality in your life is in your attitude—how you look at life and whether you see the glass half full or half empty. One day two prisoners looked to the outside world through the same prison window; one saw the mud of the previous night's rain and the other the blue sky, and he praised God for another day. Their attitudes determined what they saw. You must choose whether your attitude will be your greatest asset or your greatest obstacle.

Your Spiritual Authority

You who are younger must accept the authority of the elders.
1 Peter 5:5 NLT

Let everyone be subject to the governing authorities, for there is no authority except that which God has established. The authorities that exist have been established by God.
Romans 13:1 NIV

Have confidence in your leaders and submit to their authority, because they keep watch over you as those who must give an account. Do this so that their work will be a joy, not a burden, for that would be of no benefit to you.
Hebrews 13:17 NIV

I urge you, first of all, to pray for all people. Ask God to help them; intercede on their behalf, and give thanks for them. Pray this way for kings and all who are in authority so that we can live peaceful and quiet lives marked by godliness and dignity. This is good and pleases God our Savior.
1 Timothy 2:1-3 NLT

Remind the people to be subject to rulers and authorities, to be obedient, to be ready to do whatever is good, to slander no one, to be peaceable and considerate, and always to be gentle toward everyone.
Titus 3:1-2 NIV

Power or authority is given by God and comes with great responsibility that should not be abused. All people with authority are under God, for He is the highest authority and will demand accountability from everyone. When we love God and have a relationship with Him, we accept the authority given to us. We realize that all people should be treated with love, respect, and dignity. We should practice honoring all those in authority in our country, at work, and in our families.

The Balancing Act

So be careful how you live. Don't live like fools, but like those who are wise.
Ephesians 5:15 NLT

"Seek the Kingdom of God above all else, and live righteously, and He will give you everything you need."
Matthew 6:33 NLT

A false balance is an abomination to the LORD, but a just weight is His delight.
Proverbs 11:1 ESV

You therefore, beloved, knowing this beforehand, take care that you are not carried away with the error of lawless people and lose your own stability.
2 Peter 3:17 ESV

There is a time for everything, and a season for every activity under the heavens.
Ecclesiastes 3:1 NIV

A just balance and scales are the LORD's; all the weights in the bag are His work.
Proverbs 16:11 ESV

Whatever you do, do it all in the name of the Lord Jesus.
Colossians 3:17 NIV

Most people are motivated to success because they envy their neighbors. But this, too, is meaningless. "Better to have one handful with quietness than two handfuls with hard work and chasing the wind."
Ecclesiastes 4:4, 6 NLT

As children we loved to play on the seesaw. For it to work properly you need two children who are about the same weight, otherwise the one will be kept in the air the whole time. Life is like a seesaw—we must master the art of balance, otherwise work will always weigh more and relationships will hang in the air discontented. Find a balance for everyone and everything so that when it's time for your family, they get your undivided love and attention.

Find Your Inner Beauty

He has made everything beautiful in its time.
Ecclesiastes 3:11 NIV

Charm is deceptive, and beauty is fleeting; but a woman who fears the LORD is to be praised.
Proverbs 31:30 NIV

"The LORD does not look at the things people look at. People look at the outward appearance, but the LORD looks at the heart."
1 Samuel 16:7 NIV

You are the most handsome of all. Gracious words stream from your lips. God Himself has blessed you forever.
Psalm 45:2 NLT

Your beauty should not come from outward adornment, such as elaborate hairstyles and the wearing of gold jewelry or fine clothes. Rather, it should be that of your inner self, the unfading beauty of a gentle and quiet spirit, which is of great worth in God's sight.
1 Peter 3:3-4 NIV

Women should adorn themselves in respectable apparel, with modesty and self-control, not with braided hair and gold or pearls or costly attire, but with what is proper for women who profess godliness—with good works. Let a woman learn quietly with all submissiveness.
1 Timothy 2:9-11 ESV

Hairdressers, nail technicians, day cream, night cream, diets, and whatever else—every woman longs for beauty. A beautiful car, home, and garden. Women love beautiful things. It is interesting that God also likes beauty but an inner beauty in women; someone with a gentle nature, who chooses her words well and serves Him gladly. You'll never get to be on the cover of *Vogue* Magazine, but God already has a place for you in heaven. Be a model of beauty and faith.

Failed Attempts and New Beginnings

And He who was seated on the throne said, "Behold, I am making all things new." Also He said, "Write this down, for these words are trustworthy and true."
Revelation 21:5 ESV

Therefore, if anyone is in Christ, the new creation has come: The old has gone, the new is here!
2 Corinthians 5:17 NIV

"Behold, I am doing a new thing; now it springs forth, do you not perceive it? I will make a way in the wilderness and rivers in the desert."
Isaiah 43:19 ESV

"See, I will create new heavens and a new earth. The former things will not be remembered, nor will they come to mind."
Isaiah 65:17 NIV

The steadfast love of the LORD never ceases; His mercies never come to an end; they are new every morning; great is Your faithfulness.
Lamentations 3:22-23 ESV

Do not lie to each other, since you have taken off your old self with its practices and have put on the new self, which is being renewed in knowledge in the image of its Creator.
Colossians 3:9-10 NIV

After failed attempts, divorce, or depressive circumstances people want to start anew. A new beginning is always possible with Jesus; a new beginning of hope, where His tears give dignity to yours. His arms become your shelter when you are afraid. He is the conductor when the tunnel looks dark. He announces the new season as the last leaf of your season falls to the ground. Not only does He give second chances but a brand-new beginning.

Do You Truly Believe?

"For God so loved the world that He gave His one and only Son, that whoever believes in Him shall not perish but have eternal life."
John 3:16 NIV

If you confess with your mouth that Jesus is Lord and believe in your heart that God raised Him from the dead, you will be saved. For with the heart one believes and is justified, and with the mouth one confesses and is saved.
Romans 10:9-10 ESV

"With God all things are possible."
Matthew 19:26 NIV

"And whatever you ask in prayer, you will receive, if you have faith."
Matthew 21:22 ESV

"Do not be afraid; only believe."
Mark 5:36 NKJV

"Blessed are those who have not seen and yet have believed."
John 20:29 NIV

"Anyone who believes in God's Son has eternal life."
John 3:36 NLT

We live by faith, not by sight.
2 Corinthians 5:7 NIV

Faith cannot be measured, stored, or boasted about. Faith is the result of your certainty that Jesus has already done everything for you so you can stand in a living relationship with the living God. Therefore faith is not about you. It is about putting all your hope and expectations in God. Christianity means trusting Him for the certainties and uncertainties in your life and clinging to the knowledge that nothing is impossible for Him.

A Sense of Belonging

There is neither Jew nor Gentile, neither slave nor free, nor is there male and female, for you are all one in Christ Jesus.

Galatians 3:28 NIV

You belong to God, my dear children. You have already won a victory over those people, because the Spirit who lives in you is greater than the spirit who lives in the world.

1 John 4:4 NLT

For by Him all things were created, in heaven and on earth, visible and invisible, whether thrones or dominions or rulers or authorities—all things were created through Him and for Him.

Colossians 1:16 ESV

The earth is the LORD's, and everything in it. The world and all its people belong to Him. For He laid the earth's foundation on the seas and built it on the ocean depths.

Psalm 24:1-2 NLT

Now you are the body of Christ, and each one of you is a part of it.

1 Corinthians 12:27 NIV

You, however, are not in the flesh but in the Spirit, if in fact the Spirit of God dwells in you. Anyone who does not have the Spirit of Christ does not belong to Him.

Romans 8:9 ESV

God created us for fellowship with Him, for togetherness with family and friends, and to have a place where we belong in a community of faith. The need to be committed to something greater than yourself was placed there by God Himself. Where you love, encourage and accept one another, bear one another's burdens, and become attached to one another. Do you have a women's group that you belong to? Spend time with God and thank Him for friends and a sense of belonging.

The Bible Is Key

Above all, you must understand that no prophecy of Scripture came about by the prophet's own interpretation of things. For prophecy never had its origin in the human will, but prophets, though human, spoke from God as they were carried along by the Holy Spirit.
2 Peter 1:20-21 NIV

Jesus answered, "It is written: 'Man shall not live on bread alone, but on every word that comes from the mouth of God.'"
Matthew 4:4 NIV

The entirety of Your word is truth, and every one of Your righteous judgments endures forever.
Psalm 119:160 NKJV

"Everyone then who hears these words of Mine and does them will be like a wise man who built his house on the rock. And the rain fell, and the floods came, and the winds blew and beat on that house, but it did not fall, because it had been founded on the rock. And everyone who hears these words of Mine and does not do them will be like a foolish man who built his house on the sand. And the rain fell, and the floods came, and the winds blew and beat against that house, and it fell, and great was the fall of it."
Matthew 7:24-27 ESV

The Bible is more than just a book. It is the key that unlocks the door to knowing God's heart. It's the key to the will of the Father and to your Savior who loves you and knows your name. It is a key to an intimate relationship with the Holy Spirit—to a treasure trove of gifts of gold and silver that you discover the moment your heart is ready to receive it. Sit on your favorite couch and unlock treasures today with your key, the Bible.

Bitterness Poisons the Soul

Get rid of all bitterness, rage and anger, brawling and slander, along with every form of malice.
Ephesians 4:31 NIV

Pursue peace with all people, and holiness, without which no one will see the Lord: looking carefully lest anyone fall short of the grace of God; lest any root of bitterness springing up cause trouble, and by this many become defiled.
Hebrews 12:14-15 NKJV

Behold, it was for my welfare that I had great bitterness; but in love You have delivered my life from the pit of destruction.
Isaiah 38:17 ESV

Each heart knows its own bitterness, and no one else can share its joy.
Proverbs 14:10 NIV

I realized that my heart was bitter, and I was all torn up inside. I was so foolish and ignorant—I must have seemed like a senseless animal to You. Yet I still belong to You; You hold my right hand. You guide me with Your counsel, leading me to a glorious destiny.
Psalm 73:21-24 NLT

Resentment kills a fool, and envy slays the simple.
Job 5:2 NIV

Have you heard the saying, "Bitterness is like drinking poison and waiting for the other person to die"? Bad experiences, pain, and hurt will often turn into bitterness that women will cling to. Before you even realize it, bitterness can poison you from the inside and in time completely destroy you. It is your choice whether to be bitter or not. The cross is God's answer to bitterness. Only when you forgive will you remove the poison of bitterness and find healing.

February

May the **Lord**
— of —
PEACE HIMSELF
give you
peace
AT ALL TIMES
& IN EVERY WAY.
The Lord be with all of you.

2 THESSALONIANS 3:16

Blasphemy Against the Holy Spirit

"You shall not take the name of the LORD your God in vain, for the LORD will not hold him guiltless who takes His name in vain."
Exodus 20:7 NKJV

"Anyone who speaks against the Son of Man can be forgiven, but anyone who blasphemes the Holy Spirit will not be forgiven."
Luke 12:10 NLT

Above all, my brothers, do not swear, either by heaven or by earth or by any other oath, but let your "yes" be yes and your "no" be no, so that you may not fall under condemnation.
James 5:12 ESV

"And so I tell you, every kind of sin and slander can be forgiven, but blasphemy against the Spirit will not be forgiven. Anyone who speaks a word against the Son of Man will be forgiven, but anyone who speaks against the Holy Spirit will not be forgiven, either in this age or in the age to come."
Matthew 12:31-32 NIV

You must not misuse the name of the LORD your God. The LORD will not let you go unpunished if you misuse His name.
Deuteronomy 5:11 NLT

Perhaps you have also wondered or struggled with the unforgiveable sin against the Holy Spirit. What is this sin? To slander against the Holy Spirit means to intentionally distort the truth about the Spirit and to attribute the wonderful work that the Spirit is doing to Satan. The Spirit is the one who introduces us to Jesus, so slander against the Spirit is to continually and stubbornly harden your heart, which means a lifelong rejection of Christ and His salvation.

Count Your Blessings

When God raised up His servant, Jesus, He sent Him first to you people of Israel, to bless you by turning each of you back from your sinful ways.
Acts 3:26 NLT

The LORD bless you and keep you; the LORD make His face to shine upon you and be gracious to you; the LORD lift up His countenance upon you and give you peace.
Numbers 6:24-26 ESV

Blessed is the one who trusts in the LORD, whose confidence is in Him.
Jeremiah 17:7 NIV

The LORD blesses the dwelling of the righteous.
Proverbs 3:33 ESV

"From His abundance we have all received one gracious blessing after another."
John 1:16 NLT

Praise be to the God and Father of our Lord Jesus Christ, who has blessed us in the heavenly realms with every spiritual blessing in Christ.
Ephesians 1:3 NIV

The blessing of the LORD makes one rich, and He adds no sorrow with it.
Proverbs 10:22 NKJV

Blessings crown the head of the righteous.
Proverbs 10:6 NIV

Being blessed is often associated with financial prosperity, good health, and constructive relationships. Does this mean that those who are divorced, unemployed, or don't have a home have missed God's blessing? It seems that Jesus has a different view on blessing. His blessing is when you know how dependent you are on Him, when you cry, make peace, and have a gentle and pure heart. You may be more blessed than you think.

Blatant Boastfulness

"I said to the boastful, 'Do not deal boastfully,' and to the wicked, 'Do not lift up the horn. Do not lift up your horn on high; do not speak with a stiff neck.'" For exaltation comes neither from the east nor from the west nor from the south. But God is the Judge: He puts down one, and exalts another.
Psalm 75:4-7 NKJV

You are not a God who delights in wickedness; evil may not dwell with You. The boastful shall not stand before Your eyes; You hate all evildoers. You destroy those who speak lies; the LORD abhors the bloodthirsty and deceitful man.
Psalm 5:4-6 ESV

"Be careful not to practice your righteousness in front of others to be seen by them. If you do, you will have no reward from your Father in heaven. So when you give to the needy, do not announce it with trumpets, as the hypocrites do in the synagogues and on the streets, to be honored by others. Truly I tell you, they have received their reward in full."
Matthew 6:1-2 NIV

We who are strong have an obligation to bear with the failings of the weak, and not to please ourselves. Let each of us please his neighbor for his good, to build him up.
Romans 15:1-2 ESV

Do you brag about what you have and who you are? Sometimes it's a subtle, almost spiritual boasting about how serious you are with your faith and how much you have contributed to charity. Some people boast blatantly to hurt others' feelings, offend their humanity, and to cause damage to relationships. Everything belongs to God, so if you want to boast, do it in the name of the Lord and about His salvation, love, and grace.

Be Bold!

The wicked run away when no one is chasing them, but the godly are as bold as lions.
Proverbs 28:1 NLT

In the day when I cried out, You answered me, and made me bold with strength in my soul.
Psalm 138:3 NKJV

Lord, enable Your servants to speak Your word with great boldness.
Acts 4:29 NIV

Let us come boldly to the throne of our gracious God. There we will receive His mercy, and we will find grace to help us when we need it most.
Hebrews 4:16 NLT

Because of Christ and our faith in Him, we can now come boldly and confidently into God's presence.
Ephesians 3:12 NLT

If the ministry that brought condemnation was glorious, how much more glorious is the ministry that brings righteousness! For what was glorious has no glory now in comparison with the surpassing glory. And if what was transitory came with glory, how much greater is the glory of that which lasts! Therefore, since we have such a hope, we are very bold.
2 Corinthians 3:9-12 NIV

God's heart is open to you through the blood of Jesus. You are welcome to stand in His presence with confidence and to have a personal relationship with Him. This confidence is a necessity in your relationship and contact with God, because by it you pray and persevere. The Greek word for boldness (*parrhesia*) could also be translated as courage, confidence, and openness. It is in this way that you draw near to God.

Living within Godly Boundaries

When the Most High gave the nations their inheritance, when He divided all mankind, He set up boundaries for the peoples.
Deuteronomy 32:8 NIV

The boundary lines have fallen for me in pleasant places; surely I have a delightful inheritance.
Psalm 16:6 NIV

Who has gone up to heaven and come down? Whose hands have gathered up the wind? Who has wrapped up the waters in a cloak? Who has established all the ends of the earth? What is His name, and what is the name of His Son? Surely you know!
Proverbs 30:4 NIV

Yours is the day, Yours also the night; You have established the heavenly lights and the sun. You have fixed all the boundaries of the earth; You have made summer and winter.
Psalm 74:16-17 ESV

The LORD merely spoke, and the heavens were created. He breathed the word, and all the stars were born. He assigned the sea its boundaries and locked the oceans in vast reservoirs. Let the whole world fear the LORD, and let everyone stand in awe of Him. For when He spoke, the world began! It appeared at His command.
Psalm 33:6-9 NLT

God doesn't only set boundaries for nature but also for His children. In this way He can give you a secure living space to move around in and to make decisions. To live beyond the boundaries God has set is to live like a fish out of water with the illusion that you will be free. There's no freedom beyond God's boundaries but rather death. Make your choices within His boundaries and live a fulfilling life.

Fight Against Bribery

For I know your manifold transgressions and your mighty sins: Afflicting the just and taking bribes; diverting the poor from justice at the gate.
Amos 5:12 NKJV

For the LORD your God is God of gods and Lord of lords, the great God, mighty and awesome, who shows no partiality nor takes a bribe.
Deuteronomy 10:17 NKJV

Do not accept a bribe, for a bribe blinds those who see and twists the words of the innocent.
Exodus 23:8 NIV

Though people tried to bribe me, I have kept myself from the ways of the violent through what Your lips have commanded.
Psalm 17:4 NIV

A bribe is seen as a charm by the one who gives it; they think success will come at every turn.
Proverbs 17:8 NIV

Greed brings grief to the whole family, but those who hate bribes will live.
Proverbs 15:27 NLT

Surely oppression drives the wise into madness, and a bribe corrupts the heart.
Ecclesiastes 7:7 ESV

Where jealousy and selfish ambition exist, there will be disorder and every vile practice.
James 3:16 ESV

People are tired of corruption and bribery, and yet they often consider it for personal gain. For a speeding ticket you could just pass a few bucks under the table and no one, not even your husband, has to know. For a few extra bucks, you can make sure you get the right contract so that your finances can improve. Bribery undermines and destroys communities; it does not bring glory to God. It brings your integrity into question. Don't make any compromises; keep your integrity.

He Heals the Brokenhearted

The LORD is close to the brokenhearted and saves those who are crushed in spirit.
Psalm 34:18 NIV

He heals the brokenhearted and binds up their wounds.
Psalm 147:3 NKJV

My flesh and my heart may fail, but God is the strength of my heart and my portion forever.
Psalm 73:26 NIV

I am feeble and crushed; I groan because of the tumult of my heart. Do not forsake me, O LORD! O my God, be not far from me! Make haste to help me, O LORD, my salvation!
Psalm 38:8, 21-22 ESV

"Fear not, for I am with you; be not dismayed for I am your God; I will strengthen you, I will help you, I will uphold you with My righteous right hand."
Isaiah 41:10 ESV

You have kept count of my tossings; put my tears in Your bottle. Are they not in Your book?
Psalm 56:8 ESV

LORD, sustain me as You promised that I may live! Do not let my hope be crushed.
Psalm 119:116 NLT

A glad heart makes a cheerful face, but by sorrow of heart the spirit is crushed.
Proverbs 15:13 ESV

"Humpty Dumpty had a great fall. All the King's soldiers and all the King's men couldn't put Humpty together again." Maybe you fell and got hurt, and no matter how many counselors, therapists, and psychologists tried, the hurt remained. Do you realize that the King can do what humans can't? He can recreate and make things brand new. He wants to pick you up and heal you today. Give your pain to Him.

Don't Be a Victim

"But I say to you, do not resist the one who is evil. But if anyone slaps you on the right cheek, turn to him the other also."
Matthew 5:39 ESV

The ruthless will vanish, the mockers will disappear, and all who have an eye for evil will be cut down.
Isaiah 29:20 NIV

The Spirit God gave us does not make us timid, but gives us power, love and self-discipline.
2 Timothy 1:7 NIV

"Do to others whatever you would like them to do to you."
Matthew 7:12 NLT

"My grace is sufficient for you, for My power is made perfect in weakness." Therefore I will boast all the more gladly of my weaknesses, so that the power of Christ may rest upon me. For the sake of Christ, then, I am content with weaknesses, insults, hardships, persecutions, and calamities. For when I am weak, then I am strong.
2 Corinthians 12:9-10 ESV

Be strong and courageous. Do not be afraid or terrified because of them, for the LORD your God goes with you; He will never leave you nor forsake you.
Deuteronomy 31:6 NIV

Bullies usually have a paralyzing effect on people. There is a story behind every bully's face that we don't know. They often suffer from emotional pain. Without realizing it, the bully says more about himself than his victim. Don't answer violence with violence. The Bible says, "A soft answer turns away wrath," (Prov. 15:1) and, "Stop before a dispute breaks out" (Prov. 17:14). Be a winner, not a victim!

The Dangers of Burnout

Jesus said, "Come to Me, all of you who are weary and carry heavy burdens, and I will give you rest. Take My yoke upon you. Let Me teach you, because I am humble and gentle at heart, and you will find rest for your souls. For My yoke is easy to bear, and the burden I give you is light."
Matthew 11:28-30 NLT

He makes me to lie down in green pastures; He leads me beside the still waters.
Psalm 23:2 NKJV

It is useless for you to work so hard from early morning until late at night, anxiously working for food to eat; for God gives rest to His loved ones.
Psalm 127:2 NLT

I lay down and slept; I woke again, for the LORD sustained me.
Psalm 3:5 ESV

This is what the Sovereign LORD, the Holy One of Israel, says: "Only in returning to Me and resting in Me will you be saved. In quietness and confidence is your strength."
Isaiah 30:15 NLT

Rest in the LORD, and wait patiently for Him.
Psalm 37:7 NKJV

"Come with me by yourselves to a quiet place and get some rest."
Mark 6:31 NIV

When your job is no longer something you do but has become who you are, you should watch out for signs of burnout. Rather than working harder, learn to work smarter. You have to take on several roles, because you have to be a mother, wife, and boss. When you get tired, know that God is there. Plan wisely, sleep, rest, learn to say no, and spend time with God.

A Busy Bee

"Where your treasure is, there your heart will be also."
Matthew 6:21 NIV

"No one can serve two masters. Either you will hate the one and love the other, or you will be devoted to the one and despise the other. You cannot serve both God and money."
Matthew 6:24 NIV

See then that you walk circumspectly, not as fools but as wise, redeeming the time, because the days are evil. Therefore do not be unwise, but understand what the will of the Lord is.
Ephesians 5:15-17 NKJV

"Come, all you who are thirsty, come to the waters; and you who have no money, come, buy and eat! Come, buy wine and milk without money and without cost. Why spend money on what is not bread, and your labor on what does not satisfy? Listen, listen to Me, and eat what is good, and you will delight in the richest of fare."
Isaiah 55:1-2 NIV

"Six days you shall labor, but on the seventh day you shall rest; even during the plowing season and harvest you must rest."
Exodus 34:21 NIV

What is keeping you so busy? Many women get caught up in a vortex of busyness that drains their energy, health, and emotions. Busyness traps women, making them part of the "rat race" and limiting their time with God and their families. Have you calculated the price of your busyness? It's not worth it to give up your health and relationships. Stop! Choose to be calmer and more focused on enjoying life with the people closest to you.

God Is Calling You

For He chose us in Him before the creation of the world to be holy and blameless in His sight. In love He predestined us for adoption to sonship through Jesus Christ, in accordance with His pleasure and will.
Ephesians 1:4-5 NIV

We are His workmanship, created in Christ Jesus for good works, which God prepared beforehand that we should walk in them.
Ephesians 2:10 NKJV

God is faithful, who has called you into fellowship with His Son, Jesus Christ our Lord.
1 Corinthians 1:9 NIV

"You did not choose Me, but I chose you and appointed you that you should go and bear fruit and that your fruit should abide, so that whatever you ask the Father in My name, He may give it to you."
John 15:16 ESV

"The gatekeeper opens the gate for him, and the sheep listen to his voice. He calls his own sheep by name and leads them out. When he has brought out all his own, he goes on ahead of them, and his sheep follow him because they know his voice."
John 10:3-4 NIV

We can often recognize the voice of an actor or singer instantly and yet we are unsure whether it is God's voice we hear or not. Perhaps you wish that God would speak to you through a burning bush or that a voice from heaven would reveal your great calling. God will speak to you in the language of your heart, a language you know. Be still and you may hear Him in nature, in your dreams, in the whisper of a pause, or a verse from Scripture.

Free from Captivity

So Christ has truly set us free. Now make sure that you stay free, and don't get tied up again in slavery to the law.
Galatians 5:1 NLT

"You shall know the truth, and the truth shall make you free."
John 8:32 NKJV

Jesus replied, "Very truly I tell you, everyone who sins is a slave to sin. Now a slave has no permanent place in the family, but a son belongs to it forever. So if the Son sets you free, you will be free indeed."
John 8:34-36 NIV

When you were slaves to sin, you were free from the control of righteousness. What benefit did you reap at that time from the things you are now ashamed of? Those things result in death! But now that you have been set free from sin and have become slaves of God, the benefit you reap leads to holiness, and the result is eternal life.
Romans 6:20-22 NIV

He led them from the darkness and deepest gloom; He snapped their chains.
Psalm 107:14 NLT

Are you a prisoner, enclosed within the bars of self-reproach, loneliness, anger, and unforgiveness? Have your emotions become the prison that you struggle to escape from? Calm down; today there is a hand stretched out to you, the hand that bears the marks of the nails on the cross. He can save you from your prison. His grace can open prison doors and break shackles. You don't have to be a prisoner. Jesus wants to set you free.

Caring for Others

"Blessed are the merciful, for they shall obtain mercy."
Matthew 5:7 NKJV

God comforts us in all our troubles, so that we can comfort those in any trouble with the comfort we ourselves receive from God.
2 Corinthians 1:4 NIV

Honor widows who are truly widows. But if a widow has children or grandchildren, let them first learn to show godliness to their own household and to make some return to their parents, for this is pleasing in the sight of God.
1 Timothy 5:3-4 ESV

Don't look out only for your own interests, but take an interest in others, too.
Philippians 2:4 NLT

Whoever shuts their ears to the cry of the poor will also cry out and not be answered.
Proverbs 21:13 NIV

This makes for harmony among the members, so that all the members care for each other.
1 Corinthians 12:25 NLT

This is the message you have heard from the beginning: We should love one another.
1 John 3:11 NLT

Caring means choosing to make other people's problems and joys your problems and joys. It's choosing to walk with someone at their pace, to laugh with them, and to cry together. Caring doesn't mean having all the answers; it is showing love, compassion, respect, and community. Placing yourself and everything at your disposal in service to others will show that you truly care.

A Reason to Celebrate

Serve the LORD with fear and celebrate His rule with trembling.
Psalm 2:11 NIV

Rise up, O LORD, in all Your power. With music and singing we celebrate Your mighty acts.
Psalm 21:13 NLT

They rejoice in Your name all day long; they celebrate Your righteousness.
Psalm 89:16 NIV

The LORD's fame will be celebrated in Zion, His praises in Jerusalem, when multitudes gather together and kingdoms come to worship the LORD.
Psalm 102:21-22 NLT

Praise the LORD, for the LORD is good; celebrate His lovely name with music.
Psalm 135:3 NLT

They celebrate Your abundant goodness and joyfully sing of Your righteousness.
Psalm 145:7 NIV

Praise the LORD! Praise God in His sanctuary; praise Him in His mighty heaven!
Psalm 150:1 ESV

For everything there is a season, a time for every activity under heaven...a time to laugh...A time to embrace.
Ecclesiastes 3:1, 4-5 NLT

Usually we celebrate big events. We celebrate birthdays and wedding anniversaries, and we also have the privilege of celebrating the birth of Jesus, His crucifixion, His resurrection, His ascension, and Pentecost. Are these celebrations just another public holiday to you, or did you decide that because "pagans" hijacked these holidays you no longer celebrate them? Without any guilt, celebrate Jesus and the impact His life has—the reason for your salvation that leads to another reason for celebration.

Change Is the Only Constant

He turned the rock into a pool of water; yes, a spring of water flowed from solid rock.
Psalm 114:8 NLT

He who is the Glory of Israel does not lie or change His mind; for He is not a human being, that He should change His mind.
1 Samuel 15:29 NIV

So all of us who have had that veil removed can see and reflect the glory of the Lord. And the Lord—who is the Spirit—makes us more and more like Him as we are changed into His glorious image.
2 Corinthians 3:18 NLT

"I tell you the truth, unless you turn from your sins and become like little children, you will never get into the Kingdom of Heaven."
Matthew 18:3 NLT

Do not conform to the pattern of this world, but be transformed by the renewing of your mind.
Romans 12:2 NIV

To everything there is a season, a time for every purpose under heaven: A time to be born, and a time to die; a time to plant, and a time to pluck what is planted.
Ecclesiastes 3:1-2 NKJV

Change makes people uncomfortable. They feel safe with familiar things. Horses worked, so why would we want to buy cars? Fixed phone lines worked, so why do we need mobile phones? Change is necessary for growth and prosperity. God changes and renews your mind and your lifestyle, so you can grow into the image of Christ. Every change to a new season brings its own blessings and joys. Trust the unchanging God with each new season.

A Character Analysis

"Before I formed you in the womb I knew you."
Jeremiah 1:5 NIV

"Everyone who exalts himself will be humbled, and he who humbles himself will be exalted."
Luke 14:11 ESV

God is working in you, giving you the desire and the power to do what pleases Him.
Philippians 2:13 NLT

When your faith is tested, your endurance has a chance to grow. So let it grow, for when your endurance is fully developed, you will be perfect and complete, needing nothing.
James 1:3-4 NLT

"God blesses those whose hearts are pure, for they will see God."
Matthew 5:8 NLT

The Holy Spirit produces this kind of fruit in our lives: love, joy, peace, patience, kindness, goodness, faithfulness, gentleness, and self-control. There is no law against these things!
Galatians 5:22-23 NLT

The LORD bestows favor and honor; no good thing does He withhold from those whose walk is blameless.
Psalm 84:11 NIV

How can a young person stay pure? By obeying Your word.
Psalm 119:9 NLT

A woman of good character is someone who does what is right, as the Word convicts her, no matter the cost. Because you know who you are in Christ, you can be of service at all levels. This means sometimes bending the knee so that others can stand on your shoulders to see further into the future. True character is allowing others to stand on your shoulders even if that makes them more visible than you.

Charity Begins at Home

Whoever is kind to the poor lends to the LORD, and He will reward them for what they have done.

Proverbs 19:17 NIV

Share your food with the hungry, and give shelter to the homeless. Give clothes to those who need them, and do not hide from relatives who need your help. Then your salvation will come like the dawn, and your wounds will quickly heal. Your godliness will lead you forward, and the glory of the LORD will protect you from behind.

Isaiah 58:7-8 NLT

"Sell your possessions and give to the poor. Provide purses for yourselves that will not wear out, a treasure in heaven that will never fail, where no thief comes near and no moth destroys."

Luke 12:33 NIV

"When you give a feast, invite the poor, the maimed, the lame, the blind. And you will be blessed, because they cannot repay you; for you shall be repaid at the resurrection of the just."

Luke 14:13-14 NKJV

"You will always have the poor among you, but you will not always have Me."

Matthew 26:11 NLT

Poverty and hardship will stay with us until the second coming; that's why you have to choose what charity looks like for you. When you give in abundance, remember that everything you have actually belongs to God. You are blessed and often receive much more than you can give. Give what you have even if it may seem like little. In God's hands your little becomes a lot, just like the little boy's five loaves of bread and two fish.

The Gift of a Child

Children are a heritage from the LORD, offspring a reward from Him. Like arrows in the hands of a warrior are children born in one's youth. Blessed is the man whose quiver is full of them.
Psalm 127:3-5 NIV

Blessed are those who fear the LORD, who find great delight in His commands. Their children will be mighty in the land; the generation of the upright will be blessed.
Psalm 112:1-2 NIV

Children's children are a crown to the aged, and parents are the pride of their children.
Proverbs 17:6 NIV

Jesus called them to Him and said, "Let the little children come to Me, and do not forbid them; for of such is the kingdom of God."
Luke 18:16 NKJV

"Take heed that you do not despise one of these little ones, for I say to you that in heaven their angels always see the face of My Father who is in heaven."
Matthew 18:10 NKJV

"Whoever welcomes one of these little children in My name welcomes Me; and whoever welcomes Me does not welcome Me but the one who sent Me."
Mark 9:37 NIV

What is the greatest gift, next to Jesus, that you have ever received from God? I remember mine was the day my newborn baby lay in my arms, defenseless and at the mercy of my care. I realized that from then on my heart would live outside my body. The day God entrusted you with one of His children, you got one of the greatest blessings and responsibilities. Everything changes—your lifestyle, sleep patterns, way of seeing and making decisions—just so this child can know God.

Chosen by God

You are a chosen generation, a royal priesthood, a holy nation, His own special people, that you may proclaim the praises of Him who called you out of darkness into His marvelous light.

1 Peter 2:9 NKJV

For He chose us in Him before the creation of the world to be holy and blameless in His sight. In love He predestined us for adoption to sonship through Jesus Christ, in accordance with His pleasure and will—to the praise of His glorious grace, which He has freely given us in the One He loves.

Ephesians 1:4-6 NIV

In Him we were also chosen, having been predestined according to the plan of Him who works out everything in conformity with the purpose of His will, in order that we, who were the first to put our hope in Christ, might be for the praise of His glory.

Ephesians 1:11-12 NIV

"You did not choose Me, but I chose you and appointed you that you should go and bear fruit and that your fruit should abide, so that whatever you ask the Father in My name, He may give it to you."

John 15:16 ESV

What a privilege to know that even before you were able to make decisions, while you were still stained with sin, God chose you to belong to Him. He knew it would be at the cost of His Son's life and that through His blood this grace would be unaffordable. God chose you, wherever you are, so your life could become part of His plan, so you could glorify Him, and so your life could be a song to the glory of His name.

Being More Like Jesus

"I have set you an example that you should do as I have done for you."
John 13:15 NIV

God knew His people in advance, and He chose them to become like His Son, so that His Son would be the firstborn among many brothers and sisters.
Romans 8:29 NLT

Whoever claims to live in Him must live as Jesus did.
1 John 2:6 NIV

I have been crucified with Christ; it is no longer I who live, but Christ lives in me; and the life which I now live in the flesh I live by faith in the Son of God, who loved me and gave Himself for me.
Galatians 2:20 NKJV

You must have the same attitude that Christ Jesus had.
Philippians 2:5 NLT

I urge you, brothers and sisters, to offer your bodies as a living sacrifice, holy and pleasing to God—this is your true and proper worship. Do not conform to the pattern of this world, but be transformed by the renewing of your mind. Then you will be able to test and approve what God's will is—His good, pleasing and perfect will.
Romans 12:1-2 NIV

"The student is not above the teacher, but everyone who is fully trained will be like their teacher."
Luke 6:40 NIV

Jesus' footsteps started with baby steps on earth. He left peculiar footprints in places where we least expected—against an animal's feeding trough, in the street, among the sinners, with children and the sick, on the way to Calvary, against a cross, and beyond the grave into the hearts of people. I pray that you will not only walk in Jesus' footsteps but that He will be visible in yours.

The Church of God

We will speak the truth in love, growing in every way more and more like Christ, who is the head of His body, the church.
Ephesians 4:15 NLT

You yourselves like living stones are being built up as a spiritual house, to be a holy priesthood, to offer spiritual sacrifices acceptable to God through Jesus Christ.
1 Peter 2:5 ESV

Keep watch over yourselves and all the flock of which the Holy Spirit has made you overseers. Be shepherds of the church of God, which He bought with His own blood.
Acts 20:28 NIV

All who believed were together and had all things in common. And they were selling their possessions and belongings and distributing the proceeds to all, as any had need. And day by day, attending the temple together and breaking bread in their homes, they received their food with glad and generous hearts, praising God and having favor with all the people. And the LORD added to their number day by day those who were being saved.
Acts 2:44-47 ESV

Let us aim for harmony in the church and try to build each other up.
Romans 14:19 NLT

Do you feel excited, enthusiastic, disappointed, or disillusioned about the church? What are you looking for in a church? Maybe you are looking for a church that hears God's heartbeat but also sees the need of the world—a church using His body as a bridge to meet other people halfway. Realize that you are the church; everything you have wished for in a church starts with you.

The Body of Christ

Christ is also the head of the church, which is His body. He is the beginning, supreme over all who rise from the dead. So He is first in everything.
Colossians 1:18 NLT

Just as a body, though one, has many parts, but all its many parts form one body, so it is with Christ. For we were all baptized by one Spirit so as to form one body—whether Jews or Gentiles, slave or free—and we were all given the one Spirit to drink. Even so the body is not made up of one part but of many.
1 Corinthians 12:12-14 NIV

All of you together are Christ's body, and each of you is a part of it.
1 Corinthians 12:27 NLT

Just as our bodies have many parts and each part has a special function, so it is with Christ's body. We are many parts of one body, and we all belong to each other.
Romans 12:4-5 NLT

Together, we are His house, built on the foundation of the apostles and the prophets. And the cornerstone is Christ Jesus Himself. We are carefully joined together in Him, becoming a holy temple for the Lord.
Ephesians 2:20-21 NLT

The church is not just a building but a community of faithful people. You and I are the church. Jesus also used the example of His body being the church on earth. He is the head of this body, and we need each other to function optimally. Maybe you got hurt in the church and that is why you are no longer involved in a congregation. An arm, leg, or kidney needs the body to survive. The church needs you to be fully functional.

Finding Comfort

Shout for joy, you heavens; rejoice, you earth; burst into song, you mountains! For the LORD comforts His people and will have compassion on His afflicted ones.
Isaiah 49:13 NIV

"As a mother comforts her child, so will I comfort you."
Isaiah 66:13 NIV

Praise be to the God and Father of our Lord Jesus Christ, the Father of compassion and the God of all comfort, who comforts us in all our troubles so that we can comfort those in any trouble with the comfort we ourselves receive from God.
2 Corinthians 1:3-4 NIV

"I, yes I, am the one who comforts you. So why are you afraid?"
Isaiah 51:12 NLT

"Blessed are those who mourn, for they will be comforted."
Matthew 5:4 NIV

Let Your unfailing love comfort me, just as You promised me.
Psalm 119:76 NLT

This is my comfort in my affliction, that Your promise gives me life.
Psalm 119:50 ESV

Have you encountered the dark side of life: the doctor's examination results, the call from the hospital, or a police officer ringing your doorbell? Do you know the place where comfort is found in someone rather than something? Comfort lies deeper than wiping away tears and handing out tissues. True comfort gives light to your darkness. Find comfort in God's presence.

The Law Is Written in Your Heart

"If you love Me, keep My commands. And I will ask the Father, and He will give you another Advocate to help you and be with you forever—the Spirit of truth."
John 14:15-17 NIV

Jesus replied, "All who love Me will do what I say. My Father will love them, and We will come and make Our home with each of them."
John 14:23 NLT

The one who keeps God's commands lives in Him, and He in them. And this is how we know that He lives in us: We know it by the Spirit He gave us.
1 John 3:24 NIV

So Christ has truly set us free. Now make sure that you stay free, and don't get tied up again in slavery to the law.
Galatians 5:1 NLT

"I will give you a new heart and put a new spirit in you; I will remove from you your heart of stone and give you a heart of flesh. And I will put My Spirit in you and move you to follow My decrees and be careful to keep My laws."
Ezekiel 36:26-27 NIV

Loving God means keeping His commandments, and His commandments are not burdensome.
1 John 5:3 NLT

The law cannot reconcile you with God; only the blood of Jesus can. After this reconciliation with God, the law is written in your heart by the Holy Spirit. This law does not become rules and regulations you have to follow, rather a lifestyle of dependence on God and guidance from the Holy Spirit. Jesus came to teach us that love is the intention of the law—love for God, love for our neighbor, and even love for our enemies.

Committed until the End

You shall walk after the LORD your God and fear Him, and keep His commandments and obey His voice; you shall serve Him and hold fast to Him.

Deuteronomy 13:4 NKJV

Only fear the LORD and serve Him faithfully with all your heart. For consider what great things He has done for you.

1 Samuel 12:24 ESV

"What does the LORD your God require of you? He requires only that you fear the LORD your God, and live in a way that pleases Him, and love Him and serve Him with all your heart and soul."

Deuteronomy 10:12 NLT

May your hearts be fully committed to the LORD our God, to live by His decrees and obey His commands.

1 Kings 8:61 NIV

You shall love the LORD your God with all your heart, with all your soul, and with all your strength.

Deuteronomy 6:5 NKJV

Into Your hands I commit my spirit; deliver me, LORD, my faithful God.

Psalm 31:5 NIV

Teach me to do Your will, for You are my God! Let Your good Spirit lead me on level ground!

Psalm 143:10 ESV

Are you really committed to the Lord and His calling for you? Being in such a relationship with Jesus requires that you get out of your comfort zone and trust Him. It asks that you give yourself completely over to Him. This kind of commitment means making the decision to go to the place that God determines for you, even if you're still not sure where it is or what the road ahead looks like. Choose to be committed until the end, even if it is no longer convenient.

Healthy Ways to Communicate

My dear brothers and sisters, take note of this: Everyone should be quick to listen, slow to speak and slow to become angry, because human anger does not produce the righteousness that God desires.
James 1:19-20 NIV

Let the words of my mouth and the meditation of my heart be acceptable in Your sight, O LORD, my rock and my redeemer.
Psalm 19:14 ESV

The mouth of the righteous speaks wisdom, and his tongue talks of justice.
Psalm 37:30 NKJV

Set a guard, O LORD, over my mouth; keep watch over the door of my lips!
Psalm 141:3 ESV

Avoid worthless, foolish talk that only leads to more godless behavior.
2 Timothy 2:16 NLT

The heart of the wise makes his speech judicious and adds persuasiveness to his lips.
Proverbs 16:23 ESV

Let your conversation be always full of grace, seasoned with salt, so that you may know how to answer everyone.
Colossians 4:6 NIV

Communication is the basis of all relationships and is much more than the sum of the words that roll over your lips. Communication consists of 7 percent words, 35 percent tone of voice and 58 percent body language. The non-verbal part of communication is extremely important, and first impressions are made before any words are spoken. Your body language and the tone of your voice play an important role, as well as truly listening. How is your communication?

Saved by Grace

As they were eating, Jesus took bread, blessed and broke it, and gave it to the disciples and said, "Take, eat; this is My body." Then He took the cup, and gave thanks, and gave it to them, saying, "Drink from it, all of you. For this is My blood of the new covenant, which is shed for many for the remission of sins."
Matthew 26:26-28 NKJV

"The true bread of God is the One who comes down from heaven and gives life to the world."
John 6:33 NLT

Whenever you eat this bread and drink this cup, you proclaim the Lord's death until He comes.
1 Corinthians 11:26 NIV

He took some bread and gave thanks to God for it. Then He broke it in pieces and gave it to the disciples, saying, "This is My body, which is given for you. Do this in remembrance of Me." After supper He took another cup of wine and said, "This cup is the new covenant between God and His people—an agreement confirmed with My blood, which is poured out as a sacrifice for you."
Luke 22:19-20 NLT

Let your conversation be always full of grace, seasoned with salt, so that you may know how to answer everyone.
Colossians 4:6 NIV

In the upper room, Jesus instituted Communion for those who struggled. While He was washing His disciples' feet, He knew they would run away. As He was dipping His bread in the bowl, He heard the clinking of thirty coins and betrayal. Even while Peter was speaking, He could hear the sound of a rooster crowing. Jesus knew for whom His body would be broken, and yet He gave Communion. With Communion, God says *yes* to those drowning in His grace. Eat the bread, drink the wine—you are saved.

Part of God's Community

How good and pleasant it is when God's people live together in unity! It is like precious oil poured on the head, running down on the beard, running down on Aaron's beard, down on the collar of his robe.
Psalm 133:1-2 NIV

"Where two or three are gathered together in My name, I am there in the midst of them."
Matthew 18:20 NKJV

Live in harmony with each other. Don't be too proud to enjoy the company of ordinary people. And don't think you know it all!
Romans 12:16 NLT

Let us consider how to stir up one another to love and good works, not neglecting to meet together, as is the habit of some, but encouraging one another, and all the more as you see the Day drawing near.
Hebrews 10:24-25 ESV

Share each other's burdens, and in this way obey the law of Christ.
Galatians 6:2 NLT

We urge you, brothers and sisters, warn those who are idle and disruptive, encourage the disheartened, help the weak, be patient with everyone.
1 Thessalonians 5:14 NIV

As believers we form a community of faith where relationships are important and people grow closer together and to God. A community where we live without masks; where we take care of and serve each other in true love. We help to bear each other's burdens and encourage each other to be the best version of ourselves. Here you will find a safe space where you can lay down your fears and joys before the throne in prayer. It is a testimony of God's Kingdom that functions differently than the world.

Be Compassionate

The LORD is good to everyone. He showers compassion on all His creation.
Psalm 145:9 NLT

The LORD is compassionate and merciful, slow to get angry and filled with unfailing love.
Psalm 103:8 NLT

You are a forgiving God, gracious and compassionate, slow to anger and abounding in love.
Nehemiah 9:17 NIV

Through the LORD's mercies we are not consumed, because His compassions fail not.
Lamentations 3:22 NKJV

As a father has compassion on his children, so the LORD has compassion on those who fear Him.
Psalm 103:13 NIV

"The LORD your God is gracious and merciful. If you return to Him, He will not continue to turn His face from you."
2 Chronicles 30:9 NLT

Return to the LORD your God, for He is gracious and merciful, slow to anger, and of great kindness.
Joel 2:13 NKJV

You, Lord, are a compassionate and gracious God, slow to anger, abounding in love and faithfulness.
Psalm 86:15 NIV

People have a hunger and desperation for unconditional love and compassion. To have compassion is more than just caring or being touched by other people's needs; it is experiencing their pain with them. Their hurt becomes yours. Jesus had compassion for people, felt their need, and then helped them. Learn from Jesus; compassion starts in your heart but ends in an act.

March

Rejoice
in **hope,**

BE PATIENT

in tribulation,
be constant in
prayer.

Romans 12:12

Competing with Others

Pay careful attention to your own work, for then you will get the satisfaction of a job well done, and you won't need to compare yourself to anyone else.
Galatians 6:4 NLT

Let us not become conceited, provoking one another, envying one another.
Galatians 5:26 NKJV

Most people are motivated to success because they envy their neighbors. But this, too, is meaningless—like chasing the wind.
Ecclesiastes 4:4 NLT

"Many who are first will be last, and the last first."
Matthew 19:30 NKJV

Do nothing out of selfish ambition or vain conceit. Rather, in humility value others above yourselves, not looking to your own interests but each of you to the interests of the others.
Philippians 2:3-4 NIV

"Whoever desires to become great among you, let him be your servant."
Matthew 20:26 NKJV

Wherever there is jealousy and selfish ambition, there you will find disorder and evil of every kind.
James 3:16 NLT

"Mine is bigger, smarter, and better than yours. I won!" Unfortunately, every now and then, women are tempted to compete with each other. There is nothing worse in sports than a team not playing together and each player only playing for themselves. Your spouse, your children, your family, and your friends are not your competition; they are on your team. They are God's gift, so you don't have to play the game of life alone. Play as a team so that everyone wins.

Think Before You Complain

Do everything without complaining and arguing, so that no one can criticize you. Live clean, innocent lives as children of God, shining like bright lights in a world full of crooked and perverse people.

Philippians 2:14-15 NLT

Those who are wayward in spirit will gain understanding; those who complain will accept instruction.

Isaiah 29:24 NIV

Let no corrupting talk come out of your mouths, but only such as is good for building up, as fits the occasion, that it may give grace to those who hear.

Ephesians 4:29 ESV

I cry out to the LORD with my voice; with my voice to the LORD I make my supplication. I pour out my complaint before Him; I declare before Him my trouble.

Psalm 142:1-2 NKJV

Evening and morning and at noon I utter my complaint and moan, and He hears my voice.

Psalm 55:17 ESV

Not that I am speaking of being in need, for I have learned in whatever situation I am to be content.

Philippians 4:11 ESV

Don't grumble against one another, brothers and sisters.

James 5:9 NIV

Have you mastered the art of complaining? Complaining to others, to yourself, and to the Lord, about your husband, your boss, things that don't work, the weather, and so on. Ingratitude and discontentment is the source of many complaints. Before you complain about the long queue, remember you've got legs to stand on. Before you complain about the hot car you're sitting in, remember you've got transport while others don't. Swap your complaints for gratitude.

No Condemnation

Therefore, there is now no condemnation for those who are in Christ Jesus, because through Christ Jesus the law of the Spirit who gives life has set you free from the law of sin and death.
Romans 8:1-2 NIV

"God did not send His Son into the world to condemn the world, but that the world through Him might be saved."
John 3:17 NKJV

If our hearts condemn us, we know that God is greater than our hearts, and He knows everything.
1 John 3:20 NIV

Who dares accuse us whom God has chosen for His own? No one—for God Himself has given us right standing with Himself. Who then will condemn us? No one—for Christ Jesus died for us and was raised to life for us, and He is sitting in the place of honor at God's right hand, pleading for us.
Romans 8:33-34 NLT

The LORD will rescue His servants; no one who takes refuge in Him will be condemned.
Psalm 34:22 NIV

"I, even I, am He who blots out your transgressions for My own sake; and I will not remember your sins."
Isaiah 43:25 NKJV

The only One who has the right to judge is He who is without sin. Jesus could condemn you, but God's grace is much greater than the debt that you have, so He invites you to give Him everything. He took your judgment on Himself so you could walk away scot-free, without any convictions. Nobody can judge you anymore because you are a new person in Christ, a child of the King—redeemed.

Confess Your Faith

If anyone acknowledges that Jesus is the Son of God, God lives in them and they in God.
1 John 4:15 NIV

If you confess with your mouth that Jesus is Lord and believe in your heart that God raised Him from the dead, you will be saved. For with the heart one believes and is justified, and with the mouth one confesses and is saved.
Romans 10:9-10 ESV

"Therefore whoever confesses Me before men, him I will also confess before My Father who is in heaven. But whoever denies Me before men, him I will also deny before My Father who is in heaven."
Matthew 10:32-33 NKJV

Simon Peter answered, "You are the Messiah, the Son of the living God."
Matthew 16:16 NLT

So you see, faith by itself isn't enough. Unless it produces good deeds, it is dead and useless...Just as the body is dead without breath, so also faith is dead without good works.
James 2:17, 26 NLT

The only thing that counts is faith expressing itself through love.
Galatians 5:6 NIV

At the name of Jesus every knee should bow...and every tongue declare that Jesus Christ is Lord.
Philippians 2:10-11 NLT

When you confess your faith with your mouth, it becomes engraved on your heart. Then your life becomes the confession that God is your Lord. A confession of faith lived out shows greater evidence of who God is than the one recited by mouth. Maybe you should choose today to believe in spite of your doubts and struggles. Confess your faith with your mouth, keep it in your heart, and live it out every day.

Godly Confidence

"Blessed are those who trust in the LORD and have made the LORD their hope and confidence."
Jeremiah 17:7 NLT

We have placed our confidence in Him, and He will continue to rescue us.
2 Corinthians 1:10 NLT

We can say with confidence, "The LORD is my helper, so I will have no fear. What can mere people do to me?"
Hebrews 13:6 NLT

Because of Christ and our faith in Him, we can now come boldly and confidently into God's presence.
Ephesians 3:12 NLT

The LORD will be your confidence and will keep your foot from being caught.
Proverbs 3:26 ESV

The fruit of that righteousness will be peace; its effect will be quietness and confidence forever.
Isaiah 32:17 NIV

You have been my hope, Sovereign LORD, my confidence since my youth.
Psalm 71:5 NIV

Now this is the confidence that we have in Him, that if we ask anything according to His will, He hears us.
1 John 5:14 NKJV

Stephen Covey said, "Trust is the glue of life. It's the most essential ingredient in effective communication. It's the foundational principle that holds all relationships." To trust God completely means not forcing your own plans but to allow God to give you the best in His time. Trust God to take care of you then you'll remain standing, even in difficult situations. Trust Him with your heart, your marriage, your relationships, your life, and your dreams. He is faithful.

Dealing with Conflict

A gentle answer turns away wrath, but a harsh word stirs up anger.
Proverbs 15:1 NIV

You must all be quick to listen, slow to speak, and slow to get angry.
James 1:19 NLT

Bear with each other and forgive one another if any of you has a grievance against someone. Forgive as the Lord forgave you.
Colossians 3:13 NIV

Never pay back evil with more evil. Do things in such a way that everyone can see you are honorable. Do all that you can to live in peace with everyone.
Romans 12:17-18 NLT

"Blessed are the peacemakers, for they will be called children of God."
Matthew 5:9 NIV

"But I say to you who hear: Love your enemies, do good to those who hate you, bless those who curse you, and pray for those who spitefully use you."
Luke 6:27-28 NKJV

Let all bitterness, wrath, anger, clamor, and evil speaking be put away from you, with all malice. And be kind to one another, tenderhearted, forgiving one another, even as God in Christ forgave you.
Ephesians 4:31-32 NKJV

The two most prominent ways people deal with conflict are fighting and fleeing. In the Word it seems there is a better way, one that ends in a stronger and better relationship. If you choose to fight, there must be a winner and a loser. You don't always have to be fighting to win. Good conflict resolution helps both parties to walk away as winners. Unresolved conflict is an emotional weight, so fleeing won't really help you. Conflict must be dealt with as soon as possible.

Listen to Your Conscience

Let us draw near to God with a sincere heart and with the full assurance that faith brings, having our hearts sprinkled to cleanse us from a guilty conscience and having our bodies washed with pure water.
Hebrews 10:22 NIV

Cling to your faith in Christ, and keep your conscience clear. For some people have deliberately violated their consciences; as a result, their faith has been shipwrecked.
1 Timothy 1:19 NLT

I myself always strive to have a conscience without offense toward God and men.
Acts 24:16 NKJV

Keep your conscience clear. Then if people speak against you, they will be ashamed when they see what a good life you live because you belong to Christ.
1 Peter 3:16 NLT

Even Gentiles, who do not have God's written law, show that they know His law when they instinctively obey it, even without having heard it. They demonstrate that God's law is written in their hearts, for their own conscience and thoughts either accuse them or tell them they are doing right.
Romans 2:14-15 NLT

I will maintain my innocence and never let go of it; my conscience will not reproach me as long as I live.
Job 27:6 NIV

Your conscience is your inner voice that is with you throughout life. It is formed and cultivated by your parents, through culture, and through the Bible. Your conscience is not necessarily the Holy Spirit, because other factors may also play a role. When your life is devoted to God, your conscience is guided by the Holy Spirit and shaped further by the Word. Always test your conscience against the Word so that it will become another way for the Spirit to communicate with you.

Choices Have Consequences

Do not be deceived: God cannot be mocked. A man reaps what he sows.
Galatians 6:7 NIV

An evil man is ensnared in his transgression, but a righteous man sings and rejoices.
Proverbs 29:6 ESV

Death and life are in the power of the tongue, and those who love it will eat its fruit.
Proverbs 18:21 NKJV

For he, too, had done what was evil in the LORD's sight. He followed the example of Jeroboam in all the sins he had committed and led Israel to commit.
1 Kings 16:19 NLT

An evil man is held captive by his own sins; they are ropes that catch and hold him.
Proverbs 5:22 NLT

My experience shows that those who plant trouble and cultivate evil will harvest the same.
Job 4:8 NLT

"Enter through the narrow gate. For wide is the gate and broad is the road that leads to destruction, and many enter through it. But small is the gate and narrow the road that leads to life, and only a few find it."
Matthew 7:13-14 NKJV

Every choice that you make has consequences, and with every consequence comes huge responsibilities. Without realizing it, women are mathematicians that calculate daily what the consequences of their decisions will be. The choice of only working and not spending time with family causes impaired relationships. The choice not to spend time with God results in a feeling of loneliness. Do your calculations and choose wisely.

Be Content with Today

True godliness with contentment is itself great wealth.
1 Timothy 6:6 NLT

For we brought nothing into this world, and it is certain we can carry nothing out. And having food and clothing, with these we shall be content.
1 Timothy 6:7-8 NKJV

Those who love money will never have enough. How meaningless to think that wealth brings true happiness!
Ecclesiastes 5:10 NLT

Enjoy what you have rather than desiring what you don't have. Just dreaming about nice things is meaningless—like chasing the wind.
Ecclesiastes 6:9 NLT

Keep your lives free from the love of money and be content with what you have, because God has said, "Never will I leave you; never will I forsake you."
Hebrews 13:5 NIV

I have learned in whatever situation I am to be content. I know how to be brought low, and I know how to abound. In any and every circumstance, I have learned the secret of facing plenty and hunger, abundance and need.
Philippians 4:11-12 ESV

Better to have little, with godliness, than to be rich and dishonest.
Proverbs 16:8 NLT

Are you satisfied with your spouse, yourself, your kids, your finances, your home, your work, and what you have achieved? Your own discontentment and dissatisfaction is often the reason for your unhappiness. Today, count your blessings and not your shortcomings. Jesus taught us to pray for our daily bread; and yet we are not satisfied with today's bread, we want insurance for the week's bread. Maybe your dissatisfaction is caused by living for the day after tomorrow and not for today.

Learn from Your Mistakes

Whoever heeds life-giving correction will be at home among the wise. Those who disregard discipline despise themselves, but the one who heeds correction gains understanding.
Proverbs 15:31-32 NIV

Let the godly strike me! It will be a kindness! If they correct me, it is soothing medicine. Don't let me refuse it.
Psalm 141:5 NLT

For this command is a lamp, this teaching is a light, and correction and instruction are the way to life.
Proverbs 6:23 NIV

He who keeps instruction is in the way of life, but he who refuses correction goes astray.
Proverbs 10:17 NKJV

If you ignore criticism, you will end in poverty and disgrace; if you accept correction, you will be honored.
Proverbs 13:18 NLT

A fool spurns a parent's discipline, but whoever heeds correction shows prudence.
Proverbs 15:5 NIV

Whoever loves discipline loves knowledge.
Proverbs 12:1 ESV

It takes a special, emotionally intelligent woman with an inner strength and a relationship with God to be corrected in life without becoming a victim of her circumstances. See the criticism that comes your way as positive by asking how you can learn from it and how you can grow from it. Choose to be motivated by correction and to allow it to make you stronger and better.

Counsel without Google

"I will instruct you and teach you in the way you should go; I will counsel you with My eye upon you."
Psalm 32:8 ESV

I will praise the LORD, who counsels me; even at night my heart instructs me.
Psalm 16:7 NIV

You will guide me with Your counsel, and afterward receive me to glory.
Psalm 73:24 NKJV

Plans succeed through good counsel; don't go to war without wise advice.
Proverbs 20:18 NLT

Blessed is the man who walks not in the counsel of the wicked, nor stands in the way of sinners, nor sits in the seat of scoffers; but his delight is in the law of the LORD, and on His law he meditates day and night.
Psalm 1:1-2 ESV

To God belong wisdom and power; counsel and understanding are His.
Job 12:13 NIV

The way of a fool is right in his own eyes, but he who heeds counsel is wise.
Proverbs 12:15 NKJV

When was the last time you followed someone's advice or allowed someone to teach you something? We live in a world where we are self-sufficient—we don't need people's advice anymore because we have Google. Our natural, teachable spirit has decreased because information is quickly accessible when we need it. Be open to God's Word and the Holy Spirit, who is the great advisor teaching you about the things of God and about your daily life.

Courage from a Sparrow

"Fear not, for I am with you; be not dismayed, for I am your God. I will strengthen you, yes, I will help you, I will uphold you with My righteous right hand."
Isaiah 41:10 NKJV

Be on guard. Stand firm in the faith. Be courageous. Be strong.
1 Corinthians 16:13 NLT

Be of good courage, and let us be strong for our people and for the cities of our God. And may the LORD do what is good in His sight.
2 Samuel 10:12 NKJV

Take courage! I believe God. It will be just as He said.
Acts 27:25 NLT

"Are not two sparrows sold for a copper coin? And not one of them falls to the ground apart from your Father's will."
Matthew 10:29 NKJV

Be strong and courageous and do it. Do not be afraid and do not be dismayed, for the LORD God, even my God, is with you. He will not leave you or forsake you.
1 Chronicles 28:20 ESV

Do not be afraid. Stand firm and you will see the deliverance the LORD will bring you today.
Exodus 14:13 NIV

During the Second Anglo-Boer War in South Africa, Anette Marais was kept in a concentration camp in Bethulie with many other women who had lost all hope. She prayed that God would give her words of encouragement, and that morning she read Matthew 10:29. As she was reading, a tiny sparrow came and sat on her shoulder. The women stared in amazement. The sparrow became a sign of courage and hope. After the war, the sparrow appeared on the country's smallest coin. Go share your two cents of courage today.

God's Wonderful Creation

When I look at Your heavens, the work of Your fingers, the moon and the stars, which You have set in place, what is man that You are mindful of him, and the son of man that You care for him?
Psalm 8:3-4 ESV

By Him all things were created, in heaven and on earth, visible and invisible, whether thrones or dominions or rulers or authorities—all things were created through Him and for Him.
Colossians 1:16 ESV

He is the Maker of heaven and earth, the sea, and everything in them—He remains faithful forever.
Psalm 146:6 NIV

The earth is the LORD's, and everything in it, the world, and all who live in it.
Psalm 24:1 NIV

You cause the grass to grow for the livestock and plants for man to cultivate, that he may bring forth food from the earth.
Psalm 104:14 ESV

In His hand are the depths of the earth, and the mountain peaks belong to Him.
Psalm 95:4 NIV

Sometimes we get stuck on the finer details of the story of creation, but the goal has never been to give scientific answers but rather to say who the Creator is and what His intent was with creation. Let's leave the consumer mentality that asks: What do I gain from creation? God created the universe with care so you can have a place to meet Him. Take care of it and enjoy glorifying God along with creation!

Criticism and Your Emotions

If you listen to constructive criticism, you will be at home among the wise.
Proverbs 15:31 NLT

To one who listens, valid criticism is like a gold earring or other gold jewelry.
Proverbs 25:12 NLT

In the end, people appreciate honest criticism far more than flattery.
Proverbs 28:23 NLT

Whoever stubbornly refuses to accept criticism will suddenly be destroyed beyond recovery.
Proverbs 29:1 NLT

Better to be criticized by a wise person than to be praised by a fool.
Ecclesiastes 7:5 NLT

Don't speak evil against each other, dear brothers and sisters. If you criticize and judge each other, then you are criticizing and judging God's law. But your job is to obey the law, not to judge whether it applies to you.
James 4:11 NLT

"If your brother sins against you, go and tell him his fault, between you and him alone. If he listens to you, you have gained your brother."
Matthew 18:15 ESV

Criticism often generates emotions of rejection and failure, even when it is not always the intention. Determine whether the criticism you receive is valid and, if so, be open to self-improvement. All of us have weaknesses, and criticism often shows you your weaknesses. Choose to give positive criticism that will help people to improve rather than destructive criticism that could hurt people. People will forget what you've said or did, but they won't forget how you made them feel.

Hiding from Danger

Fearing people is a dangerous trap, but trusting the LORD means safety.
Proverbs 29:25 NLT

You shall not be afraid of the terror by night, nor of the arrow that flies by day. For He shall give His angels charge over you, to keep you in all your ways.
Psalm 91:5, 11 NKJV

The wise are cautious and avoid danger; fools plunge ahead with reckless confidence.
Proverbs 14:16 NLT

The prudent sees danger and hides himself, but the simple go on and suffer for it.
Proverbs 22:3 ESV

You are my rock and my fortress. For the honor of Your name, lead me out of this danger. Psalm 31:3 NLT

The LORD is my light and my salvation—so why should I be afraid? The LORD is my fortress, protecting me from danger, so why should I tremble?
Psalm 27:1 NLT

The Lord is faithful. He will establish you and guard you against the evil one.
2 Thessalonians 3:3 ESV

What are the dangers that frighten you physically (sickness, distress, violence) or mentally (temptation, discouragement, depression)? The same way a father carries his daughter, God will carry you through every danger. He will hide you under the soft feathers of His wings. He will give light within your darkness. He will protect you from danger. He never sleeps nor slumbers. He will be a safe hiding place in your darkest night.

Light Drives Out Darkness

You LORD, are my lamp; the LORD turns my darkness into light.
2 Samuel 22:29 NIV

Even the darkness will not be dark to You; the night will shine like the day, for darkness is as light to You.
Psalm 139:12 NIV

But you are a chosen people, a royal priesthood, a holy nation, God's special possession, that you may declare the praises of Him who called you out of darkness into His wonderful light.
1 Peter 2:9 NIV

For this light within you produces only what is good and right and true.
Ephesians 5:9 NLT

This is the message we have heard from Him and declare to you: God is light, in Him there is no darkness at all.
1 John 1:5 NIV

"I will turn the darkness into light before them and make the rough places smooth."
Isaiah 42:16 NIV

The light shines in the darkness, and the darkness can never extinguish it.
John 1:5 NLT

"Let your light so shine before men, that they may see your good works and glorify your Father in heaven."
Matthew 5:16 NKJV

Children sometimes experience fear of the dark, but when they stay in the dark long enough, their eyes get used to it and can start seeing silhouettes. Jesus is the light that pushes darkness aside, but He calls you to be light. Light shows you everything, and nothing can hide. Don't become discouraged when others complain about your light—perhaps they are uncomfortable with what they discovered in their darkness. Keep shining!

Death vs. Life

For we know that if the earthly tent we live in is destroyed, we have a building from God, an eternal house in heaven, not built by human hands. Now the one who has fashioned us for this very purpose is God.
2 Corinthians 5:1, 5 NIV

Our earthly bodies are planted in the ground when we die, but they will be raised to live forever. Our bodies are buried in brokenness, but they will be raised in glory. They are buried in weakness, but they will be raised in strength.
1 Corinthians 15:42-43 NLT

"God Himself will be with them. He will wipe every tear from their eyes, and there will be no more death or sorrow or crying or pain. All these things are gone forever."
Revelation 21:3-4 NLT

Jesus told her, "I am the resurrection and the life. Anyone who believes in Me will live, even after dying."
John 11:25 NLT

Since we believe that Jesus died and was raised to life again, we also believe that when Jesus returns, God will bring back with Him the believers who have died.
1 Thessalonians 4:14 NLT

The cross that was once a murder weapon became our salvation, and the resurrection changed everything about death. Jesus experienced an excrutiating day and felt as though God had left Him. All this was part of God's great treasure of grace. Jesus died but was not abandoned, because the Father knew what He was doing. Jesus died trusting God that He would live again, so we may one day die trusting God for new life too—death becomes the gateway to an eternity with God.

Spiritual Deception

No one who trusts in You will ever be disgraced, but disgrace comes to those who try to deceive others.
Psalm 25:3 NLT

Blessed is the one whose sin the LORD does not count against them and in whose spirit is no deceit.
Psalm 32:2 NIV

Vindicate me, O God, and defend my cause against an ungodly people, from the deceitful and unjust man deliver me!
Psalm 43:1 ESV

You destroy those who speak lies; the LORD abhors the bloodthirsty and deceitful man.
Psalm 5:6 ESV

You, God, will bring down the wicked into the pit of decay; the bloodthirsty and deceitful will not live out half their days. But as for me, I trust in You.
Psalm 55:23 NIV

Who may ascend into the hill of the LORD? Or who may stand in His holy place? He who has clean hands and a pure heart, who has not lifted up his soul to an idol, nor sworn deceitfully.
Psalm 24:3-4 NKJV

The integrity of the upright guides them, but the crookedness of the treacherous destroys them.
Proverbs 11:3 ESV

The marketing world can easily mislead people. Just think of how many women were deceived with pills and creams that promised to melt away fat. But after tons of money spent, they still look the same. These days spiritual deception is growing, deceiving the world into thinking that all religions are equal. The Bible is placed into disrepute because it's no longer considered to be the inspired Word of God. Allow the Holy Spirit to guide you and to give you spiritual discernment in this world filled with deception.

Decisions, Decisions

Wisdom will enter your heart, and knowledge will fill you with joy. Wise choices will watch over you. Understanding will keep you safe.
Proverbs 2:10-11 NLT

The precepts of the Lord are right, giving joy to the heart. The commands of the LORD are radiant, giving light to the eyes.
Psalm 19:8 NIV

Trust in the LORD with all your heart; do not depend on your own understanding.
Proverbs 3:5 NLT

Let the Holy Spirit guide your lives. Then you won't be doing what your sinful nature craves.
Galatians 5:16 NLT

If any of you lacks wisdom, let him ask of God, who gives to all liberally and without reproach, and it will be given to him.
James 1:5 NKJV

Wise choices will watch over you. Understanding will keep you safe.
Proverbs 2:11 NLT

"My decisions are true, because I am not alone. I stand with the Father, who sent Me."
John 8:16 NIV

If it is true that today is the result of yesterday's choices, it means that tomorrow will be the result of today's choices. Therefore every choice is important. Even if you think you don't have to make choices, it already implies a choice. Ask yourself: Is my choice violating anything in the Word? Can I choose it with integrity even if no-one knows about it? How would I feel if it were somebody else's decision? Choose well because it affects your future.

Dedicated to God

Show me Your ways, LORD, teach me Your paths.
Psalm 25:4 NIV

Teach me to do Your will, for You are my God. May Your gracious Spirit lead me forward on a firm footing.
Psalm 143:10 NLT

Search me, O God, and know my heart; try me, and know my anxieties; and see if there is any wicked way in me, and lead me in the way everlasting.
Psalm 139:23-24 NKJV

"Anyone who wants to do the will of God will know whether My teaching is from God or is merely My own."
John 7:17 NLT

Without faith it is impossible to please God, because anyone who comes to Him must believe that He exists and that He rewards those who earnestly seek Him.
Hebrews 11:6 NIV

For God saved us and called us to live a holy life.
2 Timothy 1:9 NLT

You have six days each week for your ordinary work, but the seventh day must be a Sabbath day of complete rest, a holy day dedicated to the LORD.
Exodus 31:15 NLT

Is a dedicated life to the Lord possible, and how do I measure it? You may need to ask yourself: how important is God to me? The ideal priority list puts God first, but if you were honest it looks somewhat different. A dedicated life means He is your whole life, not simply now and then when you have a moment. At every opportunity, you live your relationship with Him, and you and your abilities are at His disposal.

Faith and Deeds

Now may our Lord Jesus Christ Himself and God our Father, who loved us and by His grace gave us eternal comfort and a wonderful hope, comfort you and strengthen you in every good thing you do and say.
2 Thessalonians 2:16-17 NLT

Whatever you do, whether in word or deed, do it all in the name of the Lord Jesus, giving thanks to God the Father through Him.
Colossians 3:17 NIV

For in Christ Jesus neither circumcision nor uncircumcision avails anything, but faith working through love.
Galatians 5:6 NKJV

Keep your conduct among the Gentiles honorable, so that when they speak against you as evildoers, they may see your good deeds and glorify God on the day of visitation.
1 Peter 2:12 ESV

Let them give thanks to the LORD for His unfailing love and His wonderful deeds for mankind.
Psalm 107:8 NIV

You see, His faith and His actions worked together. His actions made His faith complete.
James 2:22 NLT

Faith and deeds are like the head and tail of a coin; inseparable. True faith eventually turns into action, so your actions confirm what you believe and will be one of the strongest testimonies about your faith. There is a famous quote that says we should proclaim the gospel and if necessary use words. Good deeds are not done to impress and satisfy someone; they are driven by the spirit of gratitude and want to honor God and His Name.

Defended by God

Let all those rejoice who put their trust in You; let them ever shout for joy, because You defend them; let those also who love Your name be joyful in You.
Psalm 5:11 NKJV

You, Lord, took up my case; You redeemed my life.
Lamentations 3:58 NIV

Thus says your Lord, the LORD and your God, who pleads the cause of His people: "See, I have taken out of your hand the cup of trembling."
Isaiah 51:22 NKJV

For the angel of the LORD is a guard; He surrounds and defends all who fear Him.
Psalm 34:7 NLT

To You, O my Strength, I will sing praises; for God is my defense, my God of mercy.
Psalm 59:17 NKJV

A father to the fatherless, a defender of widows, is God in His holy dwelling.
Psalm 68:5 NIV

So be strong and courageous! Do not be afraid and do not panic before them. For the LORD your God will personally go ahead of you. He will neither fail you nor abandon you.
Deuteronomy 31:6 NLT

When God says He will defend and protect you, it means that He is close to you. This doesn't mean that the mountain before you is simply going to disappear or the cross you're carrying is just going to crumble. It means that He is standing in the middle of your crises and fighting on your behalf. This doesn't mean that you will always be without scars, but the scars will remind you of who defended you and secured the victory for you.

An Instrument in His Hands

Christ Himself gave the apostles, the prophets, the evangelists, the pastors and teachers, to equip His people for works of service, so that the body of Christ may be built up until we all reach unity in the faith and in the knowledge of the Son of God and become mature, attaining to the whole measure of the fullness of Christ.
Ephesians 4:11-13 NIV

You have heard me teach things that have been confirmed by many reliable witnesses. Now teach these truths to other trustworthy people who will be able to pass them on to others.
2 Timothy 2:2 NLT

Jesus called His twelve disciples together and gave them authority to cast out evil spirits and to heal every kind of disease and illness. Jesus sent out the twelve apostles with these instructions: "Don't go to the Gentiles or the Samaritans, but only to the people of Israel—God's lost sheep. Go and announce to them that the Kingdom of Heaven is near."
Matthew 10:1, 5-7 NLT

Select capable men from all the people—men who fear God, trustworthy men who hate dishonest gain—and appoint them as officials over thousands, hundreds, fifties and tens.
Exodus 18:21 NIV

A woman was standing with her alabaster jar before Jesus and poured out her expensive perfume on Him. Everything she was and owned was given to serving Him. You also received an alabaster jar full of gifts and talents, so you can serve Him, His children, and the world. This doesn't mean anything if you leave it standing somewhere as an ornament for everyone to see. Share what's in your jar, but also allow others to share their jars. Become instruments for Him.

Delight in the Lord

The LORD your God is with you, the Mighty Warrior who saves. He will take great delight in you; in His love He will no longer rebuke you, but will rejoice over you with singing.
Zephaniah 3:17 NIV

The LORD takes delight in His people; He crowns the humble with victory.
Psalm 149:4 NIV

The LORD directs the steps of the godly. He delights in every detail of their lives.
Psalm 37:23 NLT

The LORD's delight is in those who fear Him, those who put their hope in His unfailing love.
Psalm 147:11 NLT

I was in distress, but the LORD supported me. He led me to a place of safety; He rescued me because He delights in me.
Psalm 18:18-19 NLT

The LORD corrects those He loves, just as a father corrects a child in whom he delights.
Proverbs 3:12 NLT

The LORD detests lying lips, but He delights in people who are trustworthy.
Proverbs 12:22 NIV

The LORD delights in the prayers of the upright.
Proverbs 15:8 NLT

How would you describe God to someone who doesn't know Him? Perhaps as your Father, Savior, Creator, Conqueror, Shelter, or Light. Zephaniah said that God takes great delight in you. He is the God who finds joy in His creation. He is the source of joy and therefore, He plants His seed of joy through the fruit of the Spirit in you. Joy is not only a gift; it is a divine characteristic.

God Will Deliver You

Then they cried out to the LORD in their trouble, and He delivered them from their distress.
Psalm 107:6 NIV

The LORD is my rock and my fortress and my deliverer; my God, my strength, in whom I will trust; my shield and the horn of my salvation, my stronghold. I will call upon the LORD, who is worthy to be praised; so shall I be saved from my enemies.
Psalm 18:2-3 NKJV

I sought the LORD, and He answered me; He delivered me from all my fears.
Psalm 34:4 NIV

"Call upon Me in the day of trouble; I will deliver you, and you shall glorify Me."
Psalm 50:15 NKJV

"Do not be afraid, for I have ransomed you. I have called you by name; you are Mine. When you go through deep waters, I will be with you. When you go through rivers of difficulty, you will not drown. When you walk through the fire of oppression, you will not be burned up; the flames will not consume you. For I am the LORD, your God, the Holy One of Israel, your Savior."
Isaiah 43:1-3 NLT

When you find yourself in a dark hole of despair with no way out, it's the exact place where God's salvation—His love for you and His power—are revealed. In your distress, call to Him, and He will save you. It is He who can rebuke the storm and calm the waves. God wants to save you from your pit of sorrow, difficulties, and fears. Trust Him; He will not let you down.

Depend on God

The LORD is good to those who depend on Him, to those who search for Him.
Lamentations 3:25 NLT

They all depend on You to give them food as they need it. When You supply it, they gather it. You open Your hand to feed them, and they are richly satisfied.
Psalm 104:27-28 NLT

What sorrow awaits those who look to Egypt for help, trusting their horses, chariots, and charioteers and depending on the strength of human armies instead of looking to the LORD, the Holy One of Israel.
Isaiah 31:1 NLT

Trust in the LORD with all your heart; do not depend on your own understanding. Seek His will in all you do, and He will show you which path to take.
Proverbs 3:5-6 NLT

My salvation and my honor depend on God; He is my mighty rock, my refuge.
Psalm 62:7 NIV

Come back to your God. Act with love and justice, and always depend on Him.
Hosea 12:6 NLT

"I am the vine, you are the branches. He who abides in Me, and I in him, bears much fruit; for without Me you can do nothing."
John 15:5 NKJV

God knows you. He planned you in the finest detail and wove you together with a piece of frailty and vulnerability, so you will always be aware of your dependence on Him. In your dependence you will realize and acknowledge that He is the one who gives you power, gifts, and talents. You will realize that everything comes from His hand. To fully depend on God and live a humble life means to get just enough for today and await His advice and guidance for tomorrow.

The Dark Hole of Depression

Why, my soul, are you downcast? Why so disturbed within me? Put your hope in God, for I will yet praise Him, my Savior and my God.
Psalm 42:11 NIV

You, O LORD, are a shield for me, my glory and the One who lifts up my head.
Psalm 3:3 NKJV

The eternal God is your refuge, and underneath are the everlasting arms.
Deuteronomy 33:27 NKJV

The LORD Himself goes before you and will be with you; He will never leave you nor forsake you. Do not be afraid; do not be discouraged.
Deuteronomy 31:8 NIV

I waited patiently for the LORD to help me, and He turned to me and heard my cry. He lifted me out of the pit of despair, out of the mud and the mire. He set my feet on solid ground and steadied me as I walked along. He has given me a new song to sing, a hymn of praise to our God. Many will see what He has done and be amazed. They will put their trust in the LORD.
Psalm 40:1-3 NLT

The LORD hears His people when they call to Him for help. He rescues them from all their troubles.
Psalm 34:17 NLT

Depression is not a new disease. In the Bible, Elijah, Moses, and David showed signs of depression. It is remarkable that every time someone finds themselves in a deep pit, God doesn't give explanations and instructions, but rather promises and love. We don't live by explanations but by promises. If you ever find yourself in a deep, dark hole, do not look for answers, rather seek God's promises. Exchange your depression for God's promises.

Desert Times

He split open the rocks in the wilderness to give them water, as from a gushing spring.
Psalm 78:15 NLT

"I cared for you in the wilderness, in the land of burning heat."
Hosea 13:5 NIV

Our fathers ate the manna in the wilderness; as it is written, "He gave them bread from heaven to eat."
John 6:31 ESV

For forty years You sustained them in the wilderness, and they lacked nothing. Their clothes did not wear out, and their feet did not swell!
Nehemiah 9:21 NLT

The desert and the parched land will be glad; the wilderness will rejoice and blossom. It will burst into bloom; it will rejoice greatly and shout for joy. They will see the glory of the LORD, the splendor of our God. Strengthen the feeble hands, steady the knees that give way; say to those with fearful hearts, "Be strong, do not fear; your God will come, He will come with vengeance; with divine retribution He will come to save you."
Isaiah 35:1-4 NIV

The wilderness is untouched and isolated; the place where God and His children are in confrontation but also where encounters with Him take place. For many, the desert is the place of calling, like Moses, John, and later Jesus. It is also the place where people once again discover their dependence on God and His care, like manna, quail, and water from the rock. Don't be negative about your desert; it brings you one step closer to your promised land.

The Desires of Your Heart

What the wicked dread will overtake them; what the righteous desire will be granted.
Proverbs 10:24 NIV

He will fulfill the desire of those who fear Him; He also will hear their cry and save them.
Psalm 145:19 NKJV

Desire without knowledge is not good, and whoever makes haste with his feet misses his way.
Proverbs 19:2 ESV

You, LORD, hear the desire of the afflicted; You encourage them, and You listen to their cry.
Psalm 10:17 NIV

Delight yourself also in the LORD, and He shall give you the desires of your heart.
Psalm 37:4 NKJV

Praise the LORD, my soul; all my inmost being, praise His holy name. Praise the LORD, my soul, and forget not all His benefits—who forgives all your sins and heals all your diseases, who redeems your life from the pit and crowns you with love and compassion, who satisfies your desires with good things so that your youth is renewed like the eagle's.
Psalm 103:1-5 NIV

Desires have a way of getting stuck in your heart. Before you realize it, you are trapped in dissatisfaction and desire your neighbor's husband or the money your friend has. This evil desire for things and possessions is prohibited. In contrast the Spirit gives us good desires—to be wise, to be a good wife and mother, a yearning to always be in God's presence, and to make a difference in the Kingdom. These desires are fulfilled by God.

A Woman with Determination

They were just trying to intimidate us, imagining that they could discourage us and stop the work. So I continued the work with even greater determination.
Nehemiah 6:9 NLT

Jesus replied, "No one who puts a hand to the plow and looks back is fit for service in the kingdom of God."
Luke 9:62 NIV

It gives us new life to know that you are standing firm in the LORD.
1 Thessalonians 3:8 NLT

As for you, brethren, do not grow weary in doing good.
2 Thessalonians 3:13 NKJV

Fight the good fight of the faith. Take hold of the eternal life to which you were called and about which you made the good confession in the presence of many witnesses.
1 Timothy 6:12 ESV

Don't you realize that in a race everyone runs, but only one person gets the prize? So run to win! All athletes are disciplined in their training. They do it to win a prize that will fade away, but we do it for an eternal prize. So I run with purpose in every step. I am not just shadowboxing. I discipline my body like an athlete, training it to do what it should.
1 Corinthians 9:24-27 NLT

Ruth was determined to stay with Naomi and accepted her God despite their circumstances. She stood firm and later became the great-grandmother of David, an ancestor of Jesus. Esther was determined to stand up for her people and saved them. Mary was determined to anoint Jesus' feet with her perfume despite the disciples' comments and the culture that didn't want her gift. Like these women, we must remain determined to submit ourselves to God's use.

A Truly Devoted Heart

Jesus replied: "'Love the LORD your God with all your heart and with all your soul and with all your mind.'"
Matthew 22:37 NIV

Search me, O God, and know my heart; try me, and know my anxieties.
Psalm 139:23 NKJV

My soul yearns, even faints, for the courts of the LORD; my heart and my flesh cry out for the living God.
Psalm 84:2 NIV

I will praise You, O LORD, with my whole heart; I will tell of all Your marvelous works.
Psalm 9:1 NKJV

Let us draw near with a true heart in full assurance of faith, having our hearts sprinkled from an evil conscience and our bodies washed with pure water.
Hebrews 10:22 NKJV

May He strengthen your hearts so that you will be blameless and holy in the presence of our God and Father when our Lord Jesus comes with all His holy ones.
1 Thessalonians 3:13 NIV

Only fear the LORD, and serve Him in truth with all your heart; for consider what great things He has done for you.
1 Samuel 12:24 NKJV

The Lord Jesus often withdrew Himself from the masses of people to pray in solitary places. The modern woman makes little effort to set aside time to be truly alone with God. We can "multi-task," so we think we are still before the Lord while we're sorting out other things. But it is precisely in the silence of solitude where you are able to truly listen to your own heart, become cleansed by Jesus, and hear and see God.

April

Be
COMPLETELY
humble
& *gentle;*
BE PATIENT,
bearing with
one another in
love.

Ephesians 4:2

Miracles in Tough Times

"For I am the LORD your God who takes hold of your right hand and says to you, 'Do not fear, I will help you.'"
Isaiah 41:13 NIV

When troubles of any kind come your way, consider it an opportunity for great joy. For you know that when your faith is tested, your endurance has a chance to grow.
James 1:2-3 NLT

Blessed is the one who perseveres under trial because, having stood the test, that person will receive the crown of life.
James 1:12 NIV

The LORD is my strength and my shield; my heart trusts in Him, and He helps me.
Psalm 28:7 NIV

"When you go through deep waters, I will be with you. When you go through rivers of difficulty, you will not drown. When you walk through the fire of oppression, you will not be burned up; the flames will not consume you."
Isaiah 43:2 NLT

"Don't let your hearts be troubled. Trust in God, and trust also in Me."
John 14:1 NLT

Glory in tribulations, knowing that tribulation produces perseverance; and perseverance, character; and character, hope.
Romans 5:3-4 NKJV

In difficult times it can often feel like your faith is challenged, and yet this is when you have the greatest opportunity to testify. God has always used tough times for His glory, especially in the crucifixion. When you find yourself in difficult times, it is in that moment that God showcases His full strength. This is where Emmanuel, God with you, who is closer than your skin, your Refuge and Protector, also becomes your miracle worker.

Dreadful Disappointment

Why are you cast down, O my soul? And why are you disquieted within me? Hope in God, for I shall yet praise Him for the help of His countenance.
Psalm 42:5 NKJV

The LORD directs the steps of the godly. He delights in every detail of their lives. Though they stumble, they will never fall, for the LORD holds them by the hand.
Psalm 37:23-24 NLT

"Those who hope in Me will not be disappointed."
Isaiah 49:23 NIV

The LORD is close to the brokenhearted; He rescues those whose spirits are crushed.
Psalm 34:18 NLT

We know that in all things God works for the good of those who love Him, who have been called according to His purpose.
Romans 8:28 NIV

Let them thank the LORD for His steadfast love, for His wondrous works to the children of man! For He satisfies the longing soul, and the hungry soul He fills with good things.
Psalm 107:8-9 ESV

Let us not grow weary while doing good, for in due season we shall reap if we do not lose heart.
Galatians 6:9 NKJV

Disappointment is a reality that comes after expectations have not been met. Good Friday was a dark day; a lot of dreams and hopes came to a halt, and people were disappointed because they expected that He would deliver them. After each disappointment God creates a new beginning, a resurrection moment. Spend time with God and stay positive. Your disappointment might be the announcement of a new, better future and a satisfaction that only God can give.

Striving for Godly Discernment

I am Your servant; give me discernment that I may understand Your statutes.
Psalm 119:125 NIV

O LORD, listen to my cry; give me the discerning mind You promised.
Psalm 119:169 NLT

These proverbs will give insight to the simple, knowledge and discernment to the young.
Proverbs 1:4 NLT

If you cry out for discernment, and lift up your voice for understanding; then you will understand the fear of the LORD, and find the knowledge of God.
Proverbs 2:3, 5 NKJV

Wisdom is found on the lips of the discerning, but a rod is for the back of one who has no sense.
Proverbs 10:13 NIV

Let the wise listen and add to their learning, and let the discerning get guidance.
Proverbs 1:5 NIV

It is my prayer that your love may abound more and more, with knowledge and all discernment, so that you may approve what is excellent, and so be pure and blameless for the day of Christ, filled with the fruit of righteousness that comes through Jesus Christ, to the glory and praise of God.
Philippians 1:9-10 ESV

To live with discernment is no longer a luxury but a necessity. There is an increase in knowledge everywhere, but people's discernment has decreased. Discernment is to seek God's plan by having a personal relationship with Him and sensitivity to the Holy Spirit. Prayer plays an important role in this listening process as you have to weigh and sieve everything to distinguish what is really from God and what is not.

Follow Jesus

"As it is written in the Scriptures, 'They will all be taught by God.' Everyone who listens to the Father and learns from Him comes to Me."
John 6:45 NLT

God called you to do good, even if it means suffering, just as Christ suffered for you. He is your example, and you must follow in His steps.
1 Peter 2:21 NLT

"Let your light so shine before men, that they may see your good works and glorify your Father in heaven."
Matthew 5:16 NKJV

"Look, these are My mother and brothers. Anyone who does God's will is My brother and sister and mother."
Mark 3:34-35 NLT

"Take My yoke upon you and learn from Me, for I am gentle and lowly in heart, and you will find rest for your souls."
Matthew 11:29 NKJV

"Your love for one another will prove to the world that you are My disciples."
John 13:35 NLT

"Whoever does not take up their cross and follow Me is not worthy of Me."
Matthew 10:38 NIV

Discipleship requires a commitment from you that is more than just following Jesus. It requires that you be the difference that the world needs; that you will know God's heart and make some sacrifices for others. To be a disciple requires that you be the salt of the earth and not constantly judge people over previous mistakes. Disciples are people who can't wait to spread God's good news.

I Give Up!

The LORD Himself goes before you and will be with you; He will never leave you nor forsake you. Do not be afraid; do not be discouraged.
Deuteronomy 31:8 NIV

Be strong and courageous, and do the work. Don't be afraid or discouraged, for the LORD God, my God, is with you. He will not fail you or forsake you.
1 Chronicles 28:20 NLT

Do not be afraid or discouraged. Go out against them tomorrow, for the LORD is with you!
2 Chronicles 20:17 NLT

He himself went a day's journey into the wilderness and came and sat down under a broom tree. And he asked that he might die, saying, "It is enough; now, O LORD, take away my life, for I am no better than my fathers."
1 Kings 19:4 ESV

Fathers, do not aggravate your children, or they will become discouraged.
Colossians 3:21 NKJV

For consider Him who endured such hostility from sinners against Himself, lest you become weary and discouraged in your souls.
Hebrews 12:3 NKJV

Do you feel discouraged, hopeless, and despondent today? You wonder which way to go and feel overwhelmed by life. Under the broom tree, Elijah also felt discouraged, tired, and burned out. He just wanted to die. When Elijah was at his lowest, God came to meet him where he was and provided him with exactly what he needed—water, food, rest, care, and another calling and purpose. The same God, through His Spirit, wants to provide for you and lift you out of despair. Don't give up.

No Excuse for Dishonesty

Do not lie to each other, since you have taken off your old self with its practices and have put on the new self, which is being renewed in knowledge in the image of its Creator.
Colossians 3:9-10 NIV

"You shall not bear false witness against your neighbor."
Exodus 20:16 NKJV

A dishonest man spreads strife, and a whisperer separates close friends.
Proverbs 16:28 ESV

The LORD detests lying lips, but He delights in people who are trustworthy.
Proverbs 12:22 NIV

There are six things the LORD hates—no, seven things He detests: haughty eyes, a lying tongue, hands that kill the innocent, a heart that plots evil, feet that race to do wrong, a false witness who pours out lies, a person who sows discord in a family.
Proverbs 6:16-19 NLT

Therefore each of you must put off falsehood and speak truthfully to your neighbor, for we are all members of one body.
Ephesians 4:25 NIV

Honesty guides good people; dishonesty destroys treacherous people.
Proverbs 11:3 NLT

Women of God must live with integrity and honesty. Honesty begins with you. Where do I stand in my relationship with God? How do I feel about my neighbor and myself? It spills over into your family, where you can hide your dishonesty only for so long, setting an example for your children with your life. Avoid dishonest business practices despite the benefits you think it might have for you. God will reward you for your honesty.

When in Doubt

"Stop doubting and believe."
John 20:27 NLT

Jesus immediately reached out His hand and took hold of him, saying, "O you of little faith, why did you doubt?"
Matthew 14:31 ESV

When doubts filled my mind, Your comfort gave me renewed hope and cheer.
Psalm 94:19 NLT

Then Jesus told him, "You believe because you have seen Me. Blessed are those who believe without seeing Me."
John 20:29 NLT

Jesus said to the disciples, "Have faith in God. I tell you the truth, you can say to this mountain, 'May you be lifted up and thrown into the sea,' and it will happen. But you must really believe it will happen and have no doubt in your heart."
Mark 11:22-23 NLT

Jesus replied, "Truly I tell you, if you have faith and do not doubt, not only can you do what was done to the fig tree, but also you can say to this mountain, 'Go, throw yourself into the sea,' and it will be done. If you believe, you will receive whatever you ask for in prayer."
Matthew 21:21-22 NIV

When you're in doubt, stretch your trembling hand out to God to save you from the stormy seas. All of us experience doubt, and we catch ourselves acting like Thomas. We want to put our finger in the nail marks on Jesus' hands. We want to see evidence of the promises of tomorrow's providence or the forgiveness of sin. We are desperately clinging to the thought that love will heal our broken hearts. May your doubts drive you into the arms of God where His peace will drive away your doubts like a gentle breeze.

Chasing Your Dreams

"It shall come to pass afterward that I will pour out My Spirit on all flesh; your sons and your daughters shall prophesy, your old men shall dream dreams, your young men shall see visions."
Joel 2:28 NKJV

Now to Him who is able to do immeasurably more than all we ask or imagine, according to His power that is at work within us.
Ephesians 3:20 NIV

Hope deferred makes the heart sick, but a dream fulfilled is a tree of life.
Proverbs 13:12 NLT

Take courage! Do not let your hands be weak, for your work shall be rewarded.
2 Chronicles 15:7 ESV

Every good gift and every perfect gift is from above, coming down from the Father of lights, with whom there is no variation or shadow due to change.
James 1:17 NIV

Blessed is the man whose strength is in You, whose heart is set on pilgrimage.
Psalm 84:5 ESV

"I am the LORD your God, who teaches you what is best for you, who directs you in the way you should go."
Isaiah 48:17 NIV

On Good Friday it seemed that Jesus blew out the candle of everyone's dreams, and it literally and figuratively became dark. At that moment everyone forgot about God's power and His miracles. But on Resurrection Sunday, Jesus relit the candles of people's dreams and rekindled their hope. Suddenly scared fishermen, His disciples, changed into evangelists who lived every dream of God, even at the cost of their own lives. Hold on to your dreams, even if it feels dark, "Sunday" is coming.

Seeking God in All Earnest

He who earnestly seeks good finds favor, but trouble will come to him who seeks evil.
Proverbs 11:27 NKJV

You, God, are my God, earnestly I seek You; I thirst for You, my whole being longs for You, in a dry and parched land where there is no water.
Psalm 63:1 NIV

Then He said to His disciples, "The harvest is plentiful, but the laborers are few; therefore pray earnestly to the LORD of the harvest to send out laborers into His harvest."
Matthew 9:37-38 ESV

"And it shall be that if you earnestly obey My commandments which I command you today, to love the LORD your God and serve Him with all your heart and with all your soul, then I will give you the rain for your land in its season, the early rain and the latter rain, that you may gather in your grain, your new wine, and your oil."
Deuteronomy 11:13-14 NKJV

In the night I search for You; in the morning I earnestly seek You. For only when You come to judge the earth will people learn what is right.
Isaiah 26:9 NLT

We need to understand the seriousness of God's call—He is waiting for His lost children to return. Like a loving Father with arms wide open, He is welcoming each one back. We should seek after Him with the same earnest heart. And through the Holy Spirit, we learn that there is only one way to find Him and that is through Jesus. Through Him we discover the omnipresent God. Seek God, because everything that you need is found in Him.

Mixed Emotions

Fools vent their anger, but the wise quietly hold it back.
Proverbs 29:11 NLT

A merry heart makes a cheerful countenance, but by sorrow of the heart the spirit is broken.
Proverbs 15:13 NKJV

Rejoice with those who rejoice; mourn with those who mourn.
Romans 12:15 NIV

Everyone should be quick to listen, slow to speak and slow to become angry, because human anger does not produce the righteousness that God desires.
James 1:19-20 NIV

Better to be patient than powerful; better to have self-control than to conquer a city.
Proverbs 16:32 NLT

If our hearts condemn us, we know that God is greater than our hearts, and He knows everything.
1 John 3:20 NIV

A hot-tempered man stirs up strife, but he who is slow to anger quiets contention.
Proverbs 15:18 ESV

A merry heart does good, like medicine, but a broken spirit dries the bones.
Proverbs 17:22 NKJV

The more you experience trauma and rejection, the more you tend to deny or suppress those experiences. Later you battle to identify them. Nobody can make you feel a certain way without your consent. You can always control your emotions. Don't make important decisions when experiencing strong emotions like anger or sadness. Look to God when you feel depressed or sad; then you will be able to think more clearly. Take deep breaths, and listen to relaxing music to help calm you down.

Be Encouraged

"Be strong and courageous! Do not be afraid or discouraged. For the LORD your God is with you wherever you go."
Joshua 1:9 NLT

You, LORD, hear the desire of the afflicted; You encourage them, and You listen to their cry, defending the fatherless and the oppressed.
Psalm 10:17-18 NIV

May our LORD Jesus Christ Himself and God our Father, who loved us and by His grace gave us eternal encouragement and good hope, encourage your hearts and strengthen you in every good deed and word.
2 Thessalonians 2:16-17 NIV

The humble will see their God at work and be glad. Let all who seek God's help be encouraged. For the LORD hears the cries of the needy.
Psalm 69:32-33 NLT

Encourage one another and build each other up, just as in fact you are doing.
1 Thessalonians 5:11 NIV

Your words have supported those who were falling; you encouraged those with shaky knees.
Job 4:4 NLT

Worry weighs a person down; an encouraging word cheers a person up.
Proverbs 12:25 NLT

Children make us do things we never thought possible. You decided long ago that you will never cheer and scream like a lunatic during sports until your five-year old runs her first race and shouting loudly comes naturally. Every day we are engaged in a spiritual journey, and you have to choose whether to be a spectator or an encourager. You have to decide whether to allow others to encourage you so you can endure to the end or not. Do not yell at those who feel discouraged; encourage them with a passionate heart!

The End Times

There will be terrible times in the last days. People will be lovers of themselves, lovers of money, boastful, proud, abusive, disobedient to their parents, ungrateful, unholy, without love, unforgiving, slanderous, without self-control, brutal, not lovers of the good, treacherous, rash, conceited, lovers of pleasure rather than lovers of God—having a form of godliness but denying its power. Have nothing to do with such people.
2 Timothy 3:1-5 NIV

God, who at various times and in various ways spoke in time past to the fathers by the prophets, has in these last days spoken to us by His Son.
Hebrews 1:1 NKJV

"In the last days," God says, "I will pour out My Spirit on all people. Your sons and daughters will prophesy, your young men will see visions, your old men will dream dreams."
Acts 2:17 NIV

Dear children, the last hour is here. You have heard that the Antichrist is coming, and already many such antichrists have appeared. From this we know that the last hour has come.
1 John 2:18 NLT

On that day living water will flow out from Jerusalem...The LORD will be king over the whole earth. On that day there will be one LORD, and His name the only name.
Zechariah 14:8-9 NIV

Are the disasters of our day announcing the end times? No. Jesus' ascension announced it, and therefore we are living in the end times already. The Bible teaches us that the end times are at hand. God speaks to us through Jesus, and He poured out His Spirit on us to help us. Jesus and the outpouring of the Spirit were the first signs of the end times. Let us pray that His Kingdom will come soon, and may you be ready for it.

Endure to the End

Let us throw off everything that hinders and the sin that so easily entangles. And let us run with perseverance the race marked out for us, fixing our eyes on Jesus, the pioneer and perfecter of faith. For the joy set before Him He endured the cross scorning its shame, and sat down at the right hand of God.
Hebrews 12:1-2 NIV

I press on toward the goal to win the prize for which God has called me.
Philippians 3:14 NIV

You need to persevere so that when you have done the will of God, you will receive what He has promised.
Hebrews 10:36 NIV

May the God of endurance and encouragement grant you to live in such harmony with one another, in accord with Christ Jesus, that together you may with one voice glorify the God and Father of our Lord Jesus Christ.
Romans 15:5-6 ESV

We rejoice in our sufferings, knowing that suffering produces endurance, and endurance produces character, and character produces hope, and hope does not put us to shame, because God's love has been poured into our hearts through the Holy Spirit who has been given to us.
Romans 5:3-5 ESV

All of us show endurance until the demands of life test us. And not all of us pass the test. You can say to the world today: This is not easy, but even the worst thing will not get the better of me. I will continue, no matter how difficult it may be. Because in Christ, I am more than a conqueror! Through His strength, not mine, I will overcome! That is why you need more of God in your life today.

Turning Enemies into Friends

"If the world hates you, keep in mind that it hated Me first. If you belonged to the world, it would love you as its own. As it is, you do not belong to the world, but I have chosen you out of the world. That is why the world hates you."
John 15:18-19 NIV

Love your enemies, do good, and lend, hoping for nothing in return; and your reward will be great, and you will be sons of the Most High. For He is kind to the unthankful and evil.
Luke 6:35 NKJV

"But I tell you, love your enemies and pray for those who persecute you."
Matthew 5:44 NIV

Rescue me from my enemies, O God. Protect me from those who have come to destroy me. Rescue me from these criminals; save me from these murderers. Fierce enemies are out there waiting, LORD. See what is happening and help me!
Psalm 59:1-4 NLT

Lead me, LORD, in Your righteousness because of my enemies—make Your way straight before me.
Psalm 5:8 NIV

Do not let your heart envy sinners, but always be zealous for the fear of the LORD.
Proverbs 23:17 NIV

None of us want to have enemies, and yet it is inevitable. The trick is not to have no enemies, but rather to act differently towards them than how the world treats its enemies. Look at them through the eyes of the Cross, where mercy makes friends of enemies. If we still lived with the viewpoint of an eye for an eye, we would all be seeking retribution. Two wrongs don't make a right, and enemies can only be won over by showering them with undeserved love.

Bottomless Energy

Do you not know? Have you not heard? The LORD is the everlasting God, the Creator of the ends of the earth. He will not grow tired or weary, and His understanding no one can fathom. He gives strength to the weary and increases the power of the weak.
Isaiah 40:28-29 NIV

Times of refreshment will come from the presence of the LORD.
Acts 3:20 NLT

Never be lacking in zeal, but keep your spiritual fervor, serving the LORD.
Romans 12:11 NIV

Refresh my heart in Christ.
Philemon 1:20 ESV

May you be strengthened with all power, according to His glorious might, for all endurance and patience with joy, giving thanks to the Father, who has qualified you to share in the inheritance of the saints in light.
Colossians 1:11-12 ESV

To this end I strenuously contend with all the energy Christ so powerfully works in me.
Colossians 1:29 NIV

He restores my soul; He leads me in the paths of righteousness for His name's sake.
Psalm 23:3 NKJV

Research has shown that a high-sugar snack won't necessarily increase your energy levels. Sometimes you think something is good for you, while the opposite is in fact true. Women often tend to draw their energy from relationships, their looks, or what they have achieved, while it is actually just adrenaline rushing through their system. Energy is found in your secret place, at the Source of all energy, during a wholesome meal and when we rest in God.

Spurred on by Enthusiasm

Enthusiasm without knowledge is no good; haste makes mistakes.
Proverbs 19:2 NLT

Work with enthusiasm, as though you were working for the LORD rather than for people. Remember that the LORD will reward each one of us for the good we do, whether we are slaves or free.
Ephesians 6:7-8 NLT

Always work enthusiastically for the LORD, for you know that nothing you do for the LORD is ever useless.
1 Corinthians 15:58 NLT

Give me an eagerness for Your laws rather than a love for money!
Psalm 119:36 NLT

I have come out to meet You, to seek You eagerly, and I have found You.
Proverbs 7:15 ESV

May I wholeheartedly follow Your decrees, that I may not be put to shame.
Psalm 119:80 NIV

Whatever your hand finds to do, do it with your might.
Ecclesiastes 9:10 NKJV

Never be lazy, but work hard and serve the Lord enthusiastically.
Romans 12:11 NLT

Martin Luther said, "What you do in your house is worth as much as if you did it up in heaven for our Lord God." Your work and what you need to do on earth is part of your destiny. Therefore we are spurred on by enthusiasm, hope, and commitment to do our work unto the Lord and for His glory. By the presence and the power of the Spirit, your job becomes your passion and the place where God's blessing is distributed to all people.

The Green-Eyed Monster

Do not let your heart envy sinners, but always be zealous for the fear of the LORD.
Proverbs 23:17 NIV

So get rid of all evil behavior. Be done with all deceit, hypocrisy, jealousy, and all unkind speech. Like newborn babies, you must crave pure spiritual milk so that you will grow into a full experience of salvation.
1 Peter 2:1-2 NLT

Let us not become conceited, provoking one another, envying one another.
Galatians 5:26 NKJV

Fret not yourself because of evildoers; be not envious of wrongdoers!
Psalm 37:1 ESV

Do not envy the wicked, do not desire their company; for their hearts plot violence, and their lips talk about making trouble.
Proverbs 24:1-2 NIV

Do not envy the oppressor, and choose none of his ways.
Proverbs 3:31 NKJV

A tranquil heart gives life to the flesh, but envy makes the bones rot.
Proverbs 14:30 ESV

Resentment kills a fool, and envy slays the simple.
Job 5:2 NIV

That green, frayed jacket doesn't belong in your closet, and yet you don't want to get rid of it. At work, church, on the sports field, and at home you occasionally wear it and hope nobody notices. But the jacket is bright green, and its name is envy. Envy can consume you, and it springs from uncertainty about who you are in Christ. Be content with what you have and count your blessings. There is always someone else wishing they had what you have.

Equal in His Sight

From one man He made all the nations, that they should inhabit the whole earth; and He marked out their appointed times in history and the boundaries of their lands.

Acts 17:26 NIV

There is neither Jew nor Greek, there is neither slave nor free, there is no male and female, for you are all one in Christ Jesus.

Galatians 3:28 ESV

For the Lord your God is God of gods and Lord of lords, the great God, mighty and awesome, who shows no partiality nor takes a bribe.

Deuteronomy 10:17 NKJV

My brothers and sisters, believers in our glorious Lord Jesus Christ must not show favoritism. Suppose a man comes into your meeting wearing a gold ring and fine clothes, and a poor man in filthy old clothes also comes in. If you show special attention to the man wearing fine clothes and say, "Here's a good seat for you," but say to the poor man, "You stand there" or "Sit on the floor by my feet," have you not discriminated among yourselves and become judges with evil thoughts?

James 2:1-4 NIV

God does not show favoritism.

Romans 2:11 NLT

In Jesus we are joined together and equal before God. In our spiritual family, Jesus is the only Head, and we are called to serve Him. No one is more important than another, so we should have respect and dignity for all. Even in marriage, husband and wife were created equal before God with distinct differences and responsibilities. Jesus came to teach us that the one who wants to be first must be last and a servant of all.

Eternity in Heaven

For the wages of sin is death, but the free gift of God is eternal life through Christ Jesus our LORD.
Romans 6:23 NLT

"For God so loved the world that He gave His one and only Son, that whoever believes in Him shall not perish but have eternal life."
John 3:16 NIV

"I give them eternal life, and they shall never perish; no one will snatch them out of My hand. My Father, who has given them to Me, is greater than all; no one can snatch them out of My Father's hand. I and the Father are one."
John 10:28-30 NIV

Because Jesus lives forever, He has a permanent priesthood. Therefore He is able to save completely those who come to God through Him, because He always lives to intercede for them.
Hebrews 7:24-25 NIV

"Teacher, what should I do to inherit eternal life?" Jesus replied, "What does the law of Moses say? How do you read it?" The man answered, "You must love the LORD your God with all your heart, all your soul, all your strength, and all your mind.' And, 'Love your neighbor as yourself.'" "Right!" Jesus told him. "Do this and you will live!"
Luke 10:25-28 NLT

Eternal life sounds like something that's supposed to happen one day in the future. There are too many things that require your attention here and now. Little do you realize that eternal life has already started for God's children. You can make phone calls with a fixed line, but smartphones exist. The new way of living is already available to God's children. Don't battle ahead with your fixed home line when you already have access to a smartphone.

Know Right from Wrong

"Do to others whatever you would like them to do to you. This is the essence of all that is taught in the law and the prophets."
Matthew 7:12 NLT

"And just as you want men to do to you, you also do to them likewise."
Luke 6:31 NKJV

Finally, all of you, be like-minded, be sympathetic, love one another, be compassionate and humble.
1 Peter 3:8 NIV

You must use accurate scales when you weigh out merchandise, and you must use full and honest measures.
Deuteronomy 25:13-14 NLT

The integrity of the upright will guide them, but the perversity of the unfaithful will destroy them.
Proverbs 11:3 NKJV

Better the poor whose walk is blameless than a fool whose lips are perverse.
Proverbs 19:1 NIV

May integrity and uprightness protect me, because my hope, LORD, is in You.
Psalm 25:21 NIV

Let love be without hypocrisy. Abhor what is evil. Cling to what is good. Be kindly affectionate to one another with brotherly love, in honor giving preference to one another.
Romans 12:9-10 NKJV

Is it right or wrong, good or bad? Is everything black and white, or are there grey areas? How will I manage to always act ethically? Suddenly this little word *ethics* raises many questions and doubts. Perhaps the better question is: Am I doing the right thing in the right way for the right reasons? Ethics is not supposed to be words on paper, but rather a lifestyle—it's God's heart and values that become ours. Ethics is the Word that lives in us.

The Bearer of Good News

For this is what the LORD has commanded us: "'I have made you a light for the Gentiles, that you may bring salvation to the ends of the earth.'"
Acts 13:47 NIV

"No one lights a lamp and then puts it under a basket. Instead, a lamp is placed on a stand, where it gives light to everyone in the house. In the same way, let your good deeds shine out for all to see, so that everyone will praise your heavenly Father."
Matthew 5:15-16 NLT

Oh, give thanks to the LORD! Call upon His name; make known His deeds among the peoples!
Psalm 105:1 NKJV

Consequently, faith comes from hearing the message, and the message is heard through the word about Christ.
Romans 10:17 NIV

God wanted them to know that the riches and glory of Christ are for you Gentiles, too. And this is the secret: Christ lives in you. This gives you assurance of sharing His glory.
Colossians 1:27 NLT

You should keep a clear mind in every situation. Don't be afraid of suffering for the LORD. Work at telling others the Good News, and fully carry out the ministry God has given you.
2 Timothy 4:5 NLT

God has called you—where you are in your town, at work, and among your friends—to be the bearer of His good news. Through your testimony and sharing God's story, you sow the seeds that He will help to grow. Later it will become easier to mingle with the people you don't see eye to eye with while at the sports field, in the shop, or while you wait at school. In time, you'll be able to share Jesus' love and tell them that He died for them.

Find Joy in the Lord

The LORD lives! Praise be to my Rock! Exalted be God my Savior!
Psalm 18:46 NIV

Be exalted, O LORD, in Your strength! We will sing and praise Your power.
Psalm 21:13 ESV

I will exalt You, LORD, for You rescued me. You refused to let my enemies triumph over me.
Psalm 30:1 NLT

I will glory in the LORD. Glorify the LORD with me; let us exalt His name together.
Psalm 34:2-3 NIV

You are my God, and I will praise You; You are my God, and I will exalt You.
Psalm 118:28 NIV

"Be still, and know that I am God; I will be exalted among the nations, I will be exalted in the earth!" The LORD of hosts is with us; the God of Jacob is our refuge.
Psalm 46:10-11 NKJV

Be exalted, O God, above the heavens; let Your glory be over all the earth.
Psalm 57:5 NIV

Your unfailing love is higher than the heavens. Your faithfulness reaches to the clouds. Be exalted, O God, above the highest heavens. May Your glory shine over all the earth.
Psalm 108:4-5 NLT

Praise the Lord, lift up His name! To praise Him is rooted in your awareness of His intense involvement in your life. How many of your conversations with God focus on Him, and how many are about you? If we desire an intimate relationship with Him, it is necessary to focus more on Him in our conversations, prayers, and worship. Let some of your prayers only glorify and exalt Him without listing your needs before Him. Find joy in Him. And praise His name.

Be a Good Example

Follow my example, as I follow the example of Christ.
1 Corinthians 11:1 NIV

Don't let anyone look down on you because you are young, but set an example for the believers in speech, in conduct, in love, in faith and in purity.
1 Timothy 4:12 NIV

Care for the flock that God has entrusted to you. Watch over it willingly, not grudgingly—not for what you will get out of it, but because you are eager to serve God. Don't lord it over the people assigned to your care, but lead them by your own good example.
1 Peter 5:2-3 NLT

Remember your leaders, those who spoke to you the word of God. Consider the outcome of their way of life, and imitate their faith.
Hebrews 13:7 ESV

In everything set them an example by doing what is good. In your teaching show integrity, seriousness and soundness of speech that cannot be condemned, so that those who oppose you may be ashamed because they have nothing bad to say about us.
Titus 2:7-8 NIV

Whatever you have learned or received or heard from me, or seen in me—put it into practice. And the God of peace will be with you.
Philippians 4:9 NIV

Albert Schweitzer said, "There are only three ways to teach a child. The first is by example, the second is by example, the third is by example." Can you say with certainty that your example can be followed in how you drive, relax, spend your quiet time, and talk to other people? A wrong example is like a crumpled piece of paper; it's hard to get all the creases out. Many young people's actions are learned behavior. Follow Jesus' example and follow in His steps.

Exceptional Excellence

Lord, our Lord, how excellent is Your name in all the earth, who have set Your glory above the heavens!
Psalm 8:1 NKJV

Ascribe strength to God; His excellence is over Israel, and His strength is in the clouds.
Psalm 68:34 NKJV

You are more glorious and excellent than the mountains of prey.
Psalm 76:4 NKJV

Praise Him for His mighty deeds; praise Him according to His excellent greatness!
Psalm 150:2 ESV

Sing to the Lord, for He has done excellent things; this is known in all the earth.
Isaiah 12:5 NKJV

In the greatness of Your excellence You have overthrown those who rose against You.
Exodus 15:7 NKJV

By His divine power, God has given us everything we need for living a godly life. We have received all of this by coming to know Him, the one who called us to Himself by means of His marvelous glory and excellence.
2 Peter 1:3 NLT

God is a God of excellence. The one who gave Himself as ransom in the place of all people; the one who seeks after the lost and downhearted. Are you Solomon with all your riches, Lazarus who took the crumbs off other people's tables, Zacchaeus who fell out of the tree into His grace, or Paul the cleric who became a man of God? This exceptional God chose to be your God, and He invites you into His Kingdom.

Reasonable Expectations

The hope of the righteous will be gladness, but the expectation of the wicked will perish.
Proverbs 10:28 NKJV

Hope deferred makes the heart sick, but a longing fulfilled is a tree of life.
Proverbs 13:12 NIV

For the needy shall not always be forgotten; the expectation of the poor shall not perish forever.
Psalm 9:18 NKJV

My soul, wait silently for God alone, for my expectation is from Him.
Psalm 62:5 NKJV

The desire of the righteous ends only in good; the expectation of the wicked in wrath.
Proverbs 11:23 ESV

The teaching of Your word gives light, so even the simple can understand. I pant with expectation, longing for Your commands.
Psalm 119:130-131 NLT

It is my eager expectation and hope that I will not be at all ashamed, but that with full courage now as always Christ will be honored in my body, whether by life or by death. For to me to live is Christ, and to die is gain.
Philippians 1:20-21 ESV

Disappointments are often the result of a woman's high expectations, and reality that just doesn't measure up. What are your expectations for your marriage, your children, your work, and your friendships? Have you shared your expectation with these key people? Is the expectation that you have of others fair and feasible? Maybe you couldn't meet other people's reasonable expectations. Go and make peace, forgive yourself, and give your weaknesses over to God in prayer.

One Step Closer to Victory

We are pressed on every side by troubles, but we are not crushed. We are perplexed, but not driven to despair. We are hunted down, but never abandoned by God. We get knocked down, but we are not destroyed.
2 Corinthians 4:8-9 NLT

The LORD upholds all who fall, and raises up all who are bowed down.
Psalm 145:14 NKJV

Thanks be to God, who in Christ always leads us in triumphal procession, and through us spreads the fragrance of the knowledge of Him everywhere.
2 Corinthians 2:14 ESV

"I will rescue those who love Me. I will protect those who trust in My name."
Psalm 91:14 NLT

The godly may trip seven times, but they will get up again. But one disaster is enough to overthrow the wicked.
Proverbs 24:16 NLT

He will not let your foot slip— He who watches over you will not slumber.
Psalm 121:3 NIV

He said to me, "My grace is sufficient for you, for my power is made perfect in weakness." Therefore I will boast all the more gladly of my weaknesses, so that the power of Christ may rest upon me.
2 Corinthians 12:9 ESV

"I have not failed. I've just found 10,000 ways that won't work." These are the words of Thomas Edison after many failed attempts before inventing the light bulb in 1879. If Edison gave up we would still be sitting in the dark. If Alexander Bell gave up after failure, we would be without telephones. Failure is an event; it doesn't define you. Keep going when you have failed and be one step closer to victory.

Being Fair and Just

God is just: He will pay back trouble to those who trouble you.
2 Thessalonians 1:6 NIV

For You have judged in my favor; from Your throne You have judged with fairness.
Psalm 9:4 NLT

He will judge the world with justice and rule the nations with fairness. Psalm 9:8 NLT

The LORD detests the use of dishonest scales, but He delights in accurate weights.
Proverbs 11:1 NLT

Do not twist justice in legal matters by favoring the poor or being partial to the rich and powerful. Always judge people fairly. Leviticus 19:15 NLT

He protects all his bones, not one of them will be broken. Evil will slay the wicked; the foes of the righteous will be condemned.
Psalm 34:20-21 NIV

Speak up and judge fairly; defend the rights of the poor and needy.
Proverbs 31:9 NIV

Reverence for the LORD is pure, lasting forever. The laws of the LORD are true; each one is fair.
Psalm 19:9 NLT

Your justice is eternal, and your instructions are perfectly true.
Psalm 119:142 NLT

When the Bible talks about being just and fair, it doesn't mean you're perfect or without sin. It is about what is in your heart, your faith in God, and your appreciation and love for Him and His promises. It's about how you deal with people. Is God fair according to our human understanding? Fortunately not, otherwise we are all lost. His thoughts are far above ours, and His heart is full of love. He looks beyond what you deserve and showers you with undeserved kindness.

Faith like a Mustard Seed

Jesus said, "All things are possible for one who believes."
Mark 9:23 ESV

"I tell you the truth, if you had faith even as small as a mustard seed, you could say to this mountain, 'Move from here to there,' and it would move. Nothing would be impossible."
Matthew 17:20 NLT

In all circumstances take up the shield of faith, with which you can extinguish all the flaming darts of the evil one.
Ephesians 6:16 ESV

Faith is the substance of things hoped for, the evidence of things not seen.
Hebrews 11:1 NKJV

What good is it if someone claims to have faith but has no deeds? Can such faith save them? Suppose a brother or a sister is without clothes and daily food. If one of you says to them, "Go in peace; keep warm and well fed," but does nothing about their physical needs, what good is it? In the same way, faith by itself, if it is not accompanied by action, is dead. But someone will say, "You have faith; I have deeds." Show me your faith without deeds, and I will show you my faith by my deeds. Likewise, was not Rahab the harlot also justified by works when she received the messengers and sent them out another way?
James 2:14-18, 25 NIV

Sometimes the labels people put on you prevent you from doing what you know you were meant to do in faith. God makes heroes of ordinary people—it doesn't matter who you are, where you come from, where you live, or the career you chose. Jesus throws a buoy to people who don't deserve it, like Rahab, Tamar, and Ruth. Those who choose to believe and live their lives in faith become an important part of God's ultimate plan of salvation. Believe it and live in faith.

God Is Faithful

The heavens praise Your wonders, LORD, Your faithfulness too, in the assembly of the holy ones.
Psalm 89:5 NIV

If we are faithless, He remains faithful; He cannot deny Himself.
2 Timothy 2:13 NKJV

God is faithful, who has called you into fellowship with His Son, Jesus Christ our LORD.
1 Corinthians 1:9 NIV

Your faithfulness extends to every generation, as enduring as the earth You created.
Psalm 119:90 NLT

Let us hold fast the confession of our hope without wavering, for He who promised is faithful.
Hebrews 10:23 ESV

The faithful love of the LORD never ends! His mercies never cease. Great is His faithfulness; His mercies begin afresh each morning.
Lamentations 3:22-23 NLT

He is the Maker of heaven and earth, the sea, and everything in them—He remains faithful forever.
Psalm 146:6 NIV

The LORD always keeps His promises; He is gracious in all He does.
Psalm 145:13 NLT

God is faithful! His actions are not determined by who we are but are inherent to His character and who He is. Even if you are unfaithful, God remains faithful. When you struggle to pray, He prays on your behalf. If you have trouble seeing God, He is dwelling amongst us. If you are weak, He is strong. He faithfully keeps every one of His promises. At the right time, He will faithfully fulfill His promises to you.

Keep the Family Together

As for me and my household, we will serve the LORD.
Joshua 24:15 NIV

"Honor your father and mother. Then you will live a long, full life in the land the LORD your God will give you."
Exodus 20:12 NLT

Direct your children onto the right path, and when they are older, they will not leave it.
Proverbs 22:6 NLT

Her children stand and bless her. Her husband praises her: "There are many virtuous and capable women in the world, but you surpass them all!"
Proverbs 31:28-29 NLT

Do not provoke your children to anger, but bring them up in the discipline and instruction of the LORD.
Ephesians 6:4 ESV

For the Christian wife brings holiness to her marriage, and the Christian husband brings holiness to his marriage. Otherwise, your children would not be holy, but now they are holy.
1 Corinthians 7:14 NLT

Blessed are those who fear the LORD, who find great delight in His commands. Their children will be mighty in the land; the generation of the upright will be blessed.
Psalm 112:1-2 NIV

As a woman, you establish the atmosphere that makes your house a home. You serve without getting credit. You sacrifice yourself for the benefit of your family. Your influence is so important. You're a big reason for your husband's success and your children feeling safe. What is better than a home where a father blesses his family, a mother prays that God's Kingdom comes, and children play and laugh joyfully? You are the glue that keeps your family together.

Fasting in Dedication to God

"When you fast, do not look somber as the hypocrites do, for they disfigure their faces to show others they are fasting. Truly I tell you, they have received their reward in full. But when you fast, put oil on your head and wash your face, so that it will not be obvious to others that you are fasting, but only to your Father, who is unseen; and your Father, who sees what is done in secret, will reward you."

Matthew 6:16-18 NIV

"Is not this the kind of fasting I have chosen?...when you see the naked, to clothe them, and not to turn away from your own flesh and blood?"

Isaiah 58:6-7 NIV

Do not deprive one another except with consent for a time, that you may give yourselves to fasting and prayer; and come together again so that Satan does not tempt you because of your lack of self-control.

1 Corinthians 7:5 NKJV

Whether you eat or drink or whatever you do, do it all for the glory of God.

1 Corinthians 10:31 NIV

"If My people who are called by My name will humble themselves, and pray and seek My face, and turn from their wicked ways, then I will hear from heaven, and will forgive their sin and heal their land."

2 Chronicles 7:14 NKJV

Fasting is a spiritual and religious discipline. It's not done for health reasons or weight loss. It is accompanied by prayer, reading the Bible, and quiet time with God. Decide to take advantage of your time of fasting and prayer; be still in His Word. When John Knox fasted and prayed, the wicked Queen Mary of Scots, known as "Bloody Mary," said she feared no weapon as much as she feared the prayers of John Knox.

Weary of Life?

He gives strength to the weary and increases the power of the weak.
Isaiah 40:29 NIV

Those who trust in the LORD will find new strength. They will soar high on wings like eagles. They will run and not grow weary. They will walk and not faint.
Isaiah 40:31 NLT

"I will refresh the weary and satisfy the faint."
Jeremiah 31:25 NIV

I am exhausted and completely crushed. My groans come from an anguished heart...Come quickly to help me, O LORD my Savior.
Psalm 38:8, 22 NLT

Take a new grip with your tired hands and strengthen your weak knees. Mark out a straight path for your feet so that those who are weak and lame will not fall but become strong.
Hebrews 12:12-13 NLT

The LORD will display His glory, the splendor of our God. With this news, strengthen those who have tired hands, and encourage those who have weak knees.
Isaiah 35:2-3 NLT

"Come to Me, all you who are weary and burdened, and I will give you rest."
Matthew 11:28 NIV

How many balls are you juggling at the moment? Has life thrown an extra ball or two your way which you have to juggle too? At night you are exhausted and have to do the same again tomorrow. Elijah was tired, exhausted, and overworked. He did not lose his faith, only his vision. Under the broom tree God did not lecture Elijah but gave him food, water, and rest. God knows what you need most, and He is ready to provide for you in abundance.

The Gift of God's Favor

The LORD God is a sun and shield; the LORD bestows favor and honor; no good thing does He withhold from those whose walk is blameless.
Psalm 84:11 NIV

Sing the praises of the LORD, you His faithful people; praise His holy name. For His anger lasts only a moment, but His favor lasts a lifetime; weeping may stay for the night, but rejoicing comes in the morning.
Psalm 30:4-5 NIV

Let all who take refuge in You be glad; let them ever sing for joy. Surely, LORD, You bless the righteous; You surround them with Your favor as with a shield.
Psalm 5:12 NIV

Glory to God in the highest heaven, and on earth peace to those on whom His favor rests.
Luke 2:14 NIV

Obviously, I'm not trying to win the approval of people, but of God. If pleasing people were my goal, I would not be Christ's servant.
Galatians 1:10 NLT

Let the favor of the Lord our God be upon us, and establish the work of our hands upon us; yes, establish the work of our hands!
Psalm 19:17 ESV

When you seek someone's favor, it often involves choosing your words carefully. You do everything to impress that person. Sometimes we wrongly think that our actions, our words, and our efforts are needed for God's favor. The wonderful thing is that you already have God's favor; you cannot earn it. Jesus paid the full price so you can receive His favor. Use it to fulfill your calling—it shows our gratitude for His undeserved grace.

No Longer Slaves to Fear

He will cover you with His pinions, and under His wings you will find refuge; His faithfulness is a shield and buckler. You will not fear the terror of the night, nor the arrow that flies by day, nor the pestilence that stalks in darkness, nor the destruction that wastes at noonday.

Psalm 91:4-6 ESV

Be strong, and do not fear, for your God is coming to destroy your enemies. He is coming to save you.

Isaiah 35:4 NLT

"For I am the LORD your God who takes hold of your right hand and says to you, 'Do not fear; I will help you.'"

Isaiah 41:13 NIV

God has not given us a spirit of fear and timidity, but of power, love, and self-discipline.

2 Timothy 1:7 NLT

There is no fear in love. But perfect love drives out fear, because fear has to do with punishment. The one who fears is not made perfect in love.

1 John 4:18 NIV

All who are led by the Spirit of God are children of God. So you have not received a spirit that makes you fearful slaves. Instead, you received God's Spirit when He adopted you as His own children. Now we call Him, "Abba, Father."

Romans 8:14-15 NLT

Fear has many faces—fear of disease, failure, retirement or financial stress. If you don't overcome fear, you will struggle to reach your full potential. It paralyzes you and keeps you from enjoying the full power of the Spirit. Fear blinds you to God and His power and makes us forget all about the victories He has given in the past. Although the shadow of fear is very big, fear itself is small. He hasn't given us a spirit of fear but of victory.

Fellowship of Believers

Let us think of ways to motivate one another to acts of love and good works. And let us not neglect our meeting together, as some people do, but encourage one another, especially now that the day of His return is drawing near.
Hebrews 10:24-25 NLT

If we walk in the light, as He is in the light, we have fellowship with one another, and the blood of Jesus His Son cleanses us from all sin.
1 John 1:7 ESV

Be devoted to one another in love. Honor one another above yourselves.
Romans 12:10 NIV

Be kind and compassionate to one another, forgiving each other, just as in Christ God forgave you.
Ephesians 4:32 NIV

Bear one another's burdens, and so fulfill the law of Christ.
Galatians 6:2 NKJV

"A new command I give you: Love one another. As I have loved you, so you must love one another. By this everyone will know that you are My disciples, if you love one another."
John 13:34-35 NIV

Cheerfully share your home with those who need a meal or a place to stay.
1 Peter 4:9 NLT

"You don't need to be part of a fellowship of believers because church attendance won't save you!" This statement deprives women of fellowship with believers, which is more than just a get-together on a Sunday—it's a life lived together in unity. Because Jesus saved you, you should honor Him with other believers and love each other, because it's His blood that binds us together. You need this kind of fellowship with others to carry, love, and support you. And they also need you.

Fighting the Good Fight

Fight the good fight of the faith. Take hold of the eternal life to which you were called when you made your good confession in the presence of many witnesses.

1 Timothy 6:12 NIV

I have fought the good fight, I have finished the race, I have kept the faith.

2 Timothy 4:7 NKJV

You therefore must endure hardship as a good soldier of Jesus Christ. No one engaged in warfare entangles himself with the affairs of this life, that he may please him who enlisted him as a soldier.

2 Timothy 2:3-4 NKJV

Our struggle is not against flesh and blood, but against the rulers, against the authorities, against the powers of this dark world and against the spiritual forces of evil in the heavenly realms.

Ephesians 6:12 NIV

They have conquered him by the blood of the Lamb and by the word of their testimony, for they loved not their lives even unto death. Therefore, rejoice, O heavens and you who dwell in them! But woe to you, O earth and sea, for the devil has come down to you in great wrath, because he knows that his time is short!

Revelation 12:11-12 ESV

Every day is a battle to keep the faith. Your opponent, Satan, is walking around like a roaring lion who wants to destroy your faith. To fight the good fight is to keep the faith, to trust God in all circumstances, and to spend lots of time in prayer. Kick off your high heels, take off your makeup, and put on the full armor of God so that you can finish the race and receive the victor's crown.

Managing Money

"Bring all the tithes into the storehouse so there will be enough food in My Temple. If you do," says the LORD Almighty, "I will open the windows of heaven for you. I will pour out a blessing so great you won't have enough room to take it in. Try it! Put Me to the test!"
Malachi 3:10 NLT

God will supply every need of yours according to His riches in glory in Christ Jesus.
Philippians 4:19 ESV

When God gives someone wealth and possessions, and the ability to enjoy them, to accept their lot and be happy in their toil—this is a gift of God.
Ecclesiastes 5:19 NIV

"When you give to someone in need, don't let your left hand know what your right hand is doing. Give your gifts in private, and your Father, who sees everything, will reward you."
Matthew 6:3-4 NLT

Those who desire to be rich fall into temptation, into a snare, into many senseless and harmful desires that plunge people into ruin and destruction. For the love of money is a root of all kinds of evils.
1 Timothy 6:9-10 ESV

"Your Father knows the things you have need of before you ask Him."
Matthew 6:8 NKJV

The Bible mentions money over 800 times and makes over 2,000 financial references. Sometimes we wonder what makes the world go round: money that is gone in an instant or an eternal God? Do you realize that your finances stand in the service of God and His plans? Finances are a spiritual matter—it's how God guides you in managing what is His. The problem is not money, but rather how important it is to you. Be content with what you have.

Finishing Well

How can a young man cleanse his way? By taking heed according to Your word.
Psalm 119:9 NKJV

I am certain that God, who began the good work within you, will continue His work until it is finally finished on the day when Christ Jesus returns.
Philippians 1:6 NLT

Look to yourselves, that we do not lose those things we worked for, but that we may receive a full reward.
2 John 1:8 NKJV

The end of a matter is better than its beginning, and patience is better than pride.
Ecclesiastes 7:8 NIV

My life is worth nothing to me unless I use it for finishing the work assigned me by the LORD Jesus—the work of telling others the Good News about the wonderful grace of God.
Acts 20:24 NLT

I press on toward the goal to win the prize for which God has called me heavenward in Christ Jesus.
Philippians 3:14 NIV

I have fought the good fight, I have finished the race, I have kept the faith. Finally, there is laid up for me the crown of righteousness, which the Lord, the righteous Judge, will give to me on that Day.
2 Timothy 4:7-8 NKJV

Maybe your life did not start off great. Your childhood years were unstable and painful. As a mother, you made a lot of mistakes when you were younger. Things at work did not start well. It's not how you start that matters but how you finish. Think of Peter. He did not have a great start. "I don't know this Man you're talking about" (Mark 14:71). But he ended well: "Lord, You know that I love You" (John 21:15). He preached and people repented. How do you want to finish?

Set Your Focus on Jesus

Blessed are those who keep His statutes and seek Him with all their heart.

Psalm 119:2 NIV

Test all things; hold fast what is good.

1 Thessalonians 5:21 NKJV

You will keep in perfect peace those whose minds are steadfast, because they trust in You.

Isaiah 26:3 NIV

Those who live according to the flesh set their minds on the things of the flesh, but those who live according to the Spirit, the things of the Spirit.

Romans 8:5 NKJV

Let your eyes look straight ahead; fix your gaze directly before you.

Proverbs 4:25 NIV

If then you have been raised with Christ, seek the things that are above, where Christ is, seated at the right hand of God. Set your minds on things that are above, not on things that are on earth.

Colossians 3:1-2 ESV

Let us run with endurance the race God has set before us. We do this by keeping our eyes on Jesus, the champion who initiates and perfects our faith.

Hebrews 12:1-2 NLT

With binoculars everything that is far away becomes beautiful and in focus. But sometimes when you look at things close up, they seem distorted. When your focus is the world, you will see all the chaos, and God will be a vague image that doesn't fit in. When your focus is set on God and His Kingdom, you can face the world that is out of focus. That's why Noah could build an ark, Daniel could stand in the lions' den, and Paul could sing in jail—their focus was on God.

What Would Jesus Do?

Jesus answered, "If you want to be perfect, go, sell your possessions and give to the poor, and you will have treasure in heaven. Then come, follow Me."
Matthew 19:21 NIV

Then He said to another, "Follow Me." But he said, "LORD, let me first go and bury my father." Jesus said to him, "Let the dead bury their own dead, but you go and preach the kingdom of God."
Luke 9:59-60 NKJV

Then Jesus said to them, "Follow Me, and I will make you become fishers of men."
Mark 1:17 NKJV

Then He said to the crowd, "If any of you wants to be My follower, you must give up your own way, take up your cross daily, and follow Me. If you try to hang on to your life, you will lose it. But if you give up your life for My sake, you will save it."
Luke 9:23-24 NLT

Jesus said to His disciples, "Whoever wants to be My disciple must deny themselves and take up their cross and follow Me."
Matthew 16:24 NIV

Jesus spoke to them again, saying, "I am the light of the world. He who follows Me shall not walk in darkness, but have the light of life."
John 8:12 NKJV

Jesus was a passionate man who didn't cling to heavenly status or worldly possessions. He stood up against injustice. He rose early and set aside time to pray. He didn't care what people were going to say as He ate with tax collectors and sinners and lepers. Jesus lived outside the box. To Him the important people were children, the poor, widows, and those who did not know God. Maybe that's exactly what you must do to follow Him.

Citizens of Heaven

We are citizens of heaven, where the LORD Jesus Christ lives. And we are eagerly waiting for Him to return as our Savior.
Philippians 3:20 NLT

"If the world hates you, you know that it hated Me before it hated you. If you were of the world, the world would love its own. Yet because you are not of the world, but I chose you out of the world, therefore the world hates you."
John 15:18-19 NKJV

Dear friends, I warn you as "temporary residents and foreigners" to keep away from worldly desires that wage war against your very souls.
1 Peter 2:11 NLT

"They are not of the world, even as I am not of it."
John 17:16 NIV

We are foreigners and strangers in your sight, as were all our ancestors. Our days on earth are like a shadow, without hope.
1 Chronicles 29:15 NIV

All these people were still living by faith when they died. They did not receive the things promised; they only saw them and welcomed them from a distance, admitting that they were foreigners and strangers on earth.
Hebrews 11:13 NIV

You can spot tourists from a distance when they visit your country. You can hear their foreign accent or language, they look different, and their behavior and culture is different. As daughters of God, we are pilgrims and strangers in this world, because we are citizens of His Kingdom. We should therefore not withdraw from the world, but we should talk, look, and act differently.

A Silver Lining

As far as the east is from the west, so far has He removed our transgressions from us.
Psalm 103:12 NIV

All the prophets testify about Him that everyone who believes in Him receives forgiveness of sins through His name.
Acts 10:43 NIV

Now there is no condemnation for those who belong to Christ Jesus. And because you belong to Him, the power of the life-giving Spirit has freed you from the power of sin that leads to death.
Romans 8:1-2 NLT

If anyone sins, we have an Advocate with the Father, Jesus Christ the righteous. And He Himself is the propitiation for our sins, and not for ours only but also for the whole world.
1 John 2:1-2 NKJV

He stooped down again and wrote in the dust...Jesus said, "Go and sin no more."
John 8:8, 11 NLT

We praise God for the glorious grace He has poured out on us who belong to His dear Son. He is so rich in kindness and grace that He purchased our freedom with the blood of His Son and forgave our sins.
Ephesians 1:6-7 NLT

Are you walking around with a heavy bag of guilt and sin, looking for the garbage dump to throw it all away? Some women carry around a lot of baggage that tires them out. The same hand that wrote the Ten Commandments on stone is the hand that writes the word *grace* on your heart. He can carry your load—after all He died on the cross for you. Give your heavy burdens over to Him, and walk away with a much lighter load.

Paid in Full

Sin is no longer your master, for you no longer live under the requirements of the law. Instead, you live under the freedom of God's grace.
Romans 6:14 NLT

"If the Son sets you free, you will be free indeed."
John 8:36 ESV

Live as people who are free, not using your freedom as a cover-up for evil, but living as servants of God.
1 Peter 2:16 ESV

Now the LORD is the Spirit, and where the Spirit of the LORD is, there is freedom.
2 Corinthians 3:17 ESV

He will keep you strong to the end so that you will be free from all blame on the day when our LORD Jesus Christ returns. God will do this, for He is faithful to do what He says, and He has invited you into partnership with His Son, Jesus Christ our LORD.
1 Corinthians 1:8-9 NLT

LORD, I am Your servant; yes, I am Your servant, born into Your household; You have freed me from my chains. I will offer You a sacrifice of thanksgiving and call on the name of the LORD.
Psalm 116:16-17 NLT

As a condemned person, you're trapped behind bars of sin, in shackles, and your accuser, the devil, is ready to spell out your sins to you. Your sentence is the death penalty. You have two lawyers defending you: Jesus and the Holy Spirit. Then Jesus came, took your punishment upon Himself, and died with the words: "Tetelestai." In Jesus' time, *tetelestai* was written on accounts that were paid in full. Jesus opens prison doors, and He makes shackles fall off. You are truly free!

Friendships Are Precious

There are "friends" who destroy each other, but a real friend sticks closer than a brother.
Proverbs 18:24 NLT

As iron sharpens iron, so a friend sharpens a friend.
Proverbs 27:17 NLT

Don't befriend angry people or associate with hot-tempered people, or you will learn to be like them and endanger your soul.
Proverbs 22:24-25 NLT

Perfume and incense bring joy to the heart, and the pleasantness of a friend springs from their heartfelt advice.
Proverbs 27:9 NIV

Love prospers when a fault is forgiven, but dwelling on it separates close friends.
Proverbs 17:9 NLT

The friendship of the LORD is for those who fear Him, and He makes known to them His covenant.
Psalm 25:14 ESV

A friend loves at all times, and a brother is born for a time of adversity.
Proverbs 17:17 NIV

Follow the steps of the good, and stay on the paths of the righteous.
Proverbs 2:20 NLT

Friendship is a priceless treasure. The word *friend*, however, has become a convenient form of address that reduces the value of friendship. A true friend enjoys the rainbow after your storm, she travels with you through winding roads and bumpy rides, and she offers more than just company at coffee shops—she prays for you. She makes sacrifices so you can reach further, encourages when you're low, and sings your praise, even though she is the reason for your success. Cherish a treasured and sincere friend.

Fruit from the Tree of Life

"Beware of false prophets, who come to you in sheep's clothing, but inwardly they are ravenous wolves. You will know them by their fruits. Every good tree bears good fruit, but a bad tree bears bad fruit. A good tree cannot bear bad fruit, nor can a bad tree bear good fruit. Every tree that does not bear good fruit is cut down and thrown into the fire. Therefore by their fruits you will know them."
Matthew 7:15-20 NKJV

The fruit of the Spirit is love, joy, peace, forbearance, kindness, goodness, faithfulness, gentleness and self-control. Against such things there is no law.
Galatians 5:22-23 NIV

"No good tree bears bad fruit, nor does a bad tree bear good fruit. Each tree is recognized by its own fruit. A good man brings good things out of the good stored up in his heart, and an evil man brings evil things out of the evil stored up in his heart. For the mouth speaks what the heart is full of."
Luke 6:43-45 NIV

May you always be filled with the fruit of your salvation—the righteous character produced in your life by Jesus Christ—for this will bring much glory and praise to God.
Philippians 1:11 NLT

To abide in Christ and bear fruit means to live in a relationship with Him. This relationship is about more than just reading the Bible and praying. It's not about how many times you have read the whole Bible from beginning to end, but whether its words have become alive in you. It's not about how many prayers you have said but how many times your prayers were intimate moments with God. Fruit grows naturally from a plant and so does your spiritual fruit if you abide in Him.

Godly Fulfillment

You make known to me the path of life; You will fill me with joy in Your presence, with eternal pleasures at Your right hand.

Psalm 16:11 NIV

"If you keep My commands, you will remain in My love, just as I have kept My Father's commands and remain in His love. I have told you this so that My joy may be in you and that your joy may be complete."

John 15:10-11 NIV

May the God of hope fill you with all joy and peace in believing, so that by the power of the Holy Spirit you may abound in hope.

Romans 15:13 ESV

The LORD will guide you always; He will satisfy your needs in a sun-scorched land and will strengthen your frame. You will be like a well-watered garden, like a spring whose waters never fail.

Isaiah 58:11 NIV

"Blessed are those who hunger and thirst for righteousness, for they shall be filled."

Matthew 5:6 NKJV

"I am coming to You now, but I say these things while I am still in the world, so that they may have the full measure of My joy within them."

John 17:13 NIV

Women often feel dissatisfied and discontent, as if there's a large cleft between them and a happy life. We try to build bridges of performance, money, and fame, and yet the gap remains. Christ Himself came to be the bridge so you can live a fulfilled life in God's presence. The same way our physical hunger is satisfied by food and our thirst is quenched by water, our deepest needs are satisfied by the Bread of Life and His living water.

Dream About the Future

"Do not worry about tomorrow, for tomorrow will worry about itself. Each day has enough trouble of its own."
Matthew 6:34 NIV

All the days ordained for me were written in Your book before one of them came to be.
Psalm 139:16 NIV

No eye has seen, no ear has heard, and no mind has imagined what God has prepared for those who love Him.
1 Corinthians 2:9 NLT

The LORD your God will personally go ahead of you. He will neither fail you nor abandon you.
Deuteronomy 31:6 NLT

"I know the thoughts that I think toward you," says the LORD, "thoughts of peace and not of evil, to give you a future and a hope."
Jeremiah 29:11 NKJV

"If God cares so wonderfully for flowers that are here today and thrown into the fire tomorrow, He will certainly care for you."
Luke 12:28 NLT

The LORD will work out His plans for my life—for Your faithful love, O LORD, endures forever.
Psalm 138:8 NLT

Many are the plans in a person's heart, but it is the LORD's purpose that prevails.
Proverbs 19:21 NIV

To trust God with your future doesn't mean you have to walk around blindly without any plans or goals. A responsible woman plans her life and her future. Planning is living for the here and now, while still dreaming about where you're heading. Obviously this planning is subordinate to God's guidance and care. The Spirit can change this at any time. Jesus has a future expectation for you; that's why He suffered and died on the cross. Trust Him with your future. He always knows best.

From One Generation to the Next

Understand, therefore, that the LORD your God is indeed God. He is the faithful God who keeps His covenant for a thousand generations and lavishes His unfailing love on those who love Him and obey His commands.

Deuteronomy 7:9 NLT

Moreover God said to Moses, "Thus you shall say to the children of Israel: 'The LORD God of your fathers, the God of Abraham, the God of Isaac, and the God of Jacob, has sent me to you."

Exodus 3:15 NKJV

They will proclaim His righteousness, declaring to a people yet unborn.

Psalm 22:31 NIV

Your faithfulness endures to all generations; You have established the earth, and it stands fast.

Psalm 119:90 ESV

You, O LORD, reign forever; Your throne endures from generation to generation.

Lamentations 5:19, ESV

The LORD is good; His mercy is everlasting, and His truth endures to all generations.

Psalm 100:5 NKJV

"I lavish unfailing love for a thousand generations to those who love Me and obey My commands."

Deuteronomy 5:10 NLT

In the Bible we often see a generation of believers who are faithful to God and serve Him. Then the next generation chose to serve all sorts of other gods and idols. That is why God encourages us to share His Word and our relationship with Him with our families and future generations (see Deuteronomy 6). This is to hand off the faith baton. What is the spiritual legacy that you're leaving behind for the next generation?

Give from Your Treasury

"Give, and you will receive. Your gift will return to you in full—pressed down, shaken together to make room for more, running over, and poured into your lap. The amount you give will determine the amount you get back."
Luke 6:38 NLT

"Truly I tell you, whatever you did for one of the least of these brothers and sisters of Mine, you did for Me."
Matthew 25:40 NIV

Do not neglect to do good and to share what you have, for such sacrifices are pleasing to God.
Hebrews 13:16 ESV

A gift opens the way and ushers the giver into the presence of the great.
Proverbs 18:16 NIV

You should remember the words of the LORD Jesus: "It is more blessed to give than to receive."
Acts 20:35

"Freely you have received, freely give."
Matthew 10:8 NKJV

Whoever is generous to the poor lends to the LORD, and He will repay him for his deed.
Proverbs 19:17 ESV

The good news is that Jesus came to earth to offer Himself as a living sacrifice. To the hungry He gave food, to the sick He offered healing, to the blind He gave sight, and to sinners He gave salvation. In order to give forgiveness, He had to give Himself. As a follower of Jesus, you must give with a cheerful heart. The easiest thing to give away is money; a little more difficult is to give of our time and ourselves. Can you give such that others can give thanks, praise, and glory to God?

Be Gentle in Spirit

Be completely humble and gentle; be patient, bearing with one another in love.
Ephesians 4:2 NIV

Let your gentleness be evident to all. The LORD is near.
Philippians 4:5 NIV

Always be prepared to give an answer to everyone who asks you to give the reason for the hope that you have. But do this with gentleness and respect, keeping a clear conscience, so that those who speak maliciously against your good behavior in Christ may be ashamed of their slander.
1 Peter 3:15-16 NIV

Therefore, as God's chosen people, holy and dearly loved, clothe yourselves with compassion, kindness, humility, gentleness and patience.
Colossians 3:12 NIV

A servant of the LORD must not quarrel but be gentle to all, able to teach, patient, in humility correcting those who are in opposition, if God perhaps will grant them repentance, so that they may know the truth.
2 Timothy 2:24-25 NKJV

A gentle answer deflects anger, but harsh words make tempers flare.
Proverbs 15:1 NLT

Gentleness is when humility, meekness, and modesty are interwoven into your being. It is not a weakness. It is to consider others above yourself and to act on their behalf. How you intervene, with a gentle spirit, is sometimes more important than intervening at all. With your attitude and how you do things, you show that the Spirit is in you. By the Spirit nothing will be able to dominate your sincere gentleness.

My Unclaimed Gifts

"Where your treasure is, there your heart will be also."
Matthew 6:21 NKJV

Remember that the LORD will reward each one of us for the good we do.
Ephesians 6:8 NLT

A gift opens the way and ushers the giver into the presence of the great.
Proverbs 18:16 NIV

No eye has seen, no ear has heard, and no mind has imagined what God has prepared for those who love Him.
1 Corinthians 2:9 NIV

We have different gifts, according to the grace given to each of us. If your gift is prophesying, then prophesy in accordance with your faith.
Romans 12:6 NIV

Every good and perfect gift is from above, coming down from the Father of the heavenly lights, who does not change like shifting shadows.
James 1:17 NIV

God has given each of you a gift from His great variety of spiritual gifts. Use them well to serve one another.
1 Peter 4:10 NLT

What is the greatest gift that you have ever received? Maybe it's people in your life: your spouse, parents, or children. Maybe it's something physical that you've been dreaming about, like a vacation to the beach? Maybe it is the day when God's grace was put before you all wrapped up, and you could not resist it. Perhaps the Bible opened up a treasure trove for you. Come today and count all of God's wonderful gifts for you. Take hold of all the gifts He has in store for you today.

Glorify God

Whether you eat or drink or whatever you do, do it all for the glory of God.
1 Corinthians 10:31 NIV

"Let your light so shine before men, that they may see your good works and glorify your Father in heaven."
Matthew 5:16 NKJV

For you were bought at a price; therefore glorify God in your body and in your spirit, which are God's.
1 Corinthians 6:20 NKJV

"Bring all who claim Me as their God, for I have made them for My glory. It was I who created them."
Isaiah 43:7 NLT

We all, who with unveiled faces contemplate the LORD's glory, are being transformed into His image with ever-increasing glory, which comes from the LORD, who is the Spirit.
2 Corinthians 3:18 NIV

You must live as God's obedient children. Don't slip back into your old ways of living to satisfy your own desires. You didn't know any better then. But now you must be holy in everything you do, just as God who chose you is holy. For the Scriptures say, "You must be holy because I am holy."
1 Peter 1:14-16 NLT

God created you to be in a relationship with Him—to glorify Him and His Majesty. This means you must live in admiration and in awe of God. You will be like a mirror reflecting God's greatness to others. You are the temple of the Holy Spirit, and through His work you're glorifying God by the way you live. When your light shines before others and they see your works, they will glorify the Father.

A Dream Come True

We make it our goal to please Him, whether we are at home in the body or away from it.
2 Corinthians 5:9 NIV

Forgetting what is behind and straining toward what is ahead, I press on toward the goal to win the prize for which God has called me heavenward in Christ Jesus.
Philippians 3:13-14 NIV

Take courage! Do not let your hands be weak, for your work shall be rewarded.
2 Chronicles 15:7 ESV

I run with purpose in every step. I am not just shadowboxing.
1 Corinthians 9:26 NLT

The one who plants and the one who waters have one purpose, and they will each be rewarded according to their own labor.
1 Corinthians 3:8 NIV

The plans of the diligent lead surely to plenty, but those of everyone who is hasty, surely to poverty.
Proverbs 21:5 NKJV

Do your planning and prepare your fields before building your house.
Proverbs 24:27 NLT

Goals don't always include the best, most beautiful, or most important things, but a dream of what could be better. It's not only physical and financial things, but also spiritual things. A goal without a plan remains a dream. What are your goals? Maybe an intimate relationship with God: What is your plan to achieve this? Get a notebook and pen, and start planning. Goals achieved bring satisfaction and more energy for greater goals.

God Is Our Father

We know that there is only one God, the Father, who created everything, and we live for Him. And there is only one LORD, Jesus Christ, through whom God made everything and through whom we have been given life.

1 Corinthians 8:6 NLT

See how very much our Father loves us, for He calls us His children, and that is what we are! But the people who belong to this world don't recognize that we are God's children because they don't know Him.

1 John 3:1 NLT

One God and Father of all, who is above all, and through all, and in you all.

Ephesians 4:6 NKJV

"I will be a Father to you, and you shall be My sons and daughters," says the LORD Almighty.

2 Corinthians 6:18 NKJV

The Spirit you received does not make you slaves, so that you live in fear again; rather, the Spirit you received brought about your adoption to sonship. And by Him we cry, *"Abba,* Father." The Spirit Himself testifies with our spirit that we are God's children. Now if we are children, then we are heirs—heirs of God and co-heirs with Christ, if indeed we share in His sufferings in order that we may also share in His glory.

Romans 8:15-17 NIV

Jesus doesn't tell us what God looks like, but rather what He is like. He reveals God's fatherly heart to you. The heart of a perfect Father—one who loves, cares, and protects. It cost Jesus His life so you could call God, Father, but do you realize that the Lord was willing to give His Son because He wanted to take away your pain and distress? The almighty God became the good Father who calls out to you, "Come, My child!"

My Hope Is in Christ

But reject profane and old wives' fables, and exercise yourself toward godliness. For bodily exercise profits a little, but godliness is profitable for all things, having promise of the life that now is and of that which is to come.

1 Timothy 4:7, 8 NKJV

Fix your thoughts on what is true, and honorable, and right, and pure, and lovely, and admirable. Think about things that are excellent and worthy of praise.

Philippians 4:8 NLT

I pray that your love will overflow more and more, and that you will keep on growing in knowledge and understanding.

Philippians 1:9 NLT

God has given us everything we need for living a godly life. We have received all of this by coming to know Him, the one who called us to Himself by means of His marvelous glory and excellence.

2 Peter 1:3 NLT

Since you excel in everything—in faith, in speech, in knowledge, in complete earnestness and in the love we have kindled in you—see that you also excel in this grace of giving.

2 Corinthians 8:7 NIV

Whether you eat or drink or whatever you do, do it all for the glory of God.

1 Corinthians 10:31 NIV

Godliness refers to the hope of salvation and how we run the race to make our salvation assured. Your salvation comes from Jesus, who paid for you with His life on the cross. When you pursue godliness it means that you are setting aside sin, resisting the devil and his temptations, and renewing your mind day by day so you can obey Christ. Godliness means servitude to Him.

The Goodness of God

Give thanks to the LORD, for He is good; His love endures forever.
Psalm 107:1 NIV

The LORD is good to everyone. He showers compassion on all His creation. All of your works will thank You, LORD, and Your faithful followers will praise You.
Psalm 145:9-10 NLT

You are good, and what You do is good; teach me Your decrees.
Psalm 119:68 NIV

For You, O LORD, are good and forgiving, abounding in steadfast love to all who call upon You.
Psalm 86:5 ESV

According to Your love remember me, for You, LORD, are good. Good and upright is the LORD; therefore He instructs sinners in His ways. He guides the humble in what is right and teaches them His way.
Psalm 25:7-9 NIV

The LORD is good, a strong refuge when trouble comes. He is close to those who trust in Him.
Nahum 1:7 NLT

We know that for those who love God all things work together for good, for those who are called according to His purpose.
Romans 8:28 ESV

Is God really good if people are getting divorced, children and women are abused, and crime increases by the minute? Unfortunately, we want to measure the goodness of God against how well we're doing. Goodness is not something that God does; it is who He is. The story of creation tells of how He smiled and said that it was good. Today the heavens are still calling out: God is good. All of creation sings of His goodness. Maybe you can join the rest of creation in song: God is good!

No More Gossip

A gossip betrays a confidence; so avoid anyone who talks too much.
Proverbs 20:19 NIV

A gossip goes around telling secrets, but those who are trustworthy can keep a confidence.
Proverbs 11:13 NLT

A perverse person stirs up conflict, and a gossip separates close friends.
Proverbs 16:28 NIV

The words of a whisperer are like delicious morsels; they go down into the inner parts of the body.
Proverbs 26:22 ESV

Set a guard, O LORD, over my mouth; keep watch over the door of my lips.
Psalm 141:3 NKJV

Too much talk leads to sin. Be sensible and keep your mouth shut.
Proverbs 10:19 NLT

With their mouths the godless destroy their neighbors, but through knowledge the righteous escape.
Proverbs 11:9 NIV

The words of a gossip are like choice morsels; they go down to the inmost parts.
Proverbs 18:8 NIV

Gossip is like a lid that covers food. You give just enough details so that others want to see what's under the cover. The cover protects food from flies, but not from fire. And your gossip is burning the hearts and lives of others. Gossip can involve betraying a confidence by disclosing sensitive information or hurtful judgments. But someone who likes to talk behind people's backs will surely talk about you too. Close your ears to gossip. There's enough uplifting stories that you can tell rather than spread half-truths or lies.

God's Amazing Grace

To each one of us grace has been given as Christ apportioned it.
Ephesians 4:7 NIV

"My grace is sufficient for you, for My power is made perfect in weakness."
2 Corinthians 12:9 ESV

God saved you by His grace when you believed. And you can't take credit for this; it is a gift from God.
Ephesians 2:8 NLT

God is able to make all grace abound to you, so that having all sufficiency in all things at all times, you may abound in every good work.
2 Corinthians 9:8 ESV

Sin is no longer your master, for you no longer live under the requirements of the law. Instead, you live under the freedom of God's grace.
Romans 6:14 NLT

From His abundance we have all received one gracious blessing after another.
John 1:16 NLT

We praise God for the glorious grace He has poured out on us who belong to His dear Son.
Ephesians 1:6 NLT

For the grace of God has appeared, bringing salvation for all people.
Titus 2:11 ESV

Grace is God's power that helps us to see the bad side of life, to feel hurt, but still be able to have godly peace in our hearts. Grace is the arms that carry us in our lowest, most painful moments. Grace is dancing in the rain after a long drought. Grace is what you need, and His grace is enough for you.

A Grateful Heart

The LORD is my strength and shield. I trust Him with all my heart. He helps me, and my heart is filled with joy. I burst out in songs of thanksgiving.
Psalm 28:7 NLT

Let us come before Him with thanksgiving and extol Him with music and song.
Psalm 95:2 NIV

Enter into His gates with thanksgiving, and into His courts with praise. Be thankful to Him, and bless His name.
Psalm 100:4 NKJV

I thank You for answering my prayer and giving me victory!
Psalm 118:21 NLT

Yours, LORD, is the greatness and the power and the glory and the majesty and the splendor, for everything in heaven and earth is Yours. Yours, LORD, is the kingdom; You are exalted as head over all. Wealth and honor come from You; You are the ruler of all things. In Your hands are strength and power to exalt and give strength to all. Now, our God, we give You thanks, and praise Your glorious name.
1 Chronicles 29:11-13 NIV

I will give to the LORD the thanks due to His righteousness, and I will sing praise to the name of the LORD, the Most High.
Psalm 7:17 ESV

From a young age mothers teach their kids manners, to be polite, and to say "please" and "thank you." Interesting that when it comes to God, we use the word *please* a lot more than *thank you*. We are disgruntled and angry when God provides differently to our plea than we had asked for. An example includes: "Please help, Lord, my boss is furious with me," instead of, "Thank You, God, that I have a job." There are many things that you can thank God for today. Count your blessings, not your sorrows.

God Is Great

No one is like You, LORD; You are great, and Your name is mighty in power.
Jeremiah 10:6 NIV

Great is the LORD! He is most worthy of praise! He is to be feared above all gods.
1 Chronicles 16:25 NLT

For all the gods of the peoples are worthless idols, but the LORD made the heavens.
Psalm 96:5 ESV

Yours, LORD, is the greatness and the power and the glory and the majesty and the splendor, for everything in heaven and earth is Yours. Yours, LORD, is the kingdom; You are exalted as head over all.
1 Chronicles 29:11 NIV

For the LORD Most High is awesome; He is a great King over all the earth.
Psalm 47:2 NKJV

For the Mighty One is holy, and He has done great things for me.
Luke 1:49 NLT

Great is the LORD! He is most worthy of praise! He is to be feared above all gods.
Psalm 96:4 NLT

Who is He, this King of glory? The LORD Almighty—He is the King of glory.
Psalm 24:10 NIV

Is there a scale or measure to weigh the greatness of God? He reveals His greatness in His Word. He holds the waters of the sea in the hollow of His hand, He measures the dust of the earth with a bushel, He weighs the mountains and the hills on His scale, and the extent of the heavens is measured by the breadth of His hand. He knows every little detail—your name, thoughts, tears, fears, and hopes. And that is just the beginning of His greatness.

Greed Is Costly

He said, "Beware! Guard against every kind of greed. Life is not measured by how much you own."
Luke 12:15 NLT

Let there be no sexual immorality, impurity, or greed among you. Such sins have no place among God's people.
Ephesians 5:3 NLT

Turn my heart toward Your statutes and not toward selfish gain.
Psalm 119:36 NIV

Put to death, therefore, whatever belongs to your earthly nature: sexual immorality, impurity, lust, evil desires and greed, which is idolatry.
Colossians 3:5 NIV

Some people are always greedy for more, but the godly love to give!
Proverbs 21:26 NLT

The greedy stir up conflict, but those who trust in the LORD will prosper.
Proverbs 28:25 NIV

Whoever loves money never has enough; whoever loves wealth is never satisfied with their income. This too is meaningless.
Ecclesiastes 5:10 NIV

"What do you benefit if you gain the whole world but lose your own soul?"
Mark 8:36 NLT

When is enough really enough? Unfortunately, too many women believe that more things will make them happy. Therefore you are overworked and stressed, because more is better. Don't miss out on the life that God wants to give to you just because you're trying to live someone else's life. Greed causes discontentment, because you'll never have enough. You are truly blessed when you're happy with what you have and praise God for it.

June

A WIFE OF

NOBLE CHARACTER

— who —
can find?

She is worth

FAR MORE THAN

rubies.

Proverbs 31:10

A Ray of Light Amidst Grief

He heals the brokenhearted and bandages their wounds.
Psalm 147:3 NLT

The LORD is good to all; He has compassion on all He has made.
Psalm 145:9 NIV

For You have delivered my soul from death, yes, my feet from falling, that I may walk before God in the light of life.
Psalm 56:13 ESV

To all who mourn in Israel, He will give a crown of beauty for ashes, a joyous blessing instead of mourning, festive praise instead of despair. In their righteousness, they will be like great oaks that the LORD has planted for His own glory.
Isaiah 61:3 NLT

You, God, see the trouble of the afflicted; You consider their grief and take it in hand. The victims commit themselves to You; You are the helper of the fatherless.
Psalm 10:14 NIV

Be gracious to me, O LORD, for I am in distress; my eye is wasted from grief; my soul and my body also.
Psalm 31:9 ESV

"God will wipe away every tear from their eyes; there shall be no more death, nor sorrow, nor crying. There shall be no more pain, for the former things have passed away."
Revelation 21:4 NKJV

Grief and sorrow can be so intense that there are no words to describe it! Perhaps you recently found yourself among the ashes, like Job, and people's comfort simply caused more confusion and tears. God will not abandon you during your time of grief. Even before you ask, He already knows what you need. He writes down your tears in His book and comforts you. Trust Him to wipe the tears from your eyes.

Growing in Christ

Grow in the grace and knowledge of our LORD and Savior Jesus Christ. To Him be glory both now and forever!
2 Peter 3:18 NIV

Christ will make His home in your hearts as you trust in Him. Your roots will grow down into God's love and keep you strong.
Ephesians 3:17 NLT

Therefore, laying aside all malice, all deceit, hypocrisy, envy, and all evil speaking, as newborn babes, desire the pure milk of the word, that you may grow thereby, if indeed you have tasted that the LORD is gracious.
1 Peter 2:1-3 NKJV

Let the word of Christ dwell in you richly, teaching and admonishing one another in all wisdom, singing psalms and hymns and spiritual songs, with thankfulness in your hearts to God.
Colossians 3:16 ESV

We will speak the truth in love, growing in every way more and more like Christ, who is the head of His body, the church. He makes the whole body fit together perfectly. As each part does its own special work, it helps the other parts grow, so that the whole body is healthy and growing and full of love.
Ephesians 4:15-16 NLT

You don't make Jesus the Lord of your life. God already made Him Lord of everything. You simply acknowledge that He is the Lord exalted among the nations, and you accept that the Holy Spirit is in control of your life. Then you can grow into the woman He planned for you to be. If you wanted to list everything He had in mind for you, it is more than the sand on the shore. The Spirit will help you to grow until His thoughts for you become a reality.

Guard Against Evil

Be on your guard; stand firm in the faith; be courageous; be strong.
1 Corinthians 16:13 NIV

Resist the devil, and he will flee from you.
James 4:7 NIV

It is for freedom that Christ has set us free. Stand firm, then, and do not let yourselves be burdened again by a yoke of slavery.
Galatians 5:1 NIV

"Stand firm, and you will win life."
Luke 21:19 NIV

Let the Holy Spirit guide your lives. Then you won't be doing what your sinful nature craves.
Galatians 5:16 NLT

I urge you, brothers and sisters, to watch out for those who cause divisions and put obstacles in your way that are contrary to the teaching you have learned. Keep away from them.
Romans 16:17 NIV

Stay alert! Watch out for your great enemy, the devil. He prowls around like a roaring lion, looking for someone to devour. Stand firm against him, and be strong in your faith. Remember that your family of believers all over the world is going through the same kind of suffering you are.
1 Peter 5:8-9 NLT

When testimonies are given of war, with details about the wounds and brokenness, it is heart breaking. But little do we realize we're facing a war every day, in and around us—the war against evil. The best way to guard against evil is to take a stand against the devil. You do this by clinging to God's truth when he attacks you with his lies. The truth always wins. Study and know the Word; it's your sword of victory.

A Guide Dog to the Blind

The LORD will guide you always; He will satisfy your needs in a sun-scorched land and will strengthen your frame. You will be like a well-watered garden, like a spring whose waters never fail.
Isaiah 58:11 NIV

Jesus said, "I am the way, the truth, and the life. No one comes to the Father except through Me."
John 14:6 NKJV

Send out Your light and Your truth; let them guide me. Let them lead me to Your holy mountain, to the place where You live.
Psalm 43:3 NLT

May the LORD direct your hearts into God's love and Christ's perseverance.
2 Thessalonians 3:5 NIV

All who are led by the Spirit of God are children of God.
Romans 8:14 NLT

The LORD says, "I will guide you along the best pathway for your life. I will advise you and watch over you."
Psalm 32:8 NLT

Show me Your ways, LORD, teach me Your paths. Guide me in Your truth and teach me, for You are God my Savior, and my hope is in You all day long.
Psalm 25:4-5 NIV

Some days we just don't know where to turn. Overwhelmed by circumstances, we pray for guidance. We hope for a bright cloud by day and a pillar of fire by night to guide us. It sounds easy, and yet it was not enough for the people of Israel. They kept battling. God's cloud is no longer above us, but in us. He leads us by His Spirit, His Word, and other believers whom He sends. His guidance is here; are you willing to follow?

Burdened by Guilt

For I have kept the ways of the LORD; I am not guilty of turning from my God.
Psalm 18:21 NIV

Keep Your servant from deliberate sins! Don't let them control me. Then I will be free of guilt and innocent of great sin.
Psalm 19:13 NLT

For Your name's sake, O LORD, pardon my guilt, for it is great.
Psalm 25:11 ESV

Yes, what joy for those whose record the LORD has cleared of guilt, whose lives are lived in complete honesty!
Psalm 32:2 NLT

Declare me not guilty, O LORD my God, for You give justice.
Psalm 35:24 NLT

Have mercy on me, O God, because of Your unfailing love. Because of Your great compassion, blot out the stain of my sins. Wash me clean from my guilt. Purify me from my sin.
Psalm 51:1-2 NLT

I acknowledged my sin to You and did not cover up my iniquity. I said, "I will confess my transgressions to the LORD." And You forgave the guilt of my sin.
Psalm 32:5 NIV

If guilt, like debt, was a currency, then we would work harder to pay it off, but it's not. Guilt comes in packages of sins that you can never pay back. Fortunately, Jesus took your guilt upon Himself. Guilt comes with a feeling of condemnation, and the only way to win the battle is with love. Guilt exists in unforgiveness, and the only way to set yourself free is to accept God forgave you of your guilt when you trusted in His Son, Jesus! Trust Jesus to deliver you from your guilt.

Cultivate Good Habits

All things are lawful for me, but all things are not helpful. All things are lawful for me, but I will not be brought under the power of any.
1 Corinthians 6:12 NKJV

Do not be deceived: "Evil company corrupts good habits."
1 Corinthians 15:33 NKJV

You were taught, with regard to your former way of life, to put off your old self, which is being corrupted by its deceitful desires; to be made new in the attitude of your minds; and to put on the new self, created to be like God in true righteousness and holiness.
Ephesians 4:22-24 NIV

He said, "What comes out of a person is what defiles him. For from within, out of the heart of man, come evil thoughts, sexual immorality, theft, murder, adultery, coveting, wickedness, deceit, sensuality, envy, slander, pride, foolishness. All these evil things come from within, and they defile a person."
Mark 7:20-23 ESV

Do not conform to the pattern of this world, but be transformed by the renewing of your mind. Then you will be able to test and approve what God's will is—His good, pleasing and perfect will.
Romans 12:2 NIV

The power of habit has caused embarrassment to many people. Your habits have a way of controlling your actions and words. Learn to use your habits to your advantage. As a woman of God, you have to cultivate the habit of regular quiet time, reading your Bible, and spending time in prayer. Changing bad habits will change your life. It does, however, require hard work, dedication, perseverance, prayer, and a friend who will go on the journey with you.

Happiness Is a Choice

A happy heart makes the face cheerful.
Proverbs 15:13 NIV

Happy are the people whose God is the LORD!
Psalm 144:15 NKJV

You make known to me the path of life; You fill me with joy in Your presence.
Psalm 6:11 NIV

To the person who pleases Him, God gives wisdom, knowledge and happiness.
Ecclesiastes 2:26 NIV

He who is of a merry heart has a continual feast.
Proverbs 15:15 NKJV

When times are good, be happy; but when times are bad, consider this: God has made the one as well as the other.
Ecclesiastes 7:14 NIV

Happy are those who have the God of Israel as their helper, whose hope is in the LORD their God.
Psalm 146:5 NLT

I know that there is nothing better for people than to be happy and do good while they live.
Ecclesiastes 3:12 NIV

Happiness is more about who you are than what you have. When happiness is determined by how much money is in your wallet, what your children have achieved, and the status of your husband, life becomes an unbalanced seesaw. Accept and love yourself and choose to be happy. True happiness is found in Jesus Christ. His happiness lies in those who are dependent on Him and those who are peacemakers.

When Hard Times Come

He has delivered us from the domain of darkness and transferred us to the kingdom of His beloved Son.
Colossians 1:13 ESV

Blessed is the man who remains steadfast under trial, for when he stood the test he will receive the crown of life, which God has promised to those who love Him.
James 1:12 ESV

Nevertheless to remain in the flesh is more needful for you. And being confident of this, I know that I shall remain and continue with you all for your progress and joy of faith.
Philippians 1:24-25 NKJV

Trust in the LORD with all your heart and lean not on your own understanding; in all your ways submit to Him, and He will make your paths straight.
Proverbs 3:5-6 NLT

To console those who mourn in Zion, to give them beauty for ashes, the oil of joy for mourning, the garment of praise for the spirit of heaviness; that they may be called trees of righteousness, the planting of the LORD, that He may be glorified.
Isaiah 61:3 NKJV

It should not come as a surprise to see bad things happening to good people. In the Bible we see many examples of this: Joseph was sold by his brothers, Saul wanted to kill David, Job lost everything, Jesus' crucifixion, the disciples who were tortured, and Paul who ended up in jail. Yet these difficult times never silenced them. It became the pulpit from which they announced God's grace and mercy. Maybe your difficult circumstances can be a pulpit from which you can share the gospel.

Miracles of Healing

"I am the LORD who heals you."
Exodus 15:26 NLT

O LORD, if You heal me, I will be truly healed; if You save me, I will be truly saved. My praises are for You alone!
Jeremiah 17:14 NLT

He heals the brokenhearted and binds up their wounds.
Psalm 147:3 NIV

He personally carried our sins in His body on the cross so that we can be dead to sin and live for what is right. By His wounds you are healed.
1 Peter 2:24 NLT

Bless the LORD, O my soul, and forget not all His benefits, who forgives all your iniquity, who heals all your diseases, who redeems your life from the pit, who crowns you with steadfast love and mercy, who satisfies you with good so that your youth is renewed like the eagle's.
Psalm 103:2-5 ESV

He said, "Your faith has healed you. Go in peace and be freed from your suffering."
Mark 5:34 NIV

He was pierced for our rebellion, crushed for our sins. He was beaten so we could be whole. He was whipped so we could be healed.
Isaiah 53:5 NLT

Is it physical, emotional, or spiritual healing that you long for? We often don't think about healing enough. Jesus came to heal people, but that was the smallest part of the miracle—He made people whole again. He healed the leper and changed his rejection into acceptance. He healed the servant and increased his value. He healed women and gave them dignity. The madman was healed, forgiven, and included in the community. Jesus came to heal the sick and the broken-hearted.

Listening Intently

"If anyone has ears to hear, let him hear."
Mark 4:23 ESV

Then everyone who has eyes will be able to see the truth, and everyone who has ears will be able to hear it.
Isaiah 32:3 NLT

So then, my beloved brethren, let every man be swift to hear, slow to speak, slow to wrath.
James 1:19 NKJV

He wakens me morning by morning, wakens my ear to listen like one being instructed.
Isaiah 50:4 NIV

So faith comes from hearing, and hearing through the word of Christ.
John 10:27 ESV

"My sheep hear My voice, and I know them, and they follow Me."
John 10:27 ESV

Do not merely listen to the word, and so deceive yourselves. Do what it says.
James 1:22 NIV

"Anyone who belongs to God listens gladly to the words of God."
John 8:47 NLT

He said to me: "Son of man, receive into your heart all My words that I speak to you, and hear with your ears."
Ezekiel 3:10 NKJV

Parents often complain that their children don't listen, and yet we as adults struggle to listen. We mostly hear the Word, God's promises, and His commands, but we don't really listen. Listening takes effort and requires that you add meaning to the words you hear by taking action. Paul says that you do not truly know the truth until it changes the way you love other people (1 Cor. 8:1). So live the truth of God's Word by loving more today.

Is My Heart the Problem?

Let love and faithfulness never leave you; bind them around your neck, write them on the tablet of your heart. Then you will win favor and a good name in the sight of God and man.
Proverbs 3:3-4 NIV

Keep your heart with all diligence, for out of it spring the issues of life.
Proverbs 4:23 NKJV

As a face is reflected in water, so the heart reflects the real person.
Proverbs 27:19 NLT

Create in me a clean heart, O God, and renew a right spirit within me.
Psalm 51:10 ESV

"Blessed are the pure in heart, for they shall see God."
Matthew 5:8 NIV

I will praise You with uprightness of heart, when I learn Your righteous judgments.
Psalm 119:7 NKJV

Your beauty should not come from outward adornment, such as elaborate hairstyles and the wearing of gold jewelry or fine clothes. Rather, it should be that of your inner self, the unfading beauty of a gentle and quiet spirit, which is of great worth in God's sight.
1 Peter 3:3-4 NIV

Coronary heart disease, calcification, and hardening of the arteries deprives the heart of oxygen and causes heart attacks or strokes, which is one of the leading causes of death. What is the condition of your spiritual heart? Is it soft or hard, stone or flesh, beautiful or ugly? Unforgiveness and bitterness deprive your spiritual heart of oxygen and can lead to death. Fortunately, God does heart transplants. He gives a new heart of flesh filled with love, respect, and compassion; a heart that will live forever.

Heaven Is Real

"In My Father's house are many mansions; if it were not so, I would have told you. I go to prepare a place for you. And if I go and prepare a place for you, I will come again and receive you to Myself; that where I am, there you may be also."
John 14:2-3 NKJV

For we know that if the tent that is our earthly home is destroyed, we have a building from God, a house not made with hands, eternal in the heavens.
2 Corinthians 5:1 ESV

"No eye has seen, no ear has heard, and no mind has imagined what God has prepared for those who love Him."
1 Corinthians 2:9 NLT

"People will come from all over the world—from east and west, north and south—to take their places in the Kingdom of God. And note this: Some who seem least important now will be the greatest then, and some who are the greatest now will be least important then."
Luke 13:29-30 NLT

For our citizenship is in heaven, from which we also eagerly wait for the Savior, the LORD Jesus Christ, who will transform our lowly body that it may be conformed to His glorious body, according to the working by which He is able even to subdue all things to Himself.
Philippians 3:20-21 NKJV

Why do you want to go to heaven? Many women want to be with loved ones, live without violence and crime, be healthy, and be free of poverty in streets of gold. How much of heaven is about you and how much is about God? Heaven is heaven because God is there. He is enough to make it heavenly. Long for heaven because you want to be with God.

Help from the Lord

I lift up my eyes to the hills. From where does my help come? My help comes from the LORD, who made heaven and earth.
Psalm 121:1-2 ESV

God is our refuge and strength, always ready to help in times of trouble.
Psalm 46:1 NLT

You will call, and the LORD will answer; you will cry for help, and He will say: Here am I.
Isaiah 58:9 NIV

Let us come boldly to the throne of our gracious God. There we will receive His mercy, and we will find grace to help us when we need it most.
Hebrews 4:16 NLT

The LORD is with me; He is my helper. I look in triumph on my enemies.
Psalm 118:7 NIV

The LORD hears His people when they call to Him for help. He rescues them from all their troubles.
Psalm 34:17 NLT

Our help is in the name of the LORD, who made heaven and earth.
Psalm 124:8 NKJV

The LORD is my strength and my shield; in Him my heart trusts, and I am helped; my heart exults, and with my song I give thanks to Him.
Psalm 28:7 ESV

To some people, mountains remind them of a family vacation or a sport—a challenge to conquer—but for others it is an obstacle that must be overcome. Are you unable to see passed the height of the mountain in front of you? If you look just a little further and higher, you will see a God who saves very close by. Your mountain can become a place where you meet God and find help.

Helping Others

I have been a constant example of how you can help those in need by working hard.
Acts 20:35 NLT

If your enemy is hungry, give him bread to eat.
Proverbs 25:21 NKJV

Bear one another's burdens, and so fulfill the law of Christ.
Galatians 6:2 ESV

"Truly I tell you, whatever you did for one of the least of these brothers and sisters of Mine, you did for Me."
Matthew 25:40 NIV

Those who refresh others will themselves be refreshed.
Proverbs 11:25 NLT

"If you do good to those who do good to you, what credit is that to you?"
Luke 6:33 NKJV

God is not unjust. He will not forget how hard you have worked for Him and how you have shown your love to Him by caring for other believers, as you still do.
Hebrews 6:10 NLT

Do not neglect to do good and to share what you have, for such sacrifices are pleasing to God.
Hebrews 13:16 ESV

Do not withhold good from those to whom it is due, when it is in the power of your hand to do so.
Proverbs 3:27 NKJV

Jesus didn't come to be served but to serve. Everywhere around us there are needs that can be met by your service. Think outside the box about how you can help people. Help a single parent's child with his or her homework, make an extra sandwich and give it to a needy beggar, or visit an elderly person in your church who has few friends. Bless others and you will be blessed too.

We Have His Spirit

All praise to God, the Father of our LORD Jesus Christ. It is by His great mercy that we have been born again, because God raised Jesus Christ from the dead. Now we live with great expectation, and we have a priceless inheritance—an inheritance that is kept in heaven for you, pure and undefiled, beyond the reach of change and decay.
1 Peter 1:3-4 NLT

"Open their eyes, so that they may turn from darkness to light and from the power of Satan to God, that they may receive forgiveness of sins and a place among those who are sanctified by faith in Me."
Acts 26:18 ESV

Now I commit you to God and to the word of His grace, which can build you up and give you an inheritance among all those who are sanctified.
Acts 20:31 NIV

Remember that the LORD will give you an inheritance as your reward, and that the Master you are serving is Christ.
Colossians 3:24 NLT

"God blesses those who are humble, for they will inherit the whole earth."
Matthew 5:5 NLT

The meek shall inherit the earth, and shall delight themselves in the abundance of peace.
Psalm 37:11 NKJV

Death brings its own grief and inheritance. It's not something you have worked for, but it was given to you because someone decided in their will you should be gifted it. After Jesus' death, He chose to make us heirs of something far above material things. In excitement we await this inheritance that we will receive one day and live in the wonderful heritage of the Spirit that we have already received—the Spirit that helps us to speak with God here and now.

The Holiness of God

They were calling out to each other, "Holy, holy, holy is the LORD of Heaven's Armies! The whole earth is filled with His glory!"
Isaiah 6:3 NLT

There is no one holy like the LORD; there is no one besides You; there is no Rock like our God.
1 Samuel 2:2 NIV

For the Scriptures say, "You must be holy because I am holy."
1 Peter 1:16 NLT

Who among the gods is like You, LORD? Who is like You—majestic in holiness, awesome in glory, working wonders?
Exodus 15:11 NIV

"I am the LORD, your Holy One, Israel's Creator and King."
Isaiah 43:15 NLT

Who will not fear, O LORD, and glorify Your name? For You alone are holy. All nations will come and worship You, for Your righteous acts have been revealed.
Revelation 15:4 ESV

The LORD of Heaven's Armies will be exalted by His justice. The holiness of God will be displayed by His righteousness.
Isaiah 5:16 NLT

Exalt the LORD our God, and worship at His footstool—He is holy.
Psalm 99:5 NKJV

God's holiness expresses the essence of His whole entity. He is not like people—He is without sin, absolutely perfect, totally different. That is why the angels and the heavenly beings sing His praises: "Holy, holy, holy is the Lord!" When you enter the holy presence of God, you know He is greater than you've ever imagined. His holiness is overwhelming when you look at it. It leaves you in awe of the Holy God.

Filled with the Holy Spirit

"The Spirit gives life. The words I have spoken to you—they are full of the Spirit and life."
John 6:63 NIV

"When He, the Spirit of truth, has come, He will guide you into all truth; for He will not speak on His own authority, but whatever He hears He will speak; and He will tell you things to come."
John 16:13 NKJV

"The Helper, the Holy Spirit, whom the Father will send in My name, He will teach you all things, and bring to your remembrance all things that I said to you."
John 14:26 NKJV

The Holy Spirit produces this kind of fruit in our lives: love, joy, peace, patience, kindness, goodness, faithfulness, gentleness, and self-control.
Galatians 5:22-23 NLT

The Holy Spirit helps us in our weakness. For example, we don't know what God wants us to pray for. But the Holy Spirit prays for us with groanings that cannot be expressed in words. And the Father who knows all hearts knows what the Spirit is saying, for the Spirit pleads for us believers in harmony with God's own will.
Romans 8:26-27 NLT

A friend of mine always says that you are always full, either of yourself or of the Holy Spirit. Too many of us want to use the Holy Spirit as a tool to complete a specific task, while we are actually the tool in the Spirit's hands. It is His Spirit that brings your heart and God's heart together. It is His Spirit that lays your prayer before the throne when you don't know what to pray. The Spirit is a healing, gentle breeze that blows over you.

Home Is Where the Heart Is

Through wisdom a house is built, and by understanding it is established; by knowledge the rooms are filled with all precious and pleasant riches.
Proverbs 24:3-4 NKJV

The house of the righteous contains great treasure, but the income of the wicked brings ruin.
Proverbs 15:6 NIV

As for me and my family, we will serve the LORD.
Joshua 24:15 NLT

Whoever troubles his own household will inherit the wind, and the fool will be servant to the wise of heart.
Proverbs 11:29 ESV

Unless the LORD builds the house, those who build it labor in vain. Unless the LORD watches over the city, the watchman stays awake in vain.
Psalm 127:1 ESV

The wise woman builds her house, but with her own hands the foolish one tears hers down.
Proverbs 14:1 NIV

The LORD's curse is on the house of the wicked, but He blesses the home of the righteous.
Proverbs 3:33 NIV

Do you remember the smell of your mother's home? Maybe it was the smell of cinnamon and freshly baked bread, or the smell of roses. What is the smell that your family will remember about your home? Women create more than just a house; they create a home. Home is the place where you wisely build with the smell of safety, space and love; where you fill the rooms with precious things. Create a home where grace, patience, acceptance, and hospitality are welcome.

You Can Believe Me!

May integrity and honesty protect me, for I put my hope in You.
Psalm 25:21 NLT

Pour out Your unfailing love on those who love You; give justice to those with honest hearts.
Psalm 36:10 NLT

Look at those who are honest and good, for a wonderful future awaits those who love peace.
Psalm 37:37 NLT

He grants a treasure of common sense to the honest. He is a shield to those who walk with integrity.
Proverbs 2:7 NLT

Honesty guides good people; dishonesty destroys treacherous people.
Proverbs 11:3 NLT

The godly are directed by honesty; the wicked fall beneath their load of sin.
Proverbs 11:5 NLT

Lying lips are an abomination to the LORD, but those who act faithfully are his delight.
Proverbs 12:22 ESV

Better to be poor and honest than to be dishonest and a fool.
Proverbs 19:1 NLT

Honesty is like perfume that you pour out on others, yet a few drops will always land on you. A woman who is honest is a pleasant aroma in her home, among her friends, and in God's presence. Choose to be honest, especially in your marriage. Sometimes dishonesty starts with little things, but if we can lie about the little things in life, we eventually learn to be dishonest in the bigger things that could destroy our relationships.

Soli Deo Gloria!

"Sacrifice thank offerings to God, fulfill your vows to the Most High, and call on Me in the day of trouble; I will deliver you, and you will honor Me."

Psalm 50:14-15 NIV

You who fear the LORD, praise Him! All you descendants of Jacob, honor Him! Revere Him, all you descendants of Israel!

Psalm 22:23 NIV

Honor the LORD, you heavenly beings; honor the LORD for His glory and strength. Honor the LORD for the glory of His name. Worship the LORD in the splendor of His holiness.

Psalm 29:1-2 NLT

"Be still, and know that I am God! I will be honored by every nation. I will be honored throughout the world."

Psalm 46:10 NLT

Teach me Your ways, O LORD, that I may live according to Your truth! Grant me purity of heart, so that I may honor You.

Psalm 86:11 NLT

"Giving thanks is a sacrifice that truly honors Me. If you keep to My path, I will reveal to you the salvation of God."

Psalm 50:23 NLT

Honor and majesty are before Him; strength and gladness are in His place.

1 Chronicles 16:27 NKJV

Women tend to run around from sunrise to sunset, trying to get everything done. It is a great skill to leave certain things undone in order to get the more important things done. Whatever you do, do it all to the glory of God. This means that you will reflect the light of God. Whatever you do, be a living testimony of His glory. *Soli Deo Gloria*—for the glory of God alone!

Hope for the Future

Those who hope in the LORD will renew their strength. They will soar on wings like eagles; they will run and not grow weary, they will walk and not be faint.
Isaiah 40:31 NIV

Blessed are those whose hope is in the LORD their God.
Psalm 146:5 NIV

May the God of hope fill you with all joy and peace as you trust in Him, so that you may overflow with hope by the power of the Holy Spirit.
Romans 15:13 NIV

Having hope will give you courage. You will be protected and will rest in safety.
Job 11:18 NLT

Hope in the LORD! For with the LORD there is steadfast love, and with Him is plentiful redemption.
Psalm 130:7 ESV

I saw the LORD always before me...therefore my heart is glad and my tongue rejoices; my body also will live in hope.
Acts 2:25-26 NIV

The needy shall not always be forgotten, and the hope of the poor shall not perish forever.
Psalm 9:18 ESV

Hope deferred makes the heart sick, but a dream fulfilled is a tree of life.
Proverbs 13:12 NLT

Hope makes the future possible. Hope is the beacon that enables us to look past today and see beyond where we are now. Hope is not the absence of problems, but rather the presence of God amist the problems. Karl Barth said that hope is the ability to hear the music of tomorrow today, and faith is to dance to the beat of that music. May you find hope, not because of changing circumstances, but because Jesus is present in your life.

The Heart of Hospitality

Share with the LORD's people who are in need. Practice hospitality.
Romans 12:13 NIV

Be hospitable to one another without grumbling.
1 Peter 4:9 NKJV

Don't forget to show hospitality to strangers, for some who have done this have entertained angels without realizing it!
Hebrews 13:2 NLT

Dear friend, you are faithful in what you are doing for the brothers and sisters, even though they are strangers to you.
3 John 1:5 NIV

Share your food with the hungry, and give shelter to the homeless. Give clothes to those who need them, and do not hide from relatives who need your help.
Isaiah 58:7 NLT

Do not neglect to do good and to share what you have, for such sacrifices are pleasing to God.
Hebrews 13:16 ESV

Be hospitable, one who loves what is good, who is self-controlled, upright, holy and disciplined.
Titus 1:8 NIV

Hospitality is not to give someone a meal or to invite them to dinner, hospitality is to open your heart to others. In Greek it means to have love for a stranger. When you invite an outsider into your home and treat them humbly as a guest, they may become a friend of God. During mealtimes Jesus spoke about God's Kingdom, and many people were converted. May you be kind to a stranger and perhaps make them a friend of God as well.

The Beauty of Humility

Humble yourselves in the sight of the LORD, and He will lift you up.
James 4:10 NKJV

Clothe yourselves, all of you, with humility toward one another, for "God opposes the proud but gives grace to the humble." Humble yourselves, therefore, under the mighty hand of God so that at the proper time He may exalt you.
1 Peter 5:5-6 ESV

"He who is greatest among you shall be your servant. And whoever exalts himself will be humbled, and he who humbles himself will be exalted."
Matthew 23:11-12 NKJV

He has shown you, O mortal, what is good. And what does the LORD require of you? To act justly and to love mercy and to walk humbly with your God.
Micah 6:8 NIV

Do nothing out of selfish ambition or vain conceit. Rather, in humility value others above yourselves, not looking to your own interests but each of you to the interests of the others.
Philippians 2:3-4 NIV

The LORD supports the humble, but He brings the wicked down into the dust.
Psalm 147:6 NLT

Rick Warren once said, "Humility is not thinking less of yourself; it is thinking of yourself less. Humility is thinking more of others." Pride creates distance between people and builds walls that are hard to break down. Humility on the other hand builds bridges and breaks down walls. The Lord Jesus came to show humility and subservience on earth not by erecting statues of Himself, but rather washing His disciples' feet.

A Bandage for the Pain

He will order His angels to protect you wherever you go. They will hold you up with their hands so you won't even hurt your foot on a stone.
Psalm 91:11-12 NLT

We know that in all things God works for the good of those who love Him.
Romans 8:28 NIV

Though I walk in the midst of trouble, You preserve my life; You stretch out Your hand against the wrath of my enemies, and Your right hand delivers me.
Psalm 138:7 ESV

The LORD upholds all who fall, and raises up all who are bowed down.
Psalm 145:14 NKJV

Weeping may endure for a night, but joy comes in the morning.
Psalm 30:5 NKJV

Though You have made me see troubles, many and bitter, You will restore my life again; from the depths of the earth You will again bring me up. You will increase my honor and comfort me once more.
Psalm 71:20-21 NIV

"He will wipe every tear from their eyes, and there will be no more death or sorrow or crying or pain. All these things are gone forever."
Revelation 21:4 NLT

The tough questions that have come from your pain don't always have easy and simple answers. If only there was a quick response that could ease the pain and make you feel better. Sometimes your hurt and pain seems like a 2-meter-high wave that overwhelms you. There is only One who can calm this storm: Jesus, who knows everything about pain—He wants to and can ease your pain.

My Husband, My Hero

Let each one of you love his wife as himself, and let the wife see that she respects her husband.
Ephesians 5:33 ESV

This is how the holy women of old made themselves beautiful. They put their trust in God and accepted the authority of their husbands.
1 Peter 3:5 NLT

A wife of noble character who can find? She is worth far more than rubies. Her husband has full confidence in her and lacks nothing of value. She brings him good, not harm, all the days of her life.
Proverbs 31:10-12 NIV

Wives, submit to your own husbands, as to the LORD. For the husband is head of the wife, as also Christ is head of the church; and He is the Savior of the body. Therefore, just as the church is subject to Christ, so let the wives be to their own husbands in everything. Husbands, love your wives, just as Christ also loved the church and gave Himself for her.
Ephesians 5:22-25 NKJV

Wives, submit to your husbands, as is fitting in the LORD. Husbands, love your wives, and do not be harsh with them.
Colossians 3:18-19 ESV

When God established marriage in Genesis, the woman was her husband's helper and his equal. Becoming one means bringing out the best in each other so they can function better together than alone. Although you have different roles, you must serve one another, love, and act in each other's best interests. Submission (wife) and sacrificial love (man) are always used together, because in your unity, His Kingdom will be displayed through your marriage.

Don't Be a Hypocrite

Whoever claims to love God yet hates a brother or sister is a liar. For whoever does not love their brother and sister, whom they have seen, cannot love God, whom they have not seen.
1 John 4:20 NIV

If anyone among you thinks he is religious, and does not bridle his tongue but deceives his own heart, this one's religion is useless.
James 1:26 NKJV

"You hypocrite, first take the log out of your own eye, and then you will see clearly to take the speck out of your brother's eye."
Matthew 7:5 ESV

Anyone who claims to be in the light but hates a brother or sister is still in the darkness.
1 John 2:9 NIV

"When you pray, don't be like the hypocrites who love to pray publicly on street corners and in the synagogues where everyone can see them. I tell you the truth, that is all the reward they will ever get."
Matthew 6:5 NLT

The hypocrite with his mouth destroys his neighbor, but through knowledge the righteous will be delivered.
Proverbs 11:9 NKJV

The Greek word *hipokrites* used for hypocrisy literally means actor or actress. It describes someone who does all the right things to catch the lime light and status, and God is completely removed from the picture. You have a closet full of masks and various roles to play. When you constantly live your life wearing a mask, you become your mask and lose your true self in the process. Do people see and know the real you, or are you always trying to Photoshop your life?

A Loafer's Manifesto

A sluggard buries his hand in the dish; he will not even bring it back to his mouth!
Proverbs 19:24 NIV

The sluggard does not plow in the autumn; he will seek at harvest and have nothing.
Proverbs 20:4 ESV

The hand of the diligent will rule, while the slothful will be put to forced labor.
Proverbs 12:24 ESV

Go to the ant, you sluggard; consider its ways and be wise!
Proverbs 6:6 NIV

The soul of the sluggard craves and gets nothing, while the soul of the diligent is richly supplied.
Proverbs 13:4 ESV

In all labor there is profit, but idle chatter leads only to poverty.
Proverbs 14:23 NKJV

A lazy person is as bad as someone who destroys things.
Proverbs 18:9 NLT

Through laziness, the rafters sag; because of idle hands, the house leaks.
Ecclesiastes 10:18 NIV

Despite their desires, the lazy will come to ruin, for their hands refuse to work.
Proverbs 21:25 NLT

Billy Graham said, "Only those who want everything done for them are bored." God uses the example of an ant full of energy and passion. Although he is not strong like Samson, he is as wise and dedicated as Solomon was, working with consistency and diligence. Ask busy people to do things for you and they do it better than those who are idle.

You Become What You Worship

Therefore, my dear friend, flee from idolatry.
1 Corinthians 10:14 NIV

Put to death, therefore, whatever belongs to your earthly nature: sexual immorality, impurity, lust, evil desires and greed, which is idolatry.
Colossians 3:5 NIV

The acts of the flesh are obvious: sexual immorality, impurity and debauchery; idolatry and witchcraft; hatred, discord, jealousy, fits of rage, selfish ambition, dissensions, factions.
Galatians 5:19-20 NIV

Dear children, keep yourselves from idols.
1 John 5:21 NIV

But the cowardly, unbelieving, abominable, murderers, sexually immoral, sorcerers, idolaters, and all liars shall have their part in the lake which burns with fire and brimstone, which is the second death.
Revelation 21:8 NLT

"I am the LORD; that is My name; My glory I give to no other, nor My praise to carved idols."
Isaiah 42:8 ESV

"Do not put your trust in idols or make metal images of gods for yourselves. I am the LORD your God."
Leviticus 19:4 NLT

We easily excuse ourselves of idolatry, because we don't worship golden statues and don't offer sacrifices to gods, yet we place more confidence in our salary to survive than in God. When your satisfaction lies in something other than your relationship with God, there is an idol lurking somewhere. Idols are much more dangerous than what is visible to the eye; it is an attitude that takes root in your heart. Fight against it because it wants to steal God's place in your life.

Changing Ignorance into Wisdom

The prudent sees danger and hides himself, but the simple go on and suffer for it.
Proverbs 22:3 ESV

Truly, these times of ignorance God overlooked, but now commands all men everywhere to repent.
Acts 17:30 NKJV

Desire without knowledge is not good—how much more will hasty feet miss the way!
Proverbs 19:2 NIV

For it is God's will that by doing good you should silence the ignorant talk of foolish people.
1 Peter 2:15 NIV

My people are destroyed for lack of knowledge.
Hosea 4:6 NKJV

Live no longer as the Gentiles do, for they are hopelessly confused. Their minds are full of darkness; they wander far from the life God gives because they have closed their minds and hardened their hearts against Him. They have no sense of shame. They live for lustful pleasure and eagerly practice every kind of impurity. But that isn't what you learned about Christ.
Ephesians 4:17-20 NLT

The prudent sees danger and hides himself, but the simple go on and suffer for it.
Proverbs 27:12 ESV

Sometimes you talk about something ignorantly, only to discover much later that you were actually completely wrong. However, everyone around you was too afraid of conflict to correct you. It is important that you have a mentor, someone who will help and educate you in times of ignorance. It also means that you should have a teachable spirit and dig into the Word daily to change your ignorance into wisdom.

The Quest to Live Forever

To those who by persistence in doing good seek glory, honor and immortality, He will give eternal life.
Romans 2:7 NIV

In the way of righteousness there is life; along that path is immortality.
Proverbs 12:28 NIV

For the perishable must clothe itself with the imperishable, and the mortal with the immortality.
1 Corinthians 15:53 NIV

...and the mortal with immortality, then the saying that is written will come true: "Death has been swallowed up in victory."
1 Corinthians 15:54 NIV

It has now been revealed through the appearing of our Savior, Christ Jesus, who has destroyed death and has brought life and immortality to light through the gospel.
2 Timothy 1:10 NIV

But God will redeem me from the realm of the dead; He will surely take me to Himself.
Psalm 49:15 NIV

"Don't be afraid of those who want to kill your body; they cannot touch your soul. Fear only God, who can destroy both soul and body in hell."
Matthew 10:28 NLT

We are all fighting for survival. When we face bad news such as a vague test result or a hard diagnosis, we are fighting for our lives. If death seems to have prevailed, the final say and victory is on this side of life, because your immortal soul leaves your body to be with Christ forever. If you believe, you don't have to fear death. Because it is only the gateway to eternal life. You will live with Him forever in the life hereafter.

July

She is clothed
with
strength
& dignity,
and she laughs
without fear
of the **future.**

Proverbs 31:25

The Psychology behind Persuasion

Good comes to those who lend money generously and conduct their business fairly. Such people will not be overcome by evil. Those who are righteous will be long remembered...They share freely and give generously to those in need. Their good deeds will be remembered forever. They will have influence and honor.
Psalm 112:5-6, 9 NLT

This is how the LORD responds: "If you return to Me, I will restore you so you can continue to serve Me. If you speak good words rather than worthless ones, you will be My spokesman. You must influence them; do not let them influence you!"
Jeremiah 15:19 NLT

As iron sharpens iron, so one person sharpens another.
Proverbs 27:17 NIV

Dear friend, don't let this bad example influence you. Follow only what is good. Remember that those who do good prove that they are God's children, and those who do evil prove that they do not know God.
3 John 1:11 NLT

One who is righteous is a guide to his neighbor, but the way of the wicked leads them astray.
Proverbs 12:26 ESV

Sorrow is better than laughter, for sadness has a refining influence on us.
Ecclesiastes 7:3 NLT

People's choices, words, and actions have an impact on you. However, you can choose to what extent you allow people to influence your life. Your way of doing things, your speech, and the way you live influence those around you. Jesus had a great and important impact on people's lives. He impacted people with His love, gifts of hope, healing, and His presence. Now He sends you to do the same and to have an even greater influence on people's lives, so God can be glorified.

Overcoming Your Insecurities

God has not given us a spirit of fear, but of power and of love and of a sound mind.
2 Timothy 1:7 NKJV

Look, I go forward, but He is not there, and backward, but I cannot perceive Him; when He works on the left hand, I cannot behold Him; when He turns to the right hand, I cannot see Him. But He knows the way that I take; when He has tested me, I shall come forth as gold.
Job 23:8-10 NKJV

Listen! The LORD's arm is not too weak to save you, nor is His ear too deaf to hear you call.
Isaiah 59:1 NLT

"All things are possible for one who believes."
Mark 9:23 ESV

He will not let your foot slip—He who watches over you will not slumber; indeed, He who watches over Israel will neither slumber nor sleep. The LORD watches over you—the LORD is your shade at your right hand; the sun will not harm you by day, nor the moon by night.
Psalm 121:3-8 NIV

Trust in the LORD with all your heart, and lean not on your own understanding; in all your ways acknowledge Him, and He shall direct your paths.
Proverbs 3:5-6 NKJV

Women tend to be insecure and uncertain about their finances, work, health, relationships, and what the future holds. It's interesting to see what lengths people will go to find more security and assurance. Insurance policies are taken out to cover your retirement and medical insurance to cover your hospital expenses. What does your relationship with God look like? Have you responded to His call of love for you? He promises that the unknown is known to Him and that He will be with you when you feel unsure. He is your surety.

Insight into the Joys of Life

My son, pay attention to my wisdom, turn your ear to my words of insight, that you may maintain discretion and your lips may preserve knowledge.
Proverbs 5:1, 2 NIV

Say to wisdom, you are my sister, and to insight you are my relative.
Proverbs 7:4 NIV

And this is my prayer: that your love may abound more and more in knowledge and depth of insight.
Philippians 1:9 NIV

Reflect on what I am saying, for the LORD will give you insight into all this.
2 Timothy 2:7 NIV

I have more insight than all my teachers, for I meditate on Your statutes.
Psalm 119:99 NIV

God gave Solomon wisdom and very great insight, and a breadth of understanding as measureless as the sand on the seashore.
1 Kings 4:29 NIV

Tune your ears to wisdom, and concentrate on understanding. Cry out for insight, and ask for understanding. Search for them as you would for silver; seek them like hidden treasures. Then you will understand what it means to fear the Lord, and you will gain knowledge of God.
Proverbs 2:2-5 NLT

A woman with wisdom and insight is a precious gift to her family and friends. Wisdom is being able to identify the puzzle pieces, and insight is knowing how to put the pieces together to complete the bigger picture. Wisdom and insight also bring joy and hope to others. Through your relationship with God you receive the gift of wisdom, which brings joy and impacts your life positively. It also influences how you think, speak, and act.

The Spirit Ignites the Fire

Those who live at the ends of the earth stand in awe of Your wonders. From where the sun rises to where it sets, You inspire shouts of joy.
Psalm 65:8 NLT

The angel said to me, "These words are trustworthy and true. The LORD, the God who inspires the prophets, sent His angel to show His servants the things that must soon take place."
Revelation 22:6 NIV

But there is a spirit in man, and the breath of the Almighty gives him understanding.
Job 32:8 NKJV

"Even on My servants, both men and women, I will pour out My Spirit in those days, and they will prophesy."
Acts 2:18 NIV

All Scripture is given by inspiration of God, and is profitable for doctrine, for reproof, for correction, for instruction in righteousness.
2 Timothy 3:16 NKJV

We remember before our God and Father your work produced by faith, your labor prompted by love, and your endurance inspired by hope in our LORD Jesus Christ.
1 Thessalonians 1:3 NIV

Inspiration comes from the Holy Spirit. His Spirit ignites the fire within you. The Spirit inspires us to live the life Christ requires of us: service with respect and love, even for your enemies. Live in such a way that someone might say, "Because of you, I have not given up hope." The Spirit inspires your time together with God and makes you grow spiritually. Do you need inspiration? Be still, and experience the gentle breeze of the Spirit blowing over you.

A Godly Character

Joyful are people of integrity, who follow the instructions of the Lord. Joyful are those who search for Him with all their hearts.

Psalm 119:1-2 NLT

May integrity and honesty protect me, for I put my hope in You.

Psalm 25:21 NLT

The integrity of the upright will guide them.

Proverbs 11:3 NKJV

The Lord grants a treasure of common sense to the honest. He is a shield to those who walk with integrity.

Proverbs 2:7 NLT

I know, my God, that You test the heart and are pleased with integrity. All these things I have given willingly and with honest intent.

1 Chronicles 29:17 NIV

The godly walk with integrity; blessed are their children who follow them.

Proverbs 20:7 NLT

In everything set them an example by doing what is good. In your teaching show integrity, seriousness and soundness of speech that cannot be condemned, so that those who oppose you may be ashamed because they have nothing bad to say about us.

Titus 2:7-8 NIV

Integrity is what you do and who you are when no one is watching. It is who you are when you think that no one will find out. It is to glorify God in everything you do, whether you are alone or in a crowd. When integrity is important to you, you do what you say and what you know is right. If your family is important to you, spend enough time with them. If God is important to you, surrender yourself completely over to Him. Be a woman of integrity, one who keeps her word and who is not easily corrupted.

Intimate Moments with God

Draw near to God and He will draw near to you. Cleanse your hands, you sinners; and purify your hearts, you double-minded.

James 4:8 NKJV

"Here I am! I stand at the door and knock. If anyone hears My voice and opens the door, I will come in and eat with that person, and they with Me."

Revelation 3:20 NIV

"And this is the way to have eternal life—to know You, the only true God, and Jesus Christ, the one You sent to earth."

John 17:3 NLT

"Remain in Me, as I also remain in you. No branch can bear fruit by itself; it must remain in the vine. Neither can you bear fruit unless you remain in Me."

John 15:4 NIV

Now in Christ Jesus you who once were far off have been brought near by the blood of Christ.

Ephesians 2:13 NKJV

If then you were raised with Christ, seek those things which are above, where Christ is, sitting at the right hand of God.

Colossians 3:1 NKJV

Intimate moments between you and God are when the world becomes still for a while as you hear, smell, and experience God. Maybe it's the smell of Chai Tea while relaxing on your couch or your grandmother's knitted blanket with the well-known hymn *Amazing Grace* playing in the background. These are the moments where your spirit connects with God's Spirit and your heart and God's heart come together. In these quiet moments you experience that God loves you, and that He is truly with you, always.

A Jealous God

"You shall not make for yourself a carved image. You shall not bow down to them or serve them, for I the LORD your God am a jealous God."
Exodus 20:4-5 ESV

Do not worship any other god, for the LORD, whose name is Jealous, is a jealous God.
Exodus 34:14 NIV

"Nevertheless I have this against you, that you have left your first love."
Revelation 2:4 NKJV

Be careful not to forget the covenant of the LORD your God that He made with you. For the LORD your God is a consuming fire, a jealous God.
Deuteronomy 4:23-24 NIV

You must not worship any of the gods of neighboring nations, for the LORD your God, who lives among you, is a jealous God. His anger will flare up against you, and He will wipe you from the face of the earth.
Deuteronomy 6:14-15 NLT

The LORD is a jealous God.
Nahum 1:2 NLT

How long, LORD? Will You be angry forever? How long will Your jealousy burn like fire?
Psalm 79:5 NIV

God is a holy and jealous God. He gives everything, but He also asks everything of you. He gave His Son as a sacrifice for your sins, and now He asks you to give your life as an offering to Him. He wants to be first in your life. You're the apple of His eye, and He wants to be your first love. He wants you to serve Him alone, and not to worship idols like money and status.

Jesus Christ, King of Judah

For unto us a Child is born, unto us a Son is given; and the government will be upon His shoulder. And His name will be called Wonderful, Counselor, Mighty God, Everlasting Father, Prince of Peace.

Isaiah 9:6 NKJV

"I give them eternal life, and they will never perish. No one can snatch them away from Me, for My Father has given them to Me, and He is more powerful than anyone else. No one can snatch them from the Father's hand. The Father and I are one."

John 10:28-30 NLT

Then the angel said to them, "Do not be afraid, for behold, I bring you good tidings of great joy which will be to all people. For there is born to you this day in the city of David a Savior, who is Christ the LORD."

Luke 2:10-11 NKJV

He was pierced for our transgressions, He was crushed for our iniquities; the punishment that brought us peace was on Him, and by His wounds we are healed.

Isaiah 53:5 NIV

God showed how much He loved us by sending His one and only Son into the world so that we might have eternal life through Him.

1 John 4:9 NLT

Who is Jesus to you? The vulnerable Baby in the manger whom you wish could stay small so that you can control Him when you want to? Or the Knight in shining armor on His white horse, the one with the victor's crown? Jesus is more than the words we use to describe Him. In His DNA we find the love that willed Him to sacrifice Himself, peace that surpasses all understanding, and a heart for the lost and weary. Jesus is the Lord and Leader of servants. Do you know this Jesus?

The Thief of Joy

This is the day that the LORD has made; let us rejoice and be glad in it.
Psalm 118:24 ESV

In Him our hearts rejoice, for we trust in His holy name.
Psalm 33:21 NIV

The joy of the LORD is your strength.
Nehemiah 8:10 NKJV

Those who look to Him for help will be radiant with joy; no shadow of shame will darken their faces.
Psalm 34:5 NLT

Light shines on the godly, and joy on those whose hearts are right.
Psalm 97:11 NLT

The LORD has done great things for us, and we are filled with joy.
Psalm 126:3 NIV

The precepts of the LORD are right, giving joy to the heart. The commands of the LORD are radiant, giving light to the eyes.
Psalm 19:8 NIV

Honor and majesty are before Him; strength and gladness are in His place.
1 Chronicles 16:27 NKJV

Shouts of joy and victory resound in the tents of the righteous: "The LORD's right hand has done mighty things!"
Psalm 118:15 NIV

Achievements, circumstances, and people cannot bring lasting joy. Joy is a gift from God irrespective of your circumstances. Joy happens in the heart; it's something inside you that no one can take away from you. It is the full assurance that God is in control, that you can trust Him, and that you can praise Him for this gift. Contentment and joy are twin sisters that cannot be separated. Accept responsibility for your own joy. Don't count on someone else or circumstances to bring you joy.

The Danger of Playing God

"Do not judge others, and you will not be judged. For you will be treated as you treat others. The standard you use in judging is the standard by which you will be judged."
Matthew 7:1-2 NLT

Do not pervert justice; do not show partiality to the poor or favoritism to the great, but judge your neighbor fairly.
Leviticus 19:15 NIV

"Do not judge, and you will not be judged. Do not condemn, and you will not be condemned. Forgive, and you will be forgiven."
Luke 6:37 NIV

Do not speak evil against one another, brothers. The one who speaks against a brother or judges his brother, speaks evil against the law and judges the law. But if you judge the law, you are not a doer of the law but a judge. There is only one lawgiver and judge, He who is able to save and to destroy. But who are you to judge your neighbor?
James 4:11-12 ESV

"So when they continued asking Him, He raised Himself up and said to them, "He who is without sin among you, let him throw a stone at her first."
John 8:7 NKJV

When we judge someone, we make him or her "smaller," because we ourselves are insecure and unhappy. Pride and jealousy are the main reasons for judging others. When you're hurting, you sometimes believe the lie that judgment will make you feel better, but the opposite is true. Before highlighting someone else's mistakes for all to see, stop and acknowledge your own weaknesses and flaws, then deal with it by talking to God about it.

The Right Thing to Do

Truly, God will not do wrong. The Almighty will not twist justice.
Job 34:12 NLT

Blessed are they who observe justice, who do righteousness at all times!
Psalm 106:3 ESV

He is the LORD our God. His justice is seen throughout the land.
1 Chronicles 16:14 NLT

LORD, You always give me justice when I bring a case before You.
Jeremiah 12:1 NLT

The righteous LORD loves justice. The virtuous will see His face.
Psalm 11:7 NLT

Follow justice and justice alone, so that you may live and possess the land the LORD your God is giving you.
Deuteronomy 16:20 NIV

The LORD will not reject His people; He will never forsake His inheritance. Judgment will again be founded on righteousness, and all the upright in heart will follow it.
Psalm 94:14-15 NIV

Your justice is eternal, and Your instructions are perfectly true.
Psalm 119:142 NLT

The breastplate of justice protects your most important organ, your heart. The heart is where our thoughts and actions originate. Justice heals—it creates a path of hope for people. Justice wants to take you further and higher than where you are currently. Justice will take you from fear to hope, from revenge to reconciliation, and from hatred to forgiveness. Righteousness is a godly characteristic that God gives His children who received righteousness in Christ.

Random Acts of Kindness

Those who are kind benefit themselves, but the cruel bring ruin on themselves.
Proverbs 11:17 NIV

Anxiety weighs down the heart, but a kind word cheers it up.
Proverbs 12:25 NIV

Give thanks to the LORD, for He is good! For His mercy endures forever.
Psalm 118:1 NKJV

Whoever is kind to the poor lends to the LORD, and He will reward them for what they have done.
Proverbs 19:17 NIV

When the kindness and love of God our Savior appeared, He saved us, not because of righteous things we had done, but because of His mercy.
Titus 3:4-5 NIV

Since God chose you to be the holy people whom He loves, you must clothe yourselves with tenderhearted mercy, kindness, humility, gentleness, and patience. Make allowance for each other's faults, and forgive anyone who offends you. Remember, the LORD forgave you, so you must forgive others.
Colossians 3:12-13 NLT

God's mercies and kindness are new every morning and always enough for the day. Kindness is a characteristic of God—it is who He is and what He does. Sometimes you miss God's kindness because He revealed it in a different way than you anticipated. It can be in the form of salvation, answered prayers, redemption, and many other ways. Search for it, because it is right there. When you receive His kindness, go out and share it. The satisfaction and reward of being kind to others is indescribable.

The Kingdom of Heaven

"The kingdom of heaven is like a mustard seed, which a man took and planted in his field. Though it is the smallest of all seeds, yet when it grows, it is the largest of garden plants and becomes a tree, so that the birds come and perch in its branches."
Matthew 13:31-32 NIV

"The kingdom of heaven is like leaven, which a woman took and hid in three measures of meal till it was all leavened."
Matthew 13:33 NKJV

"Seek the kingdom of God above all else, and live righteously, and He will give you everything you need."
Matthew 6:33 NIV

"Again, the kingdom of heaven is like a merchant seeking beautiful pearls, who, when he had found one pearl of great price, went and sold all that he had and bought it."
Matthew 13:45-46 NKJV

Set your minds on things above, not on earthly things.
Colossians 3:2 NIV

For the kingdom of God is not a matter of eating and drinking but of righteousness and peace and joy in the Holy Spirit.
Romans 14:17 ESV

To focus on the Kingdom of God should not be an excuse to hide in an idealistic dream world. When you think about the things in heaven above, it helps to think in a new way about earthly things. On earth it changes the rules and relationships of marriage, parenting, and the workplace. Your hands get dirty because you serve others, and your heart breaks for those in distress and pain, because you're embodying God's kingdom values.

Knowledge Gives Power

Intelligent people are always ready to learn. Their ears are open for knowledge.
Proverbs 18:15 NLT

The fear of the LORD is the beginning of knowledge, but fools despise wisdom and instruction.
Proverbs 1:7 NKJV

Choose my instruction rather than silver, and knowledge rather than pure gold.
Proverbs 8:10 NLT

Teach me knowledge and good judgment, for I trust Your commands.
Psalm 119:66 NIV

My people are destroyed for lack of knowledge.
Hosea 4:6 ESV

"I desire mercy and not sacrifice, and the knowledge of God more than burnt offerings."
Hosea 6:6 NKJV

Enthusiasm without knowledge is no good; haste makes mistakes.
Proverbs 19:2 NLT

Blessed be the name of God forever and ever, to whom belong wisdom and might. He gives wisdom to the wise and knowledge to those who have understanding.
Daniel 2:20-21 ESV

The one who has knowledge uses words with restraint, and whoever has understanding is even-tempered.
Proverbs 17:27 NIV

What is the difference between knowledge and wisdom? Knowledge is knowing a tomato is a fruit. Wisdom is knowing not to put a tomato in fruit salad. Knowledge begins with the servitude of the Lord, where we allow Him to reveal Himself to us. Sometimes we are like Job and his friends speculating about God for thirty-seven chapters before He came to say something about Himself and Job cried out: Now I know You!

Work Hard

You shall eat the fruit of the labor of your hands; you shall be blessed, and it shall be well with you.
Psalm 128:2 ESV

The labor of the righteous leads to life, the wages of the wicked to sin.
Proverbs 10:16 NKJV

Unless the LORD builds the house, the builders labor in vain. Unless the LORD watches over the city, the guards stand watch in vain.
Psalm 127:1 NIV

You will enjoy the fruit of your labor. How joyful and prosperous you will be!
Psalm 128:2 NKJV

In all labor there is profit, but idle chatter leads only to poverty.
Proverbs 14:23 NKJV

The appetite of laborers works for them; their hunger drives them on.
Proverbs 16:26 NIV

Stand firm. Let nothing move you. Always give yourselves fully to the work of the LORD, because you know that your labor in the LORD is not in vain.
1 Corinthians 15:58 NIV

The one who plants and the one who waters have one purpose, and they will each be rewarded according to their own labor.
1 Corinthians 3:8 NIV

We spend most of our waking moments at work. Many women are negative about their work, boss, colleagues, hours, and salary. Work is a curse! Or maybe not. Maybe there are numerous Scripture verses describing work as a blessing, but the devil wants to convince you otherwise and steal your joy. God enjoyed His work of creation. Be grateful for your job. Enjoy your work, it's a privilege, but also know when to say no and to set boundaries.

Learn from the Ant!

A lazy person is as bad as someone who destroys things.
Proverbs 18:9 NLT

The way of the lazy man is like a hedge of thorns, but the way of the upright is a highway.
Proverbs 15:19 NKJV

The lazy do not roast any game, but the diligent feed on the riches of the hunt.
Proverbs 12:27 NIV

Lazy people irritate their employers, like vinegar to the teeth or smoke in the eyes.
Proverbs 10:26 NLT

Lazy hands make for poverty, but diligent hands bring wealth.
Proverbs 10:4 NIV

You, lazybones, how long will you sleep? When will you wake up? A little extra sleep, a little more slumber, a little folding of the hands to rest—then poverty will pounce on you like a bandit; scarcity will attack you like an armed robber.
Proverbs 6:9-11 NLT

Go to the ant, you sluggard; consider its ways and be wise!
Proverbs 6:6 NIV

Laziness is more than driving around looking for parking near the entrance while there are many open spaces in the parking lot. Or leaving your shoes where you took them off or not putting your plates in the dishwasher. Laziness is failing to do what should be done when it needs to be done. Jesus, our example, got up early to pray, and yet we are spiritually lazy—too lazy to read the Bible, pray, or attend church activities. Get off the couch and get moving. Learn from the ant.

Lead by Example

Be an example to all believers in what you say, in the way you live, in your love, your faith, and your purity.
1 Timothy 4:12 NLT

Remember your leaders, who spoke the word of God to you. Consider the outcome of their way of life and imitate their faith.
Hebrews 13:7 NIV

In everything set them an example by doing what is good. In your teaching show integrity, seriousness and soundness of speech.
Titus 2:7-8 NIV

Humble yourselves before the LORD, and He will lift you up.
James 4:10 NLT

The LORD says, "It is the one who is least among you all who is the greatest."
Luke 9:48 NIV

"Since I, your LORD and Teacher, have washed your feet, you ought to wash each other's feet."
John 13:14 NLT

Be careful to live properly among your unbelieving neighbors. Then even if they accuse you of doing wrong, they will see your honorable behavior, and they will give honor to God when He judges the world.
1 Peter 2:12 NLT

Leaders remind us of frontrunners, the influential ones with lapels and badges. God's leaders appear somewhat different to the world. His leaders are the least, the ones who lead without badges. God's leaders lead with compassion, care, love, and integrity, because God is in front. He is the greatest. He is the King and we as servant leaders are His shadows. A leader is a woman standing in God's presence and then turning around or stepping aside so His rays can shine on others.

Mindful Learning

A wise man will hear and increase learning, and a man of understanding will attain wise counsel.
Proverbs 1:5 NKJV

Instruct the wise and they will be wiser still; teach the righteous and they will add to their learning.
Proverbs 9:9 NIV

As for you, the anointing you received from Him remains in you, and you do not need anyone to teach you. But as His anointing teaches you about all things and as that anointing is real, not counterfeit—just as it has taught you, remain in Him.
1 John 2:27 ESV

You, however, have followed my teaching, my conduct, my aim in life, my faith, my patience, my love, my steadfastness.
2 Timothy 3:10 ESV

Show me Your ways, LORD, teach me Your paths. Guide me in Your truth and teach me, for You are God my Savior, and my hope is in You all day long.
Psalm 25:4-5 NIV

Get wisdom; develop good judgment. Don't forget my words or turn away from them. Don't turn your back on wisdom, for she will protect you. Love her, and she will guard you.
Proverbs 4:5-6 NLT

John Calvin said that God had removed his spirit of self-sufficiency and given him a teachable spirit. Are you like Calvin, willing to be taught and corrected by the Bible? This means that you allow the Word to live inside your heart and mind. You allow it to transform you and then live like a whole new person. Your Teacher, the Holy Spirit, will guide you into all truth. He will remind you of who Jesus is and how to live out this truth.

Live the Life You Love

Whoever finds me finds life and receives favor from the LORD.
Proverbs 8:35 NIV

Hear, my son, and receive my sayings, and the years of your life will be many.
Proverbs 4:10 NKJV

"Man shall not live by bread alone, but by every word that comes from the mouth of God."
Matthew 4:4 ESV

Now I call on heaven and earth to witness the choice you make. Oh, that you would choose life, so that you and your descendants might live!
Deuteronomy 30:19 NLT

"I have come that they may have life, and have it to the full."
John 10:10 NKJV

You make known to me the path of life; You will fill me with joy in Your presence, with eternal pleasures at Your right hand.
Psalm 16:11 NIV

I will praise the LORD as long as I live; I will sing praises to my God while I have my being.
Psalm 146:2 ESV

The path of the righteous is like the morning sun, shining ever brighter till the full light of day.
Proverbs 4:18 NIV

Do you merely breathe and survive, or are you truly living life? Too many women are just surviving without experiencing the fullness of life that Jesus planned for them. Do you realize that you are a miracle, and He came to give you the gift of life? What are you doing with this gift? Warm up your feet next to the fire place, your hands with a hot cup of tea, and your heart with God's Word. Choose life and thrive!

A Light in the Darkness

Your word is a lamp to my feet and a light to my path.
Psalm 119:105 ESV

If we walk in the light, as He is in the light, we have fellowship with one another, and the blood of Jesus, His Son, purifies us from all sin.
1 John 1:7 NIV

"I am the light of the world. Whoever follows Me will never walk in darkness, but will have the light of life."
John 8:12 NIV

"Let your light shine before others, that they may see your good deeds and glorify your Father in heaven."
Matthew 5:16 NIV

You, LORD, are my lamp; the LORD turns my darkness into light.
2 Samuel 22:29 NIV

Light shines on the righteous and joy on the upright in heart. Rejoice in the LORD, you who are righteous, and praise His holy name.
Psalm 97:11-12 NIV

You are a chosen people, a royal priesthood, a holy nation, God's special possession, that you may declare the praises of Him who called you out of darkness into His wonderful light.
1 Peter 2:9 NIV

Every day we face a battle between light and darkness. Sometimes it feels like the darkness is winning, and victory seems impossible. In the darkest places a small light will always drive out the darkness. Jesus came as the Light to dispel evil and destruction. After three hours on the cross, He finally conquered all. Therefore, you never have to fear Satan or the dark. Let Jesus' light shine through you so that people can see His beautiful light shining in a dark world.

Change Limitations into Strengths

No king is saved by the size of his army; no warrior escapes by his great strength. A horse is a vain hope for deliverance; despite all its great strength it cannot save. But the eyes of the LORD are on those who fear Him, on those whose hope is in His unfailing love.
Psalm 33:16-18 NIV

"For nothing will be impossible with God."
Luke 1:37 ESV

Jesus replied, "What is impossible with man is possible with God."
Luke 18:27 NIV

With Your help I can advance against a troop; with my God I can scale a wall.
Psalm 18:29 NIV

For I can do everything through Christ, who gives me strength.
Philippians 4:13 NLT

I know that You can do anything, and no one can stop You.
Job 42:2 NLT

"Humanly speaking, it is impossible. But with God everything is possible."
Matthew 19:26 NLT

What limits you to live your life to the full? Many times we view circumstances and events as limitations that deter us from our goal in life. Nick Vujicic, the man without arms and legs, is truly an inspiration and lives according to the motto: "I truly believe my life is without limitations." Can it really be, or is he in denial? Maybe he just realizes his limitations are in God's hands. God takes your limitations and turns it into victory and contentment.

Listen with Your Heart

"My sheep listen to My voice; I know them, and they follow Me."
John 10:27 NIV

"Anyone who belongs to God listens gladly to the words of God."
John 8:47 NLT

He said to me: "Son of man, receive into your heart all My words that I speak to you, and hear with your ears."
Ezekiel 3:10 NKJV

"Whoever has ears, let them hear what the Spirit says to the churches."
Revelation 3:22 NIV

Faith comes from hearing, that is, hearing the Good News about Christ.
Romans 10:17 NLT

Do not merely listen to the word, and so deceive yourselves. Do what it says.
James 1:22 NIV

For merely listening to the law doesn't make us right with God. It is obeying the law that makes us right in His sight.
Romans 2:13 NLT

Serve only the LORD your God and fear Him alone. Obey His commands, listen to His voice, and cling to Him.
Deuteronomy 13:4 NLT

There is a big difference between hearing and receiving information, and really listening and using the information. Jesus is God's anthem of love to us, but sometimes we struggle to hear it because of certain filters like our own opinions, preconceived ideas, egos, and will. Because of this we sometimes don't hear God's Word. A woman with a closed Bible is a woman who does not listen to God. Listen with your heart and really hear what God wants to tell you.

Alone or Lonely?

"Surely I am with you always, to the very end of the age."
Matthew 28:20 NIV

"No, I will not abandon you as orphans—I will come to you."
John 14:18 NLT

If I go up to the heavens, You are there; if I make my bed in the depths, You are there. If I rise on the wings of the dawn, if I settle on the far side of the sea, even there Your hand will guide me, Your right hand will hold me fast.
Psalm 139:8-10 NIV

"I will never leave you nor forsake you."
Hebrews 13:5 ESV

"I am with you, and I will protect you wherever you go. One day I will bring you back to this land. I will not leave you until I have finished giving you everything I have promised you."
Genesis 28:15 NLT

"I will ask the Father, and He will give you another Advocate, who will never leave you. He is the Holy Spirit, who leads into all truth...He lives with you now and later will be in you."
John 14:16-17 NLT

You shall call, and the LORD will answer; you shall cry, and He will say, "Here I am."
Isaiah 58:9 NKJV

Loneliness can leave a person cold. Even in a room full of people, one can feel isolated and alone. There is no one who cares, no one who is interested in you or who loves you, and surely no one who knows how you feel. Jesus knows how it feels to be lonely—He was terrified in Gethsemane. He was all alone; even His Father left Him. In Gethsemane He also took your loneliness on Himself, so you never have to be without Him.

That Fabulous Look

The Lord does not see as man sees; for man looks at the outward appearance, but the Lord looks at the heart.
1 Samuel 16:7 NKJV

God is working in you, giving you the desire and the power to do what pleases Him.
Philippians 2:13 NLT

"Physical training is good, but training for godliness is much better, promising benefits in this life and in the life to come."
1 Timothy 4:8 NLT

"Blessed are the pure in heart, for they shall see God."
Matthew 5:8 ESV

Your beauty...should be that of your inner self, the unfading beauty of a gentle and quiet spirit, which is of great worth in God's sight.
1 Peter 3:3-4 NIV

Charm is deceptive, and beauty is fleeting; but a woman who fears the Lord is to be praised.
Proverbs 31:30 NIV

I praise You because I am fearfully and wonderfully made.
Psalm 139:14 NIV

Know that the Lord is God. It is He who made us, and we are His; we are His people, the sheep of His pasture.
Psalm 100:3 NIV

Which qualities do you look for in a friend or marriage partner? Do you look at their achievements, where they live, their personality, age, status, and how other people see them? The way we see people so often determines our relationship with them. But God looks at us differently. He looks at the heart, your beliefs, and thoughts—the things that cannot be seen with the eye. You might be able to spot a good friend or husband when you look at others as God does.

Lost, But Found

"What man of you, having a hundred sheep, if he has lost one of them, does not leave the ninety-nine in the open country, and go after the one that is lost, until he finds it? And when he has found it, he lays it on his shoulders, rejoicing. And when he comes home, he calls together his friends and his neighbors, saying to them, 'Rejoice with me, for I have found my sheep that was lost.' Just so, I tell you, there will be more joy in heaven over one sinner who repents than over ninety-nine righteous persons who need no repentance."
Luke 15:4-7 ESV

"For the Son of Man came to seek and save those who are lost."
Luke 19:10 NLT

"I tell you, there is rejoicing in the presence of the angels of God over one sinner who repents."
Luke 15:10 NIV

"These twelve Jesus sent out with the following instructions: "Do not go among the Gentiles or enter any town of the Samaritans. Go rather to the lost sheep of Israel. As you go, proclaim this message: 'The kingdom of heaven has come near.' Heal the sick, raise the dead, cleanse those who have leprosy, drive out demons. Freely you have received; freely give."
Matthew 10:5-8 NIV

Did you ever get lost as a child, or were your parents ever suddenly nowhere to be seen when you turned around at the mall? At first you're a little unsure, then you start to panic, and then you call out to them with a trembling voice. Later you are crying hysterically: "Help, I'm lost!" Or you hear a mother anxiously calling her lost child's name. God heard the solitude of man and answered our cry of distress. He will continue searching until He finds you.

The Love of God

"I have loved you with an everlasting love; I have drawn you with unfailing kindness."
Jeremiah 31:3 NIV

Give thanks to the God of gods. His love endures forever.
Psalm 136:2 NIV

For I am convinced that neither death nor life, neither angels nor demons, neither the present nor the future, nor any powers, neither height nor depth, nor anything else in all creation, will be able to separate us from the love of God.
Romans 8:38-39 NIV

See how very much our Father loves us, for He calls us His children, and that is what we are!
1 John 3:1 NLT

The faithful love of the LORD never ends! His mercies never cease. Great is His faithfulness; His mercies begin afresh each morning.
Lamentations 3:22-23 NLT

"For God so loved the world that He gave His one and only Son, that whoever believes in Him shall not perish but have eternal life."
John 3:16 NIV

"I have loved you even as the Father has loved Me. Remain in My love."
John 15:9 NLT

Are you battling with the question of whether God really loves you? Well, His answer is 1,000 times yes! With every sunrise and bright moon, with every blooming flower and soft rain falling, He sings a love song to you. He opens the floodgates of His heart and overflowing love out on you. When you allow Him to live inside you, He will fill you with His undeserved love and grace.

Love Your Enemies

"I tell you, love your enemies and pray for those who persecute you, that you may be children of your Father in heaven. He causes His sun to rise on the evil and the good, and sends rain on the righteous and the unrighteous."
Matthew 5:44-45 NIV

"I say to you who hear, love your enemies, do good to those who hate you, bless those who curse you, pray for those who abuse you. To one who strikes you on the cheek, offer the other also, and from one who takes away your cloak do not withhold your tunic either."
Luke 6:27-29 ESV

Bless those who persecute you. Don't curse them; pray that God will bless them.
Romans 12:14 NLT

Do not repay evil with evil or insult with insult. On the contrary, repay evil with blessing, because to this you were called so that you may inherit a blessing.
1 Peter 3:9 NIV

If your enemy is hungry, feed him; if he is thirsty, give him a drink; for in so doing you will heap coals of fire on his head.
Romans 12:20 NKJV

Don't let evil conquer you, but conquer evil by doing good.
Romans 12:21 NLT

Peace and reconciliation between two enemies come when God's children fight the darkness with light and expel hatred with love. The change doesn't start with your enemy, but with you. After your character and attitude toward your enemy changes, your circumstances will change too. To love and forgive your enemy, even though you feel they don't deserve it, is the greatest gift you can give yourself. Only then will the chains of anger, hatred, and injustice fall off. Then you are free indeed.

Love Your Neighbor

If we love each other, God lives in us, and His love is brought to full expression in us.
1 John 4:12 NLT

Love each other deeply, because love covers a multitude of sins.
1 Peter 4:8 ESV

"Love your neighbor as yourself."
Matthew 19:19 NLT

"Love each other as I have loved you."
John 15:12 NIV

Love one another deeply, from the heart.
1 Peter 1:22 NLT

Pursue righteousness, faith, love, peace.
2 Timothy 2:22 NKJV

"A new commandment I give to you, that you love one another; as I have loved you, that you also love one another."
John 13:34 NKJV

If I speak in the tongues of men or of angels, but do not have love, I am only a resounding gong or a clanging cymbal. If I have the gift of prophecy and can fathom all mysteries and all knowledge, and if I have a faith that can move mountains, but do not have love, I am nothing. If I give all I possess to the poor and give over my body to hardship that I may boast, but do not have love, I gain nothing.
1 Corinthians 13:1-3 NIV

Love is more than an emotion or a feeling; love is a choice. Mother Teresa once said that the biggest killer in the world is a lack of love. The Lord commanded us to love because we are His image bearers. Your confession that you love God becomes visible through your love for others. Love that wears an apron, washes feet, and makes time for people—that is love in action. People will not care how much you know until they know how much you care and love.

A Loyal Servant

Love the LORD, all you godly ones! For the LORD protects those who are loyal to Him.
Psalm 31:23 NLT

Loyalty makes a person attractive. It is better to be poor than dishonest.
Proverbs 19:22 NLT

Many will say they are loyal friends, but who can find one who is truly reliable?
Proverbs 20:6 NLT

Let your heart therefore be loyal to the LORD our God, to walk in His statutes and keep His commandments.
1 Kings 8:61 NKJV

Never let loyalty and kindness leave you! Tie them around your neck as a reminder. Write them deep within your heart.
Proverbs 3:3 NLT

The LORD leads with unfailing love and faithfulness all who keep His covenant and obey His demands.
Psalm 25:10 NLT

Let us hold fast the confession of our hope without wavering, for He who promised is faithful.
Hebrews 10:23 NKJV

A friend is always loyal, and a brother is born to help in time of need.
Proverbs 17:17 NLT

We expect loyalty from others, yet we struggle to be loyal. Loyalty is not a feeling or something that someone imposes on you; it comes from a place of love, dedication, and commitment that is a deliberate choice. Loyalty acts with integrity, even if it is difficult. Loyalty protects relationships and supports others emotionally and physically through thick and thin.

The Devil in Disguise

"I know your deeds, that you are neither cold nor hot. I wish you were either one or the other! So, because you are lukewarm—neither hot nor cold—I am about to spit you out of My mouth."
Revelation 3:15-16 NIV

"Anyone who isn't with Me opposes Me, and anyone who isn't working with Me is actually working against Me."
Matthew 12:30 NLT

"You are the salt of the earth; but if the salt loses its flavor, how shall it be seasoned? It is then good for nothing but to be thrown out and trampled underfoot by men."
Matthew 5:13 NKJV

Blessed is the one who reads aloud the words of this prophecy, and blessed are those who hear it and take to heart what is written in it, because the time is near.
Revelation 1:3 NIV

What does it profit, my brethren, if someone says he has faith but does not have works? Can faith save him? If a brother or sister is naked and destitute of daily food, and one of you says to them, "Depart in peace, be warmed and filled," but you do not give them the things which are needed for the body, what does it profit? Thus also faith by itself, if it does not have works, is dead.
James 2:14-17 NKJV

On cold days a warm cup of coffee helps to warm you up, while an ice cold drink cools you down on a scorching day. Nobody orders a cup of lukewarm tea or a glass of lukewarm soda, yet we are often satisfied with lukewarm faith. We often talk about God with a flaming desire, while our hearts are like lukewarm water. We confess the name of Jesus, but He doesn't hold exclusive rights in our lives. We serve as long as it suits us. What is the temperature of your heart and your faith today?

A Moral Choice

Lead me, LORD, in Your righteousness because of my enemies—make Your way straight before me. Not a word from their mouth can be trusted; their heart is filled with malice. Their throat is an open grave; with their tongues they tell lies. Declare them guilty, O God! Let their intrigues be their downfall. Banish them for their many sins, for they have rebelled against You.
Psalm 5:8-10 NIV

The wicked conceive evil; they give birth to lies. They dig a deep pit to trap others, then fall into it themselves.
Psalm 7:14-15 NLT

Their mouths are full of cursing, lies, and threats. Trouble and evil are on the tips of their tongues. The wicked think, "God isn't watching us! He has closed His eyes and won't even see what we do!" Arise, O LORD! Punish the wicked, O God! Do not ignore the helpless!
Psalm 10:7, 11-12 NLT

"He (the Devil) does not stand in the truth, because there is no truth in him. When he lies, he speaks out of his own character, for he is a liar and the father of lies."
John 8:44 ESV

How many times have you exchanged the truth for a lie, even little white lies, to keep the peace or prevent you from getting into trouble? The price tag that you cut off the "old dress" this morning, the empty promises of prayer, and lying about your age—you hear lies everywhere and still the naked truth is better than the best dressed lie. Research shows that when a lie is told often enough, you start to believe it. Choose the truth, because the truth will always set you free.

August

Above all these
—— put on ——

love
which binds
everything together in

perfect
harmony.

Colossians 3:14

More than Just a Ring

Love each other with genuine affection, and take delight in honoring each other.
Romans 12:10 NLT

Love is patient, love is kind. It does not envy, it does not boast, it is not proud. It does not dishonor others, it is not self-seeking, it is not easily angered, it keeps no record of wrongs. Love does not delight in evil but rejoices with the truth. It always protects, always trusts, always hopes, always perseveres.
1 Corinthians 13:4-7 NIV

Each one of you also must love his wife as he loves himself, and the wife must respect her husband.
Ephesians 5:33 NIV

Be like-minded, be sympathetic, love one another, be compassionate and humble. Do not repay evil with evil or insult with insult. On the contrary, repay evil with blessing, because to this you were called so that you may inherit a blessing.
1 Peter 3:8-9 NIV

Let marriage be held in honor among all, and let the marriage bed be undefiled.
Hebrews 13:4 ESV

The believing wife brings holiness to her marriage, and the believing husband brings holiness to his marriage. Otherwise, your children would not be holy, but now they are holy.
1 Corinthians 7:14 NLT

"For better or worse" has changed to "outwit and outlast" in marriages these days. Instead of the husband and wife living together in perfect unity where they complement each other and become stronger together, marriage has become a competition. Marriage is a godly institution—a flame lit by God that starts with butterflies in your stomach and stars in your eyes. Pray together, otherwise you leave your marriage open to attack by the devil. Marital bliss starts with a choice. Choose happiness and love.

A Magnificent Masterpiece

Thank You for making me so wonderfully complex! Your workmanship is marvelous—how well I know it.
Psalm 139:14 NLT

You formed my inward parts; You knitted me together in my mother's womb. I praise You, for I am fearfully and wonderfully made. Wonderful are Your works; my soul knows it very well. My frame was not hidden from You, when I was being made in secret, intricately woven in the depths of the earth. Your eyes saw my unformed substance; in Your book were written, every one of them, the days that were formed for me, when as yet there was none of them.
Psalm 139:13-16 ESV

We are God's masterpiece. He has created us anew in Christ Jesus, so we can do the good things He planned for us long ago.
Ephesians 2:10 NLT

You, LORD, are our Father. We are the clay, You are the potter; we are all the work of Your hand.
Isaiah 64:8 NIV

God created man in His own image; in the image of God He created him; male and female He created them.
Genesis 1:27 NKJV

Know that the LORD, He is God! It is He who made us, and we are His; we are His people, and the sheep of His pasture.
Psalm 100:3 ESV

What is your first thought when you wake up and look in the mirror? You are God's masterpiece, destined for heaven, made in His image, the one in whom His mystery and treasures are locked up. Realize the Potter is still busy molding His clay—in control, with love and compassion, He gently but firmly shapes you into a work of art. For a moment He takes a step back to look at you and admire you; His masterpiece is good.

The High Price of Materialism

Keep your life free from love of money, and be content with what you have, for He has said, "I will never leave you nor forsake you."
Hebrews 13:5 ESV

Better to have little, with fear for the LORD, than to have great treasure and inner turmoil.
Proverbs 15:16 NLT

"Sell your possessions and give to the poor. Provide purses for yourselves that will not wear out, a treasure in heaven that will never fail, where no thief comes near and no moth destroys. For where your treasure is, there your heart will be also."
Luke 12:33-34 NIV

If someone has enough money to live well and sees a brother or sister in need but shows no compassion—how can God's love be in that person?
1 John 3:17 NLT

Godliness with contentment is great gain. For we brought nothing into the world, and we can take nothing out of it.
1 Timothy 6:6-7 NIV

He said to them, "Take heed and beware of covetousness, for one's life does not consist in the abundance of the things he possesses."
Luke 12:15 NKJV

People's desire for more and more things is the result of an achievement-driven society. Materialism has a very high price, and I am not talking about currency that is dependent on the stock markets. I'm talking about the toll stress takes on us. We are overworked, we have too little time to spend on relationships, and it affects our health. Materialism is addictive. Once you get caught in its trap, you just have to get more and more to feel satisfied, and then it takes complete control of your life.

Experiencing the Presence of God

Keep this Book of the Law always on your lips; meditate on it day and night, so that you may be careful to do everything written in it. Then you will be prosperous and successful.
Joshua 1:8 NIV

I will meditate on Your precepts, and contemplate Your ways.
Psalm 119:15 NKJV

Cause me to understand the way of Your precepts, that I may meditate on Your wonderful deeds.
Psalm 119:27 NIV

On the glorious splendor of Your majesty, and on Your wondrous works, I will meditate.
Psalm 145:5 ESV

O God, we meditate on Your unfailing love as we worship in Your Temple.
Psalm 48:9 NLT

I will ponder all Your work, and meditate on Your mighty deeds. Psalm 77:12 ESV

Look, I go forward, but He is not there, and backward, but I cannot perceive Him; when He works on the left hand, I cannot behold Him; when He turns to the right hand, I cannot see Him. But He knows the way that I take; when He has tested me, I shall come forth as gold. Job 23:8-10 NKJV

You have hedged me behind and before, and laid Your hand upon me.
Psalm 139:5 NKJV

Many people think the Bible is a magical book that you can quickly open and close, and it produces quick answers, indicating the road to follow and predicting the future. But the Word comes to life through the Spirit's work in you. Therefore you have to spend time reading and meditating on it, so the words can be engraved on your heart. Make it your goal to think about the Scripture verses you've read each day.

Strength in Meekness

The meek will inherit the land and enjoy peace and prosperity.
Psalm 37:11 NIV

In Your majesty ride out victoriously for the cause of truth and meekness and righteousness; let Your right hand teach You awesome deeds!
Psalm 45:4 ESV

"God blesses those who are humble, for they will inherit the whole earth."
Matthew 5:5 NLT

Therefore, as the elect of God, holy and beloved, put on tender mercies, kindness, humility, meekness, longsuffering.
Colossians 3:12 NKJV

A man's pride will bring him low, but the humble in spirit will retain honor.
Proverbs 29:23 NKJV

Gently instruct those who oppose the truth. Perhaps God will change those people's hearts, and they will learn the truth.
2 Timothy 2:25 NLT

Pride leads to disgrace, but with humility comes wisdom.
Proverbs 11:2 NLT

True humility and fear of the LORD lead to riches, honor, and long life.
Proverbs 22:4 NLT

Meekness is not a weakness that turns you into a doormat. The meek are not deprived. Rather the woman who has allowed the character, nature, and love of God to saturate her heart and soften her spirit is in touch with God's plan for her life. So your meekness is a force under the control of the Spirit; it gives healing and refreshment to others, spreading the peace of God.

The Art of Mentoring

Even when I am old and gray, do not forsake me, my God, till I declare Your power to the next generation, Your mighty acts to all who are to come.
Psalm 71:18 NIV

You have heard me teach things that have been confirmed by many reliable witnesses. Now teach these truths to other trustworthy people who will be able to pass them on to others.
2 Timothy 2:2 NLT

Let no one despise your youth, but be an example to the believers in word, in conduct, in love, in spirit, in faith, in purity.
1 Timothy 4:12 NKJV

Encourage the young men to live wisely. And you yourself must be an example to them by doing good works of every kind. Let everything you do reflect the integrity and seriousness of your teaching. Teach the truth so that your teaching can't be criticized.
Titus 2:6-8 NLT

Whatever you have learned or received or heard from me, or seen in me—put it into practice. And the God of peace will be with you.
Philippians 4:9 NIV

Give instruction to a wise man, and he will be still wiser; teach a just man, and he will increase in learning.
Proverbs 9:9 NKJV

Timothy was very fortunate to have Paul, a man with knowledge and experience of God, as a mentor in his life. You also need a Paul in your life who can mentor and inspire you. Someone who will tackle life's journey with you. You are also a Paul, the mentor for your child who observes your life, wisdom, advice, and guidance. As a mentor you must remember and teach others that the Spirit of God always remains our best mentor.

A Miracle Is Possible

"Do not stop him," Jesus said. "For no one who does a miracle in My name can in the next moment say anything bad about Me."
Mark 9:39 NLT

God did extraordinary miracles through Paul.
Acts 19:11 NIV

When He came near the place where the road goes down the Mount of Olives, the whole crowd of disciples began joyfully to praise God in loud voices for all the miracles they had seen.
Luke 19:37 NIV

Sing to Him, sing praise to Him; tell of all His wonderful acts.
1 Chronicles 16:9 NIV

There are varieties of activities, but it is the same God who empowers them all in everyone.
1 Corinthians 12:6 ESV

O God, You have taught me from my youth; and to this day I declare Your wondrous works.
Psalm 71:17 NKJV

Let the hearts of those who seek the LORD rejoice! Seek the LORD and His strength; seek His presence continually! Remember the wondrous works that He has done, His miracles and the judgments He uttered. He is the LORD our God; His judgments are in all the earth.
1 Chronicles 16:10-12, 14 ESV

What is the greatest miracle that Jesus has ever performed for you? Was it physical healing, like the lepers and the blind man? Did He provide for you financially, like the disciples who took a coin out of the fish's mouth? Maybe He calmed your storm and gave you peace. The greatest miracle is that He chose you, an imperfect woman. He forgave you and made you His child. What a great miracle—the wonder of His love and forgiveness in abundance.

A Vision for Missions

Everyone who calls on the name of the LORD will be saved." How, then, can they call on the one they have not believed in? And how can they believe in the one of whom they have not heard? And how can they hear without someone preaching to them? And how can anyone preach unless they are sent? As it is written: "How beautiful are the feet of those who bring good news!"
Romans 10:13-15 NIV

For the LORD gave us this command when He said, "I have made you a light to the Gentiles, to bring salvation to the farthest corners of the earth."
Acts 13:47 NLT

Declare His glory among the nations, His wonders among all peoples.
1 Chronicles 16:24 NKJV

"You shall receive power when the Holy Spirit has come upon you; and you shall be witnesses to Me in Jerusalem, and in all Judea and Samaria, and to the end of the earth."
Acts 1:8 NKJV

"Go into all the world and preach the Good News to everyone."
Mark 16:15 NLT

Publish His glorious deeds among the nations. Tell everyone about the amazing things He does.
Psalm 96:3 NLT

All God's children are called to be witnesses and to share His Good News with others. It started in Jerusalem and spread all over the world. For the disciples Jerusalem was a place of fear—Jesus was crucified and the Jews wanted their heads too. Samaria was the location of the enemy. Jesus sent them to their enemies and frightening places, because He knew the Spirit would equip them to be brave witnesses for Him.

Making Mistakes

Who can discern their own errors? Forgive my hidden faults.
Psalm 19:12 NIV

The godly may trip seven times, but they will get up again. But one disaster is enough to overthrow the wicked.
Proverbs 24:16 NLT

The LORD directs the steps of the godly. He delights in every detail of their lives. Though they stumble, they will never fall, for the LORD holds them by the hand.
Psalm 37:23-24 NLT

"Forget the former things; do not dwell on the past."
Isaiah 43:18 NIV

We all stumble in many ways. Anyone who is never at fault in what they say is perfect, able to keep their whole body in check.
James 3:2 NIV

Enthusiasm without knowledge is no good; haste makes mistakes.
Proverbs 19:2 NLT

My flesh and my heart may fail, but God is the strength of my heart and my portion forever.
Psalm 73:26 ESV

If your boss is angry at you, don't quit! A quiet spirit can overcome even great mistakes.
Ecclesiastes 10:4 NLT

To make a mistake is easy, but to forgive yourself or someone else for a mistake is much more difficult. Yet mistakes are our teachers for the future. Because you also make mistakes and need forgiveness, you must be gentle and patient with others' mistakes. Remember that you are much more than the mistakes you make, so acknowledge them and apologize. You will earn more respect by fixing your mistakes than by trying to hide them.

The Mocking of Jesus

If you are wise, your wisdom will reward you; if you are a mocker, you alone will suffer.
Proverbs 9:12 NIV

My friends scorn me, but I pour out my tears to God.
Job 16:20 NLT

Whoever mocks the poor insults his Maker; he who is glad at calamity will not go unpunished.
Proverbs 17:5 ESV

They bowed the knee before Him and mocked Him, saying, "Hail, King of the Jews!"
Matthew 27:29 NKJV

Mockers stir up a city, but the wise turn away anger.
Proverbs 29:8 NIV

The LORD mocks the mockers but is gracious to the humble.
Proverbs 3:34 NLT

A mocker seeks wisdom and never finds it, but knowledge comes easily to those with understanding.
Proverbs 14:6 NLT

They will hand Him over to the Romans to be mocked, flogged with a whip, and crucified. But on the third day He will be raised from the dead."
Matthew 20:19 NLT

To be mocked and ridiculed is not pleasant. We keep it in our hearts to brood on later. And eventually it colors what we believe about ourselves. Jesus knows the feeling of being mocked. First they sang songs of praise to Him, then their praises changed to mockery. He was scorned, spat on, and a crown of thorns was put on His head. He could have ended it all right there, but He didn't; He died so that you will never have to endure such mockery and pain without God. Don't brood on the insults and remarks of others; give it to Him.

A Modest Heart

Do not think of yourself more highly than you ought, but rather think of yourself with sober judgment, in accordance with the faith God has distributed to each of you.
Romans 12:3 NIV

Don't demand an audience with the king or push for a place among the great. It's better to wait for an invitation to the head table than to be sent away in public disgrace.
Proverbs 25:6-7 NLT

Humility is the fear of the LORD; its wages are riches and honor and life.
Proverbs 22:4 NIV

We will not boast about things done outside our area of authority. We will boast only about what has happened within the boundaries of the work God has given us, which includes our working with you. Nor do we boast and claim credit for the work someone else has done. Instead, we hope that your faith will grow so that the boundaries of our work among you will be extended.
2 Corinthians 10:13, 15 NLT

I will not boast about myself, except about my weaknesses...I refrain, so no one will think more of me than is warranted by what I do or say.
2 Corinthians 12:5-6 NIV

Being humble can be tough sometimes. Is it pride or my identity in Christ? Am I humble or is it low self-esteem? Modesty is not about whether you think too much or too little of yourself, it's about God and His Kingdom. Modest people know who they are in Christ. They realize everything is grace, and they can take a step back so God can get the glory.

Money Matters

Whoever loves money never has enough; whoever loves wealth is never satisfied with their income. This too is meaningless.
Ecclesiastes 5:10 NIV

People who long to be rich fall into temptation and are trapped by many foolish and harmful desires that plunge them into ruin and destruction.
1 Timothy 6:9 NLT

"What good is it for someone to gain the whole world, yet forfeit their soul?"
Mark 8:36 NIV

Do not overwork to be rich; because of your own understanding, cease!
Proverbs 23:4 NKJV

Dishonest money dwindles away, but whoever gathers money little by little makes it grow.
Proverbs 13:11 NIV

The love of money is a root of all kinds of evils. It is through this craving that some have wandered away from the faith and pierced themselves with many pangs.
1 Timothy 6:10 ESV

"No one can serve two masters. Either you will hate the one and love the other, or you will be devoted to the one and despise the other. You cannot serve both God and money."
Matthew 6:24 NIV

The world says, "Money works wonders," while others say that "money is the root of all evil." The problem is not with money per se, but in how we manage it. Handle your finances well, and depend on God. Let your money be used in His service. Be happy with what you have, and store up your treasures in heaven.

The Evaluation of Morality

Do not be deceived: "Bad company ruins good morals."
1 Corinthians 15:33 ESV

Get rid of all moral filth and the evil that is so prevalent and humbly accept the word planted in you, which can save you.
James 1:21 NIV

Supplement your faith with a generous provision of moral excellence, and moral excellence with knowledge, and knowledge with self-control, and self-control with patient endurance, and patient endurance with godliness, and godliness with brotherly affection, and brotherly affection with love for everyone.
2 Peter 1:5-7 NLT

When there is moral rot within a nation, its government topples easily. But wise and knowledgeable leaders bring stability.
Proverbs 28:2 NLT

He said, "What comes out of a man, that defiles a man. For from within, out of the heart of men, proceed evil thoughts, adulteries, fornications, murders, thefts, covetousness, wickedness, deceit, lewdness, an evil eye, blasphemy, pride, foolishness. All these evil things come from within and defile a man."
Mark 7:20-23 NKJV

Walk by the Spirit, and you will not gratify the desires of the flesh.
Galatians 5:16 NIV

We live in an age of moral decay because of the gradual shift away from strict values and norms to fit in with the times. The media, especially TV and social media platforms, promote morals that are not biblical, yet we follow and implement these morals in our lives. Love and sexuality are used as and when you want to fulfill your immediate needs and desires. To develop morality, children need good examples from their parents who live according to biblical standards.

The Ministry of Motherhood

Her children stand and bless her. Her husband praises her: "There are many virtuous and capable women in the world, but you surpass them all!"
Proverbs 31:28-29 NLT

"Can a woman forget her nursing child, and not have compassion on the son of her womb? Surely they may forget, yet I will not forget you."
Isaiah 49:15 NKJV

Instead, we were like young children among you. Just as a nursing mother cares for her children.
1 Thessalonians 2:7 NIV

I am reminded of your sincere faith, a faith that dwelt first in your grandmother Lois and your mother Eunice and now, I am sure, dwells in you as well.
2 Timothy 1:5 NIV

I have calmed and quieted my soul, like a weaned child with its mother; like a weaned child is my soul within me.
Psalm 131:2 ESV

He settles the childless woman in her home as a happy mother of children. Praise the LORD.
Psalm 113:9 NIV

For nine months a miracle was developing inside you when you were pregnant. The day that your bundle of joy lies in your arms, perfectly created in mini format, your life changes completely. The way you think, talk, and act changes for good. You don't have to be super mom; just be a loving, patient, and kind mom willing to serve. A mother who is always there for her children. When you reflect on your life growing up, do you see her on her knees, encouraging you, driving you around, and feeding you? Appreciate your mother, and return the love.

Magical Music

My head will be exalted above the enemies who surround me; at His sacred tent I will sacrifice with shouts of joy; I will sing and make music to the LORD.
Psalm 27:6 NIV

It is good to give thanks to the LORD, to sing praises to Your name, O Most High; to declare Your steadfast love in the morning, and Your faithfulness by night.
Psalm 92:1-2 ESV

Sing and make music from your heart to the LORD, always giving thanks to God the Father for everything in the name of our LORD Jesus Christ.
Ephesians 5:19-20 NIV

I will praise You with the harp for Your faithfulness, my God; I will sing praise to You with the lyre, Holy One of Israel.
Psalm 71:22 NIV

My heart is confident in You, O God; no wonder I can sing Your praises with all my heart!
Psalm 108:1 NLT

Sing to God, sing in praise of His name, extol Him who rides on the clouds; rejoice before Him—His name is the LORD.
Psalm 68:4 NIV

I will praise the LORD according to His righteousness, and will sing praise to the name of the LORD Most High.
Psalm 7:17 NKJV

Music has great power and can impact your life, even when you don't realize it. Music creates good memories and different emotions. Therefore it is important that you are selective when choosing the music you listen to. Inside the church we see that music has the ability to unite people in praise, but also to cause discord regarding individual preferences. Psalms is a book of 150 songs that encourage people through all aspects of life. Sing to the glory of the Lord!

The Names of the Lord

Everyone who calls on the name of the LORD will be saved.
Romans 10:13 NLT

The name of the LORD is a fortified tower; the righteous run to it and are safe.
Proverbs 18:10 NIV

You were cleansed; you were made holy; you were made right with God by calling on the name of the LORD Jesus Christ and by the Spirit of our God.
1 Corinthians 6:11 NLT

There is none like You, O LORD; You are great, and Your name is great in might.
Jeremiah 10:6 ESV

"Whatever you ask in My name, this I will do, that the Father may be glorified in the Son. If you ask Me anything in My name, I will do it."
John 14:13-14 ESV

Moses protested, "If I go to the people of Israel and tell them, 'The God of your ancestors has sent me to you,' they will ask me, 'What is His name?' Then what should I tell them?" God replied to Moses, "I AM WHO I AM. Say this to the people of Israel: I AM has sent me to you."
Exodus 3:13-14 NLT

Names are important to people. In biblical times, it was no different. A name carried meaning linked to the person, his identity, or occupation. God's name is a revelation of who He is. Some of the names of God are *Elohay Mikarov* which means the God who is near us; *El Roi* means the God who sees everything; *Jehovah Rapha* means the God who heals; *Jehovah Shalom* is our peace, and *Jehovah Jireh* is the God provides. Discover God and praise Him in every name He has.

Your Special Needs

The LORD is my shepherd; I have all that I need.
Psalm 23:1 NLT

Fear the LORD, you His godly people, for those who fear Him will have all they need.
Psalm 34:9 NLT

Those who are righteous will be long remembered. They share freely and give generously to those in need. Their good deeds will be remembered forever. They will have influence and honor.
Psalm 112:6, 9 NLT

God will meet all your needs according to the riches of His glory in Christ Jesus.
Philippians 4:19 NIV

They all depend on You to give them food as they need it. When You supply it, they gather it. You open Your hand to feed them, and they are richly satisfied.
Psalm 104:27-28 NLT

"Therefore I say to you, do not worry about your life, what you will eat or what you will drink; nor about your body, what you will put on. Is not life more than food and the body more than clothing? Look at the birds of the air, for they neither sow nor reap nor gather into barns; yet your heavenly Father feeds them. Are you not of more value than they?"
Matthew 6:25-26 NKJV

Make a list of your greatest needs. Make sure each item on your list is a necessity and not a desire. When we nurture desires we tend to believe that they are needs and that we cannot live without them. Yet when we seek God's guidance, it is our hunger for Him that makes us realize that His heart's desire is to meet our needs. He wants to answer your spiritual needs through Jesus and by the power of the Spirit. Trust Him.

Who Is My Neighbor?

"You shall not give false testimony against your neighbor."
Exodus 20:16 NIV

Do not devise evil against your neighbor, for he dwells by you for safety's sake.
Proverbs 3:29 NKJV

"Love your neighbor as yourself."
Mark 12:31 NLT

Love does no harm to a neighbor; therefore love is the fulfillment of the law.
Romans 13:10 NKJV

"In everything, do to others what you would have them do to you, for this sums up the Law and the Prophets."
Matthew 7:12 NIV

"Now which of these three would you say was a neighbor to the man who was attacked by bandits?" Jesus asked. The man replied, "The one who showed him mercy." Then Jesus said, "Yes, now go and do the same."
Luke 10:36-37 NLT

"Teacher, what should I do to inherit eternal life?" Jesus replied, "What does the law of Moses say? How do you read it?" The man answered, "'You must love the LORD your God with all your heart, all your soul, all your strength, and all your mind.' And, 'Love your neighbor as yourself.'" "Right!" Jesus told him. "Do this and you will live!"
Luke 10:25-28 NLT

Love your neighbor as yourself. Immediately we want to know—who is my neighbor? Whom must I love and show compassion to? Jesus Himself answered this question in the story of the Good Samaritan. Do you realize that you are actually the injured person along the way and are dependent on a neighbor? Once you do, be grateful and look for neighbors to offer help to. When someone crosses your path, God shows you that they are your neighbor too.

Life-Changing Truths

Jesus Christ is the same yesterday and today and forever.
Hebrews 13:8 NIV

"For I am the LORD, I do not change; therefore you are not consumed."
Malachi 3:6 NKJV

LORD, You remain the same forever! Your throne continues from generation to generation.
Lamentations 5:19 NLT

"I am the Alpha and the Omega, the Beginning and the End, the First and the Last."
Revelation 22:13 NKJV

"You, LORD, laid the foundation of the earth in the beginning, and the heavens are the work of Your hands; they will perish, but You remain; they will all wear out like a garment, like a robe You will roll them up, like a garment they will be changed. But You are the same, and Your years will have no end."
Hebrews 1:10-12 ESV

Whatever is good and perfect is a gift coming down to us from God our Father, who created all the lights in the heavens. He never changes or casts a shifting shadow.
James 1:17 NLT

Do the changes in climate, the economy, your health, or politics make you stress and worry? I have good news: God is the same yesterday, today, and forever. He is love. In the garden of Eden He whispered it, on the cross He showed it, and today we still hear His heart beating for us. God has compassion—therefore, He sent manna and quails, He wept at Lazarus' tomb, and He sent His Spirit to comfort us today. He is your certainty in changing times.

A Life of Obedience

Peter and the other apostles replied: "We must obey God rather than human beings!"
Acts 5:29 NIV

Obey the LORD your God and follow His commands and decrees.
Deuteronomy 27:10 NIV

For merely listening to the law doesn't make us right with God. It is obeying the law that makes us right in His sight.
Romans 2:13 NLT

Thanks be to God that, though you used to be slaves to sin, you have come to obey from your heart the pattern of teaching that has now claimed your allegiance.
Romans 6:17 NIV

"Obey My voice, and I will be your God, and you shall be My people. And walk in all the ways that I have commanded you, that it may be well with you."
Jeremiah 7:23 NKJV

So Samuel said: "Has the LORD as great delight in burnt offerings and sacrifices, as in obeying the voice of the LORD? Behold, to obey is better than sacrifice, and to heed than the fat of rams."
1 Samuel 15:22 NKJV

You must love the LORD your God and always obey His requirements, decrees, regulations, and commands.
Deuteronomy 11:1 NLT

What do you think is the most important sacrifice you can bring to God today? A tithe, your precious time, your dreams and goals? The most important and greatest sacrifice He asks of you is obedience to Him. Sometimes we are caught in pious ceremonies, customs, and habits without a sincere heart. Obedience is sometimes difficult and incomprehensible, like Abraham who had to sacrifice Isaac. He lived close to God and recklessly obeyed Him. The result: a reward far greater than the present!

Returning God's Love with Offerings

Your faithful service is an offering to God.
Philippians 2:17 NLT

The LORD will have men who will bring offerings in righteousness, and the offerings of Judah and Jerusalem will be acceptable to the LORD.
Malachi 3:3-4 NIV

He gave His life to free us from every kind of sin, to cleanse us, and to make us His very own people, totally committed to doing good deeds.
Titus 2:14 NLT

Present your bodies a living sacrifice, holy, acceptable to God.
Romans 12:1 NKJV

Through Him then let us continually offer up a sacrifice of praise to God.
Hebrews 13:15 ESV

You will delight in the sacrifices of the righteous.
Psalm 51:19 NIV

Give to the LORD glory and strength. Give to the LORD the glory due His name; bring an offering, and come before Him. Oh, worship the LORD in the beauty of holiness! Tremble before Him, all the earth.
1 Chronicles 16:28-30 NKJV

Jesus made the ultimate sacrifice so we could be redeemed and called children of God. It is strange that when God asks an offering from us, we think in terms of gold and silver. Everything you have belongs to God. He doesn't need your money and possessions, therefore He asks a sacrifice that's going to cost you something more than earthly riches. Give yourself as a living sacrifice to the Lord. Give your faith and love and care as a sacrifice that is like a pleasing fragrance to God.

The Omnipotence of God

For ever since the world was created, people have seen the earth and sky. Through everything God made, they can clearly see His invisible qualities—His eternal power and divine nature.
Romans 1:20 NLT

He determines the number of the stars; He gives to all of them their names. Great is our LORD, and abundant in power; His understanding is beyond measure.
Psalm 147:4-5 ESV

"Humanly speaking, it is impossible. But with God everything is possible."
Matthew 19:26 NLT

Just as you cannot understand the path of the wind or the mystery of a tiny baby growing in its mother's womb, so you cannot understand the activity of God, who does all things.
Ecclesiastes 11:5 NLT

Yours, LORD, is the greatness and the power and the glory and the majesty and the splendor, for everything in heaven and earth is Yours. Yours, LORD, is the kingdom; You are exalted as head over all.
1 Chronicles 29:11 NIV

"I am the LORD, the God of all mankind. Is anything too hard for Me?"
Jeremiah 32:27 NIV

When looking at the wonder of Creation, the stars and the ocean, you know God is omnipotent. But when standing next to the hospital bed of a 12-year-old, you want God to prove that He is almighty. Is God only omnipotent when He heals and silences the storms of life? Or is His omnipotence also the incomprehensible seismic wave of heaven? How great is God's power? It is far greater than we can ever imagine, understand, or experience.

The Omnipresence of God

I can never escape from Your Spirit! I can never get away from Your presence! If I go up to heaven, You are there; if I go down to the grave, You are there. If I ride the wings of the morning, if I dwell by the farthest oceans, even there Your hand will guide me, and Your strength will support me.
Psalm 139:7-10 NLT

His purpose was for the nations to seek after God and perhaps feel their way toward Him and find Him—though He is not far from any one of us. For in Him we live and move and exist. As some of your own poets have said, "We are His offspring."
Acts 17:27-28 NLT

The eyes of the LORD are in every place, keeping watch on the evil and the good.
Proverbs 15:3 NKJV

For thus says the One who is high and lifted up, who inhabits eternity, whose name is holy: "I dwell in the high and holy place, and also with him who is of a contrite and lowly spirit, to revive the spirit of the lowly, and to revive the heart of the contrite."
Isaiah 57:15 ESV

God has said, "Never will I leave you; never will I forsake you."
Hebrews 13:5 NIV

In good times we say, "Yes, my God is everywhere!" In times of crises we often question God's presence. Can circumstances determine whether God is present? God was the gentle breeze that dried your tears, the soft rain that extinguished the runaway fire; He has always been there. Because Jesus came to earth, you can be confident of God's intimate involvement in your life. He is not only here, He is everywhere. What a comforting reality!

The Omniscience of God

You have searched me, LORD, and You know me. You know when I sit and when I rise; You perceive my thoughts from afar. Before a word is on my tongue You, LORD, know it completely. Such knowledge is too wonderful for me, too lofty for me to attain.
Psalm 139:1-2, 4, 6 NIV

"Blessed be the name of God forever and ever, to whom belong wisdom and might. He changes times and seasons; He removes kings and sets up kings; He gives wisdom to the wise and knowledge to those who have understanding."
Daniel 2:20-21 ESV

God is greater than our hearts, and He knows everything.
1 John 3:20 NIV

How many are Your works, LORD! In wisdom You made them all; the earth is full of Your creatures. There is the sea, vast and spacious, teeming with creatures beyond number—living things both large and small.
Psalm 104:24-25 NIV

Nothing in all creation is hidden from God's sight. Everything is uncovered and laid bare before the eyes of Him to whom we must give account.
Hebrews 4:13 NIV

Why do I still need to pray if God knows everything? Prayer is not your briefing session to get God on track with what's happening in your life. He already knows all about it. Prayer is for synchronizing your heart with God's heart through the work of the Holy Spirit. It is actually to make you aware of what God knows. Fortune tellers want to pretend to have something like God's omniscience concerning your life. May you rather trust the only omniscient God on your journey with Him on earth.

Responding to Opposition

I come to You for protection, O LORD my God. Save me from my persecutors—rescue me!
Psalm 7:1 NLT

My times are in Your hand; rescue me from the hand of my enemies and from my persecutors!
Psalm 31:15 ESV

O LORD, oppose those who oppose me. Fight those who fight against me.
Psalm 35:1 NLT

He rescues me unharmed from the battle waged against me, even though many oppose me.
Psalm 55:18 NIV

Hear my cry, for I am very low. Rescue me from my persecutors, for they are too strong for me.
Psalm 142:6 NLT

"But I say to you, love your enemies, bless those who curse you, do good to those who hate you!"
Matthew 5:44 NKJV

If God is for us, who can be against us?
Romans 8:31 NIV

When a man's ways please the LORD, He makes even his enemies to be at peace with him.
Proverbs 16:7 ESV

How do you feel when you hear the word *enemy*? Anger, hatred, fear, resentment, hostility, or pain? Maybe you're planning to take revenge. Remember how your Master treated His enemies? He spoke words of peace during the war, love in the midst of hatred, and forgiveness even when they sinned because they knew not what they were doing. God will give you victory, and until then, bless your persecutors and forgive them.

Overcoming Evil

Whatever is born of God overcomes the world. And this is the victory that has overcome the world—our faith.
1 John 5:4 NKJV

"These things I have spoken to you, that in Me you may have peace. In the world you will have tribulation; but be of good cheer, I have overcome the world."
John 16:33 NKJV

Do not be overcome by evil, but overcome evil with good.
Romans 12:21 NIV

Who is he who overcomes the world, but he who believes that Jesus is the Son of God?
1 John 5:5 NKJV

We are more than conquerors through Him who loved us.
Romans 8:37 NIV

The Word gave life to everything that was created, and His life brought light to everyone. The light shines in the darkness, and the darkness can never extinguish it.
John 1:4-5 NLT

The LORD is my strength and my song; He has given me victory.
Psalm 118:14 NLT

The LORD your God is the one who goes with you to fight for you against your enemies to give you victory.
Deuteronomy 20:4 NIV

Our strength and victory come from our relationship with Jesus who has achieved the victory on our behalf. Jesus withdrew in prayer before every major event, and prior to performing miracles He approached His Father and thanked Him. Satan's temptations are overcome by knowing the Word and being obedient to it. For you to be able to overcome the world and all its forces, you have to pray and know His Word.

The Race Called Parenthood

Grandchildren are the crowning glory of the aged; parents are the pride of their children.
Proverbs 17:16 NLT

Children, obey your parents because you belong to the LORD, for this is the right thing to do. "Honor your father and mother." This is the first commandment with a promise: If you honor your father and mother, "things will go well for you, and you will have a long life on the earth."
Ephesians 6:1-3 NLT

Fathers, do not aggravate your children, or they will become discouraged.
Colossians 3:21 NLT

He will also go before Him in the spirit and power of Elijah, "to turn the hearts of the fathers to the children," and the disobedient to the wisdom of the just, to make ready a people prepared for the LORD.
Luke 1:17 NKJV

I remember your genuine faith, for you share the faith that first filled your grandmother Lois and your mother, Eunice. And I know that same faith continues strong in you.
2 Timothy 1:5 NLT

Train up a child in the way he should go, and when he is old he will not depart from it.
Proverbs 22:6 NKJV

When a baby is born and delicately placed in your arms, you know your life is going to change forever. Some parents remain in the starting blocks because they are trapped in a bad start. They are prisoners of the past and victims of their circumstances. It is not how you start, but how you finish that counts. Hug your kids, spend time with them, and tell them how much you love them. Finish the race of parenthood strong.

Overcome Sinful Desires!

Let not sin therefore reign in your mortal body, to make you obey its passions.
Romans 6:12 ESV

For the time is coming when people will not endure sound teaching, but having itching ears they will accumulate for themselves teachers to suit their own passions, and will turn away from listening to the truth and wander off into myths.
2 Timothy 4:3-4 ESV

You ask and do not receive, because you ask amiss, that you may spend it on your pleasures.
James 4:3 NKJV

Put to death therefore what is earthly in you: sexual immorality, impurity, passion, evil desire, and covetousness, which is idolatry.
Colossians 3:5 ESV

Those who belong to Christ Jesus have crucified the flesh with its passions and desires.
Galatians 5:24 NIV

So flee youthful passions and pursue righteousness, faith, love, and peace, along with those who call on the LORD from a pure heart.
2 Timothy 2:22 ESV

"Wherever your treasure is, there the desires of your heart will also be."
Luke 12:34 NLT

A passion and fire that burns for God has special power, but a passion fueled by sin is an enemy of the Spirit and brings destruction and death. God created your desires to be in harmony with His. Desire the things that God generously and abundantly gave to you. His desire is that people will hear His Word and repent of their sins. Lustful desires make everything revolve around self and enslave you so you cannot soar in His freedom. Reignite your passion for God today.

The Strongholds of the Past

Brothers and sisters, I do not consider myself yet to have taken hold of it. But one thing I do: Forgetting what is behind and straining toward what is ahead, I press on toward the goal to win the prize for which God has called me heavenward in Christ Jesus.
Philippians 3:13-14 NIV

We were therefore buried with Him through baptism into death in order that, just as Christ was raised from the dead through the glory of the Father, we too may live a new life. Romans 6:4 NIV

Remember not the former things, nor consider the things of old. Isaiah 43:18 ESV

Jesus replied, "No one who puts a hand to the plow and looks back is fit for service in the kingdom of God."
Luke 9:62 NIV

"I, even I, am He who blots out your transgressions for My own sake; and I will not remember your sins."
Isaiah 43:25 NKJV

Therefore, if anyone is in Christ, He is a new creation. The old has passed away; behold, the new has come. All this is from God, who through Christ reconciled us to Himself and gave us the ministry of reconciliation.
2 Corinthians 5:17-18 ESV

In a way we are dependent on the past, yet we don't have to be a victim of it. Perhaps you've inherited love, protection, and care from your past, or maybe your inheritance was poverty, abuse, ridicule, and shame. Either way, you must choose today not to be a victim. You have to choose to be someone who takes responsibility for the future. A new beginning is ahead of you—a new beginning that triumphs over your past. Give your past to God, and receive a great future with Him.

The Art of Peaceful Living

The LORD is not slow in keeping His promise, as some understand slowness. Instead He is patient with you.
2 Peter 3:9 NIV

The end of a thing is better than its beginning; the patient in spirit is better than the proud in spirit.
Ecclesiastes 7:8 NKJV

Don't you see how wonderfully kind, tolerant, and patient God is with you?
Romans 2:4 NLT

I waited patiently for the LORD; He inclined to me and heard my cry.
Psalm 40:1 ESV

Be completely humble and gentle; be patient, bearing with one another in love. Make every effort to keep the unity of the Spirit through the bond of peace.
Ephesians 4:2-3 NIV

We can rejoice, too, when we run into problems and trials, for we know that they help us develop endurance. And endurance develops strength of character, and character strengthens our confident hope of salvation.
Romans 5:3-4 NLT

Better a patient person than a warrior, one with self-control than one who takes a city.
Proverbs 16:32 NIV

We live in a hectic world where everything should have happened yesterday already. There is not even time to be patient. One of the best definitions of patience is to calmly carry on with life in the knowledge that God is in control. Patience is to love under pressure. Maybe you can practice your patience this week by driving in the slow lane and showing love for your family during your busiest hour.

Peace in the Midst of War

"I am leaving you with a gift—peace of mind and heart. And the peace I give is a gift the world cannot give. So don't be troubled or afraid."
John 14:27 NLT

"Blessed are the peacemakers, for they will be called children of God."
Matthew 5:9 NIV

Those who are peacemakers will plant seeds of peace and reap a harvest of righteousness.
James 3:18 NLT

God is not a God of confusion but of peace.
1 Corinthians 14:33 ESV

Let the peace of Christ rule in your hearts.
Colossians 3:15 ESV

The work of righteousness will be peace, and the effect of righteousness, quietness and assurance forever.
Isaiah 32:17 NKJV

You will keep in perfect peace those whose minds are steadfast, because they trust in You!
Isaiah 26:3 NIV

The God of peace be with you.
Romans 15:33 NIV

Are you seeking the kind of peace that is more than a feeling and isn't dependent on good circumstances? This peace is called Jesus—the Prince of Peace. He doesn't give you peace; He wants to *be* your peace. Peace grows from your relationship with Him. Not only should you seek after peace, but you should also strive to be a peacemaker. Peace is not the absence of conflict, but the presence of God during conflict. It is not to giving up biblical principles, but living them. Peace be with you!

September

Honor her for all that her hands have done,
& let her works bring her praise.

PROVERBS 31:31

A Global Attack on Christians

"Blessed are those who are persecuted because of righteousness, for theirs is the kingdom of heaven."
Matthew 5:10 NIV

Many are my persecutors and my enemies, yet I do not turn from Your testimonies.
Psalm 119:157 NKJV

Yes, and everyone who wants to live a godly life in Christ Jesus will suffer persecution. But evil people and impostors will flourish. They will deceive others and will themselves be deceived. **2 Timothy 3:12-13 NLT**

"If the world hates you, you know that it hated Me before it hated you." **John 15:18 NKJV**

Remember, it is better to suffer for doing good, if that is what God wants, than to suffer for doing wrong!
1 Peter 3:17 NLT

"I say to you, love your enemies, bless those who curse you, do good to those who hate you, and pray for those who spitefully use you and persecute you, that you may be sons of your Father in heaven; for He makes His sun rise on the evil and on the good, and sends rain on the just and on the unjust."
Matthew 5:44-45 NKJV

Persecution! Have you ever experienced it in your life? It is the world hating Christ and taking it out on His followers. More than 42 million Christians died in the 20th century under anti-Christian governments, yet the Good News about Jesus cannot be silenced. When persecution is fiercest, masses repent. During times of persecution, may you experience the glory of God and an open sky, with the Gospel as your final words.

The Power of Perseverance

You need to persevere so that when you have done the will of God, you will receive what He has promised.
Hebrews 10:36 NIV

Let us throw off everything that hinders and the sin that so easily entangles. And let us run with perseverance the race marked out for us.
Hebrews 12:1 NIV

Blessed is the one who perseveres under trial because, having stood the test, that person will receive the crown of life that the LORD has promised to those who love Him.
James 1:12 NIV

We rejoice in our sufferings, because we know that suffering produces perseverance; perseverance, character; and character, hope. And hope does not disappoint us, because God has poured out His love into our hearts by the Holy Spirit, whom He has given us.
Romans 5:3-5 NIV

Everything that was written in the past was written to teach us, so that through the endurance taught in the Scriptures and the encouragement they provide we might have hope.
Romans 15:4 NIV

The difference between a great performance and the worst failure is the willingness to persevere. Charles Spurgeon said, "By perseverance the snail reached the ark." Perseverance requires effort; it takes time, patience, and perspiration. It is what kept Job going. He persisted in his belief about who God is, even though everything around him pulled in the opposite direction. Keep going, you are closer to your breakthrough and miracle than you think. It is always too soon to quit.

Improve Your Performance

"Do not worry about tomorrow, for tomorrow will worry about itself. Each day has enough trouble of its own."
Matthew 6:34 NIV

The LORD your God will personally go ahead of you. He will neither fail you nor abandon you.
Deuteronomy 31:6 NLT

Teach me Your way, O LORD; I will walk in Your truth.
Psalm 86:11 NKJV

"If God cares so wonderfully for flowers that are here today and thrown into the fire tomorrow, He will certainly care for you."
Luke 12:28 NLT

O LORD, You have searched me and known me! You know when I sit down and when I rise up; You discern my thoughts from afar. You search out my path and my lying down and are acquainted with all my ways.
Psalm 139:1-3 ESV

The plans of the diligent lead surely to abundance, but everyone who is hasty comes only to poverty.
Proverbs 21:5 ESV

God is mighty, but despises no one; He is mighty and firm in His purpose.
Job 36:5 NIV

There is never enough time to do everything, but there is always enough time to do what is important. Plan ahead so you don't have to set aside the important things because urgent things steal your time. Plan to spend time with God. Plan to make time for your marriage and your children. Plan to take a break and rest sometime this week. Ask yourself where your priorities aren't straight, and start planning there.

For His Pleasure

You make known to me the path of life; You will fill me with joy in Your presence, with eternal pleasures at Your right hand.
Psalm 16:11 NIV

They are abundantly satisfied with the fullness of Your house, and You give them drink from the river of Your pleasures.
Psalm 36:8 NKJV

May the glory of the LORD continue forever! The LORD takes pleasure in all He has made!
Psalm 104:31 NLT

The LORD takes pleasure in those who fear Him, in those who hope in His steadfast love.
Psalm 147:11 ESV

For the LORD takes pleasure in His people; He will beautify the humble with salvation.
Psalm 149:4 NKJV

When the LORD takes pleasure in anyone's way, He causes their enemies to make peace with them.
Proverbs 16:7 NIV

"Fear not, little flock, for it is your Father's good pleasure to give you the kingdom."
Luke 12:32 ESV

You ask and do not receive, because you ask amiss, that you may spend it on your pleasures.
James 4:3 NKJV

Do you sometimes feel unimportant and without purpose? On the day of your birth, God stood still and watched His miracle daughter being born. The one whom He carefully planned for His glory and pleasure. Do you know that? You have value and meaning, and your life is a song of praise to Him. Your purpose is to please Him. God created you for His pleasure, so you can have the pleasure of knowing Him.

Miss Popularity

Don't copy the behavior and customs of this world, but let God transform you into a new person by changing the way you think. Then you will learn to know God's will for you, which is good and pleasing and perfect.
Romans 12:2 NLT

Do you not know that friendship with the world is enmity with God? Whoever therefore wants to be a friend of the world makes himself an enemy of God.
James 4:4 NKJV

Walk with the wise and become wise, for a companion of fools suffers harm.
Proverbs 13:20 NIV

"For what does it profit a man if he gains the whole world and loses or forfeits himself?"
Luke 9:25 ESV

One who has unreliable friends soon comes to ruin, but there is a friend who sticks closer than a brother.
Proverbs 18:24 NIV

Don't befriend angry people or associate with hot-tempered people, or you will learn to be like them and endanger your soul.
Proverbs 22:24-25 NLT

Your friendships and the people you're popular with say something about who you are and how you choose to live your life. Do you choose to be popular in the eyes of the world with its customs, or with God and His body, the church? Someone once said, "Friendship is like a bank account. You can't continue to draw from it without making deposits." Where are you currently investing, spending your time, energy, and heart? Choose wisely.

More Than Just a Pretty Face

You saw me before I was born. Every day of my life was recorded in Your book. Every moment was laid out before a single day had passed.
Psalm 139:16 NLT

I pray that your hearts will be flooded with light so that you can understand the confident hope He has given to those He called—His holy people who are His rich and glorious inheritance.
Ephesians 1:18 NLT

"For I know the plans I have for you," declares the LORD, "plans to prosper you and not to harm you, plans to give you hope and a future."
Jeremiah 29:11 NIV

Teach me to do Your will, for You are my God; Your Spirit is good. Lead me in the land of uprightness.
Psalm 143:10 NKJV

I cry out to God Most High, to God who fulfills His purpose for me.
Psalm 57:2 NLT

The LORD has made everything for its purpose.
Proverbs 16:4 ESV

God has now revealed to us His mysterious will regarding Christ, which is to fulfill His own good plan. And this is the plan: At the right time He will bring everything together under the authority of Christ—everything in heaven and on earth.
Ephesians 1:9-10 NIV

Potential is when others see a shepherd boy, but God sees a king. Jesus stood before fishermen and saw the potential of witnesses—fishers of men. He held five fish and two loaves of bread and saw the potential to provide an abundance of food. God saw a young virgin and a mother for His Son. Of course you are more than what you see now—you will discover that truth when you meet Him face-to-face.

A Hole in My Pocket

The needy will not be ignored forever; the hopes of the poor will not always be crushed.
Psalm 9:18 NLT

The poor will eat and be satisfied; those who seek the LORD will praise Him—may your hearts live forever!
Psalm 22:26 NIV

This poor man called, and the LORD heard him; He saved him out of all his troubles.
Psalm 34:6 NIV

Defend the poor and fatherless; do justice to the afflicted and needy.
Psalm 82:3 NKJV

They have freely scattered their gifts to the poor, their righteousness endures forever; their horn will be lifted high in honor.
Psalm 112:9 NIV

He raises the poor from the dust and lifts the needy from the ash heap.
Psalm 113:7 ESV

With every bone in my body I will praise Him: "LORD, who can compare with You? Who else rescues the helpless from the strong? Who else protects the helpless and poor from those who rob them?"
Psalm 35:10 NLT

The world is poverty-stricken, and we don't always know where to give and where to draw the line. It is important to remember that poor people are important to God too. It's also important to remember that material things don't bring true happiness. Happiness comes from within. You can be satisfied and happy. Handle poor people with respect and dignity, rather than giving money with disrespect. Do what you can, and pray that God will do the rest.

The Power of God

One thing God has spoken, two things I have heard: "Power belongs to You, God, and with You, LORD, is unfailing love"; and, "You reward everyone according to what they have done."

Psalm 62:11-12 NIV

Proclaim the power of God, whose majesty is over Israel, whose power is in the heavens.

Psalm 68:34 NIV

The LORD is my rock, my fortress, and my Savior; my God is my rock, in whom I find protection. He is my shield, the power that saves me, and my place of safety.

Psalm 18:2 NLT

You are the God of great wonders! You demonstrate your awesome power among the nations.

Psalm 77:14 NLT

The highest angelic powers stand in awe of God. He is far more awesome than all who surround His throne.

Psalm 89:7 NLT

For God says, "I will break the strength of the wicked, but I will increase the power of the godly."

Psalm 75:10 NLT

If it is of God, you cannot overthrow it—lest you even be found to fight against God.

Acts 5:39 NKJV

How do you measure the power of God? He is so powerful that a whole universe can come to a standstill before Him. He measures the earth with His measuring tape, He knows every star's name, and gives the horse his strength. God makes the dead come back to life, He makes the deaf hear, and died on the cross to bear our sins. How do you measure the power of the Spirit that comforts and guides? It's too great. This immense power is available to you too.

Strength when I'm Weak

God chose things the world considers foolish in order to shame those who think they are wise. And he chose things that are powerless to shame those who are powerful.
1 Corinthians 1:27 NLT

For what the law was powerless to do because it was weakened by the flesh, God did by sending His own Son in the likeness of sinful flesh to be a sin offering.
Romans 8:3 NIV

If it is of God, you cannot overthrow it—lest you even be found to fight against God.
Acts 5:39 NKJV

"Abide in Me, and I in you. As the branch cannot bear fruit of itself, unless it abides in the vine, neither can you, unless you abide in Me. I am the vine, you are the branches. He who abides in Me, and I in him, bears much fruit; for without Me you can do nothing."
John 15:4-5 NKJV

When we were utterly helpless, Christ came at just the right time and died for us sinners.
Romans 5:6 NLT

The prayer of a righteous person is powerful and effective.
James 5:16 NIV

There is great need: unemployment is on the rise, diseases for which there is no cure exist, and unforeseen circumstances overwhelm. And all of it can make you feel totally helpless. What do you do when you are standing dismayed and helpless before a difficult situation? The people in the Bible discovered the power of prayer and used it. People are saved from their powerlessness through the power and strength of God.

Choose to Praise God

Sing praises to God and to His name! Sing loud praises to Him who rides the clouds. His name is the LORD—rejoice in His presence!
Psalm 68:4 NLT

Praise be to the LORD God, the God of Israel, who alone does marvelous deeds. Praise be to His glorious name forever; may the whole earth be filled with His glory.
Psalm 72:18-19 NIV

Declare His glory among the nations, His wonders among all peoples. For the LORD is great and greatly to be praised; He is also to be feared above all gods.
1 Chronicles 16:24-25 NKJV

Praise Him, you highest heavens, and you waters above the heavens! Let them praise the name of the LORD! For He commanded and they were created. And He established them forever and ever; He gave a decree, and it shall not pass away.
Psalm 148:4-6 ESV

Praise the LORD, my soul; all my inmost being, praise His holy name. Praise the LORD, my soul, and forget not all His benefits—who forgives all your sins and heals all your diseases, who redeems your life from the pit and crowns you with love and compassion.
Psalm 103:1-4 NIV

How often do you glorify the Lord? Do you praise God for who He is, the Creator, the Mighty Ruler, the Faithful One, the Most High, the Omniscient and Omnipotent, the Provider, the Holy One, Victor, Prince of Peace, Shepherd? Praise Him because He forgave your sins and saved you from eternal death. Praise Him with the intent to glorify Him! Praise is a choice that comes from within your heart. Offer your whole life as a sacrifice of praise to Him.

The Power of Prayer

"You ask and do not receive, because you ask amiss, that you may spend it on your pleasures."
James 4:3 NKJV

Do not be anxious about anything, but in every situation, by prayer and petition, with thanksgiving, present your requests to God. And the peace of God, which transcends all understanding, will guard your hearts and your minds in Christ Jesus.
Philippians 4:6-7 NIV

Devote yourselves to prayer with an alert mind and a thankful heart.
Colossians 4:2 NLT

"When you pray, don't be like the hypocrites who love to pray publicly on street corners and in the synagogues where everyone can see them. I tell you the truth, that is all the reward they will ever get."
Matthew 6:5 NLT

First of all, then, I urge that supplications, prayers, intercessions, and thanksgivings be made for all people, for kings and all who are in high positions, that we may lead a peaceful and quiet life, godly and dignified in every way. This is good, and it is pleasing in the sight of God our Savior, who desires all people to be saved and to come to the knowledge of the truth.
1 Timothy 2:1-4 ESV

The best way to learn to pray is by doing it. There is no formula for successful prayer. Prayer is your oxygen; your time with God, and His time to work in you. The secret to a full prayer life is making prayer first about God and then about you and others. Prayer is the place where you and God open your hearts and minds mutually to each other. If you don't know what to pray, the Spirit will pray on your behalf.

A King in Servant's Clothes

Therefore judge nothing before the appointed time; wait until the LORD comes. He will bring to light what is hidden in darkness and will expose the motives of the heart. At that time each will receive their praise from God.
1 Corinthians 4:5 NIV

For by the grace given to me I say to everyone among you not to think of himself more highly than he ought to think, but to think with sober judgment, each according to the measure of faith that God has assigned.
Romans 12:3 ESV

As for the one who is weak in faith, welcome him, but not to quarrel over opinions.
Romans 14:1 ESV

There is neither Jew nor Greek, there is neither slave nor free, there is no male and female, for you are all one in Christ Jesus.
Galatians 3:28 NIV

If you show partiality, you commit sin, and are convicted by the law as transgressors.
James 2:9 NKJV

"Judge not, that you be not judged."
Matthew 7:1 ESV

They say to each other, "Don't come too close! I am holier than you!" These people are a stench in my nostrils, an acrid smell that never goes away.
Isaiah 65:5-6 NLT

Even before you say a word, others judge you on face value. Being biased and prejudiced is built on insufficient information, ideas, and opinions of others. Jesus abandoned His kingship to take the form of a servant, so He could love women, tax collectors, and sinners without prejudice and show them compassion and grace. Do not just stand in someone else's shoes, wear them until you know the twists and turns of the road they walk.

Pride Over Pity

One's pride will bring him low, but he who is lowly in spirit will obtain honor.
Proverbs 29:23 ESV

The end of a matter is better than its beginning, and patience is better than pride.
Ecclesiastes 7:8 NIV

Pride leads to conflict; those who take advice are wise.
Proverbs 13:10 NLT

When pride comes, then comes disgrace, but with the humble is wisdom.
Proverbs 11:2 ESV

Let not the foot of pride come against me, and let not the hand of the wicked drive me away. Psalm 36:11 NKJV

In his pride the wicked man does not seek Him; in all his thoughts there is no room for God.
Psalm 10:4 NIV

"It is what comes from inside that defiles you. For from within, out of a person's heart, come evil thoughts, sexual immorality, theft, murder, adultery, greed, wickedness, deceit, lustful desires, envy, slander, pride, and foolishness."
Mark 7:20-22 NLT

Human pride will be brought down, and human arrogance will be humbled. Only the LORD will be exalted on that day of judgment.
Isaiah 2:11 NLT

Is all pride negative? Am I allowed to be proud of my child? Being proud of good and beautiful deeds, making the difference you prayed for, and who you are in Jesus, can be done with a humble heart. This proud feeling should, however, not become haughtiness at the expense of others. Or create a feeling of superiority. Beware pride that doesn't seek advice, can't display vulnerable emotions, or admit when it's wrong; it will steal abundant life from you.

Set Your Priorities Straight

"Where your treasure is, there your heart will be also."
Luke 12:34 NIV

"No one can serve two masters. Either you will hate the one and love the other, or you will be devoted to the one and despise the other. You cannot serve both God and money."
Matthew 6:24 NIV

See then that you walk circumspectly, not as fools but as wise, redeeming the time, because the days are evil. Therefore do not be unwise, but understand what the will of the LORD is.
Ephesians 5:15-17 NKJV

"If anyone would come after Me, let him deny himself and take up his cross and follow Me. For whoever would save his life will lose it, but whoever loses his life for My sake will find it. For what will it profit a man if he gains the whole world and forfeits his life? Or what shall a man give in return for his life?"
Matthew 16:24-26 ESV

"But seek first the kingdom of God and His righteousness, and all these things will be added to you."
Matthew 6:33 ESV

Your priorities will determine how you spend your time. Jesus was clear in His teachings that love is our first priority. Love for God and your neighbor. Love for your neighbor starts in your home with your husband and your children and your parents, where you feed them and lovingly care for them. Make time for your children—that may just save their lives—build their character, and give them peace. Set your priorities straight today!

Faith to Proclaim the Good News

Sing to the LORD, all the earth, proclaim His salvation day after day.
1 Chronicles 16:23 ESV

The heavens proclaim the glory of God. The skies display His craftsmanship.
Psalm 19:1 NLT

The LORD gave the word; great was the company of those who proclaimed it.
Psalm 68:11 NKJV

I will cut off the chariot from Ephraim and the war horse from Jerusalem; and the battle bow shall be cut off, and he shall speak peace to the nations.
Zechariah 9:10 ESV

"The Spirit of the LORD is on me, because He has anointed me to proclaim good news to the poor. He has sent me to proclaim freedom for the prisoners and recovery of sight for the blind."
Luke 4:18 NIV

He is the one we proclaim, admonishing and teaching everyone with all wisdom, so that we may present everyone fully mature in Christ.
Colossians 1:28 NIV

Give thanks to the LORD and proclaim His greatness. Let the whole world know what He has done.
Psalm 105:1 NLT

Do you realize that God did not appoint you as a director, pharmacist, secretary, freelance journalist, or doctor, but to be a proclaimer of the Gospel? Your workplace is just a field which He provided for you to witness in. The Gospel you preach is the Good News that Jesus is the Savior, that He died on the cross for your sins, and that you were bought with the blood of Jesus. Proclaim the Gospel and bring the light of God into this dark world.

The Promises of God

All of God's promises have been fulfilled in Christ with a resounding "Yes!" And through Christ, our "Amen" (which means "Yes") ascends to God for His glory.
2 Corinthians 1:20 NLT

"My covenant I will not break, nor alter the word that has gone out of My lips."
Psalm 89:34 NKJV

God is not human, that He should lie, not a human being, that He should change His mind. Does He speak and then not act? Does He promise and not fulfill?
Numbers 23:19 NIV

Not one of all the LORD's good promises to Israel failed; every one was fulfilled.
Joshua 21:45 NIV

"I am the LORD. I speak, and the word which I speak will come to pass; it will no more be postponed; I will say the word and perform it," says the LORD GOD.
Ezekiel 12:25 NKJV

The promises are pure, like silver refined in a furnace, purified seven times over.
Psalm 12:6 NLT

The LORD will cover you with His feathers. He will shelter you with His wings. His faithful promises are your armor and protection.
Psalm 91:4 NLT

Abraham and Sarah waited many years for God to fulfill His promise to them. The people had to wait a long time for the coming of the Messiah after it was foretold in Isaiah. There are thousands of promises of God in His Word and each of them is fixed and true in Christ. Just wait patiently. The Word is full of God's promises, enough to sustain for a lifetime. You can discover them anew through the Spirit every day.

God's Umbrella of Protection

The LORD keeps you from all harm and watches over your life. The LORD keeps watch over you as you come and go, both now and forever.
Psalm 121:7-8 NLT

The LORD is my fortress, protecting me from danger, so why should I tremble?
Psalm 27:1 NLT

The LORD your God will personally go ahead of you. He will neither fail you nor abandon you.
Deuteronomy 31:6 NLT

"I am the LORD your God who takes hold of your right hand and says to you, do not fear; I will help you."
Isaiah 41:13 NIV

"Fear not, for I am with you; be not dismayed, for I am your God; I will strengthen you, I will help you, I will uphold you."
Isaiah 41:10 ESV

The LORD protects all those who love Him, but He destroys the wicked.
Psalm 145:20 NLT

Even when I walk through the darkest valley, I will not be afraid, for You, LORD, are close beside me. Your rod and Your staff protect and comfort me.
Psalm 23:4 NLT

As for me, it is good to be near God. I have made the Sovereign LORD my refuge; I will tell of all Your deeds.
Psalm 73:28 NIV

God is with you. Just like a hen hides her chicks under her wings, God keeps you safe in His arms. As the wind blows gently, He sits with you in silence until you can no longer deny His presence. This can give you assurance that He will protect you. When you are under His wings, He doesn't indemnify you of danger, but His care and protection will be over you like a big umbrella. He will strengthen you and help you.

God Provides in Your Every Need

"Your Father knows what you need before you ask Him."
Matthew 6:8 NIV

God shall supply all your need according to His riches in glory by Christ Jesus.
Philippians 4:19 NKJV

"Seek the Kingdom of God above all else, and live righteously, and He will give you everything you need."
Matthew 6:33 NLT

"I will open the windows of heaven for you. I will pour out a blessing so great you won't have enough room to take it in. Try it! Put Me to the test!"
Malachi 3:10 NLT

He will give the rain for your land in its season, the early rain and the later rain, that you may gather in your grain and your wine and your oil. And He will give grass in your fields for your livestock, and you shall eat and be full.
Deuteronomy 11:14-15 NIV

"I am the LORD your God, who brought you out of the land of Egypt; open your mouth wide, and I will fill it."
Psalm 81:10 NKJV

The lions may grow weak and hungry, but those who seek the LORD lack no good thing.
Psalm 34:10 NIV

Does God always provide? We meet the God of providence in Abraham's story. What a scary assignment: to go and sacrifice your son whom you've waited for so long. Abraham does exactly as the Lord asks of him. For three days of travelling to the place of sacrifice, Abraham faithfully held on to the knowledge that God is Jehovah Jireh, the God who provides. At just the right moment, God shows up and provides. He is acutely aware of your needs. His eyes see you and in His perfect time He will provide.

A Pure Heart for God

We know that when Christ appears, we shall be like Him, for we shall see Him as He is. All who have this hope in Him purify themselves, just as He is pure.
1 John 3:2-3 NIV

"Blessed are the pure in heart, for they shall see God."
Matthew 5:8 NKJV

Truly God is good to Israel, to those whose hearts are pure.
Psalm 73:1 NLT

Create in me a pure heart, O God, and renew a steadfast spirit within me.
Psalm 51:10 NIV

Everything is pure to those whose hearts are pure. But nothing is pure to those who are corrupt and unbelieving, because their minds and consciences are corrupted.
Titus 1:15 NLT

Pure and undefiled religion before God and the Father is this: to visit orphans and widows in their trouble, and to keep oneself unspotted from the world.
James 1:27 NKJV

With the pure You will show Yourself pure; and with the devious You will show Yourself shrewd.
Psalm 18:26 NKJV

A pure heart is giving yourself completely to God without reservation, every day and every minute of your life. Cultivate a heart that would prevent itself from being polluted by the world, is washed by Jesus' blood, and allows the Spirit to make you new from the inside. A focused heart, with Jesus as the center has pure and honorable motives. With such a pure heart the Spirit will help you see God everywhere around you.

A Purpose-Driven Life

I cry out to God Most High, to God, who fulfills His purpose for me.
Psalm 57:2 NIV

The plans of the LORD stand firm forever, the purposes of His heart through all generations.
Psalm 33:11 NIV

The LORD of hosts has sworn: "As I have planned, so shall it be, and as I have purposed, so shall it stand."
Isaiah 14:24 ESV

"I have raised you up for this very purpose, that I might show you My power and that My name might be proclaimed in all the earth."
Exodus 9:16 NIV

Great are Your purposes and mighty are Your deeds. Your eyes are open to the ways of all mankind; You reward each person according to their conduct and as their deeds deserve.
Jeremiah 32:19 NIV

The LORD has made everything for its purpose.
Proverbs 16:4 ESV

We know that God causes everything to work together for the good of those who love God and are called according to His purpose for them.
Romans 8:28 NLT

Teach me to do Your will, for You are my God! Let Your good Spirit lead me on level ground!
Psalm 143:10 ESV

Your primary goal in life is to help bring God's Kingdom to earth. But maybe you have wondered what your specific purpose is. What is your calling, that thing you were born to do? The thing that only you can do and that gives meaning to your life? God has the key to the meaning of your life. You will discover the meaning in your relationship with Him through the Spirit. Discover that place where your life finds meaning, and you'll find eternal life.

Quiet Time with God

The prayer of a righteous person is powerful and effective.
James 5:16 NIV

Pray in the Spirit on all occasions with all kinds of prayers and requests. With this in mind, be alert and always keep on praying for all the LORD's people.
Ephesians 6:18 NIV

"When you pray, go into your room, close the door and pray to your Father, who is unseen. Then your Father, who sees what is done in secret, will reward you."
Matthew 6:6 NIV

Let my prayer be set before You as incense, the lifting up of my hands as the evening sacrifice.
Psalm 141:2 NKJV

Then a great and powerful wind tore the mountains apart and shattered the rocks before the LORD, but the LORD was not in the wind. After the wind there was an earthquake, but the LORD was not in the earthquake. After the earthquake came a fire, but the LORD was not in the fire. And after the fire came a gentle whisper.
1 Kings 19:11-12 NIV

The Spirit helps us in our weakness. We do not know what we ought to pray for, but the Spirit Himself intercedes for us through wordless groans.
Romans 8:26 NIV

Life has become noisy. From the time our alarm clock wakes us in the mornings until we go to sleep at night, we experience the noise of the day. At some point you need to allow God to silence the noise within you. Jesus Himself set this example when He regularly became still before the Father. God speaks at His loudest in the silence. In these silences you will discover a strange tranquility and peace.

The Race Marked Out for Us

Let us throw off everything that hinders and the sin that so easily entangles. And let us run with perseverance the race marked out for us.
Hebrews 12:1 NIV

Do you not know that in a race all the runners run, but only one gets the prize? Run in such a way as to get the prize. Everyone who competes in the games goes into strict training. They do it to get a crown that will not last, but we do it to get a crown that will last forever.
1 Corinthians 9:24-25 NIV

I press toward the goal for the prize of the upward call of God in Christ Jesus.
Philippians 3:14 NKJV

I have fought the good fight, I have finished the race, and I have remained faithful. And now the prize awaits me—the crown of righteousness, which the LORD, the righteous Judge, will give me on the day of His return. And the prize is not just for me but for all who eagerly look forward to His appearing.
2 Timothy 4:7-8 NLT

For physical training is of some value, but godliness has value for all things, holding promise for both the present life and the life to come.
1 Timothy 4:8 NIV

Every day you are running a life-long marathon. Maybe you are fighting fit or perhaps you want to give up already. It takes months and years for a spiritual training program of prayer, joy, and gratitude to yield results. There are mountains and valleys, throwing off the weight of sin so that nothing can hold you back, and then the finish line. Be the reason another Christian is able to run the race set before them well. Run today's race at full speed!

Reconciled with God

Anyone who belongs to Christ has become a new person. The old life is gone; a new life has begun! And all of this is a gift from God, who brought us back to Himself through Christ. And God has given us this task of reconciling people to Him. For God was in Christ, reconciling the world to Himself, no longer counting people's sins against them. And He gave us this wonderful message of reconciliation.

2 Corinthians 5:17-19 NLT

There is one God and one Mediator who can reconcile God and humanity—the man Christ Jesus.

1 Timothy 2:5 NLT

Once you were far away from God, but now you have been brought near to Him through the blood of Christ. For Christ Himself has brought peace to us. He united Jews and Gentiles into one people when, in His own body on the cross, He broke down the wall of hostility that separated us...Together as one body, Christ reconciled both groups to God by means of His death on the cross, and our hostility toward each other was put to death.

Ephesians 2:13-14, 16 NLT

Jesus established reconciliation between you and God. And at that moment, the heavens and earth came together. You became aware of His holiness, and like Moses you covered your face in adoration. The woman who is reconciled with God knows the aroma of Christ in the air—the fragrance of a new beginning. Before you can call out to Him, He answers, and before you can pray, He hears. May His reconciliation be your perfume today.

We Are Set Free

The LORD redeems the life of His servants; none of those who take refuge in Him will be condemned.
Psalm 34:22 ESV

He has delivered us from the power of darkness and conveyed us into the kingdom of the Son of His love, in whom we have redemption through His blood, the forgiveness of sins.
Colossians 1:13-14 NKJV

He gave His life to free us from every kind of sin, to cleanse us, and to make us His very own people, totally committed to doing good deeds.
Titus 2:14 NLT

Give thanks to the LORD, for He is good; His love endures forever. Let the redeemed of the LORD tell their story—those He redeemed from the hand of the foe, those He gathered from the lands, from east and west, from north and south.
Psalm 107:1-3 NIV

"I have blotted out, like a thick cloud, your transgressions, and like a cloud, your sins. Return to Me, for I have redeemed you."
Isaiah 44:22 NKJV

In Him we have redemption through His blood.
Ephesians 1:7 NIV

Sin created a cleft between you and God. Only when you realize how great your sin is will you realize how much you need redemption and forgiveness. Jesus, through His death on the cross, came to establish a bridge between you and God. In gratitude we would like to go further by spreading the word about this redemption with passion. We want to deliver the good news of His love letter to others, because redemption is undeserved grace!

Finding Refuge under His Wings

Let all who take refuge in You rejoice; let them ever sing for joy, and spread Your protection over them, that those who love Your name may exult in You.
Psalm 5:11 ESV

The LORD is a refuge for the oppressed, a stronghold in times of trouble.
Psalm 9:9 NIV

Show me Your unfailing love in wonderful ways. By Your mighty power You rescue those who seek refuge from their enemies.
Psalm 17:7 NLT

The LORD is the strength of His people; He is the saving refuge of His anointed.
Psalm 28:8 ESV

The LORD will rescue His servants; no one who takes refuge in Him will be condemned.
Psalm 34:22 NIV

The LORD of hosts is with us; the God of Jacob is our refuge.
Psalm 46:7 NKJV

Whoever fears the LORD has a secure fortress, and for their children it will be a refuge. The fear of the LORD is a fountain of life, turning a person from the snares of death.
Proverbs 14:26-27 NIV

The eternal God is your refuge, and underneath are the everlasting arms.
Deuteronomy 33:27 NIV

During the holidays I watched two children chase each other, while their mother acted as their "refuge." When the older brother chased the little brother, he ran for dear life, and hid underneath his mother's arm. Every now and then life gets scary and it feels like something is chasing us. Where do you run to hide? Where is your refuge? God is ready to give you refuge under the soft feathers of His wing.

Secret Regrets

For godly grief produces a repentance that leads to salvation without regret, whereas worldly grief produces death.
2 Corinthians 7:10 ESV

"If he sins against you seven times in the day, and turns to you seven times, saying, 'I repent,' you must forgive him."
Luke 17:4 ESV

If we confess our sins, He is faithful and just to forgive us our sins and to cleanse us from all unrighteousness.
1 John 1:9 NKJV

In Him we have redemption through His blood, the forgiveness of sins, according to the riches of His grace.
Ephesians 1:7 NKJV

For it is with your heart that you believe and are justified, and it is with your mouth that you profess your faith and are saved.
Romans 10:10 NIV

Even though Jesus was God's Son, He learned obedience from the things He suffered. In this way, God qualified Him as a perfect High Priest, and He became the source of eternal salvation for all those who obey Him.
Hebrews 5:8-9 NLT

You will be pleased with sacrifices offered in the right spirit.
Psalm 51:19 NLT

The Holy Spirit will reveal sin in your life, while the devil will accuse you of your sins. True repentance is much more than just a quick apology. It is the belief that what you have done, said, or even thought was wrong. You don't defend yourself, but let the Spirit renew your mind. Your words and behavior are now in line with someone who follows the example of Christ.

Dealing with Rejection

The LORD will not cast off His people, nor will He forsake His inheritance.
Psalm 94:14 NKJV

"Anyone who accepts your message is also accepting Me. And anyone who rejects you is rejecting Me. And anyone who rejects Me is rejecting God, who sent Me."
Luke 10:16 NLT

"Blessed are you when people hate you, when they exclude you and insult you and reject your name as evil, because of the Son of Man. Rejoice in that day and leap for joy, because great is your reward in heaven."
Luke 6:22-23 NIV

Therefore, anyone who refuses to live by these rules is not disobeying human teaching but is rejecting God, who gives His Holy Spirit to you.
1 Thessalonians 4:8 NLT

"I will make My dwelling among you, and My soul shall not abhor you."
Leviticus 26:11 ESV

As you come to Him, the living Stone—rejected by humans but chosen by God—you also, like living stones, are being built into a spiritual house... For in Scripture it says: "See, I lay a stone in Zion, a chosen and precious cornerstone, and the one who trusts in Him will never be put to shame."
1 Peter 2:4-6 NIV

We all want to belong, and so most of us have an underlying fear of rejection. The fear that I am not good enough—that my clothes, sunglasses, or car will not fit in with the group, and I will not be accepted. Know who you are in Christ. Be proud of who you are, and never compromise your integrity. Then when people reject you, it is their loss, not yours. Perhaps you are getting rejected because you are a swan swimming among ducks.

Rejoice in the Lord

Rejoice in the LORD always.
Philippians 4:4 NIV

Rejoice in the LORD and be glad, all you who obey Him! Shout for joy, all you whose hearts are pure!
Psalm 32:11 NLT

"Rejoice because your names are written in heaven."
Luke 10:20 NKJV

My heart rejoices in the LORD; in the LORD my horn is lifted high. My mouth boasts over my enemies, for I delight in Your deliverance. There is no one holy like the LORD; there is no one besides You; there is no Rock like our God.
1 Samuel 2:1-2 NIV

Rejoice always, pray without ceasing, give thanks in all circumstances; for this is the will of God in Christ Jesus for you.
1 Thessalonians 5:16-18 ESV

This is the day that the LORD has made; let us rejoice and be glad in it.
Psalm 118:24 ESV

Rejoice, O people of Zion! Shout in triumph, O people of Jerusalem! Look, your King is coming to you. He is righteous and victorious, yet He is humble, riding on a donkey—riding on a donkey's colt.
Zechariah 9:9 NLT

It's always nice to spend time with joyful and happy people. The problem is that some days certain circumstances don't give us much reason to be joyful or happy. It is during these days that we have to make the choice to rejoice in Jesus and not in circumstances. It is not a sudden cure or denial of circumstances, but a choice to focus on Christ and to trust and submit to Him.

The Power of Reliability

The LORD detests lying lips, but He delights in those who tell the truth.
Proverbs 12:22 NLT

"One who is faithful in a very little is also faithful in much, and one who is dishonest in a very little is also dishonest in much."
Luke 16:10 ESV

Understand, therefore, that the LORD your God is indeed God. He is the faithful God who keeps His covenant for a thousand generations and lavishes His unfailing love on those who love Him and obey His commands.
Deuteronomy 7:9 NLT

A truthful witness saves lives, but a false witness is deceitful.
Proverbs 14:25 NIV

God is not a man, that He should lie, nor a son of man, that He should repent. Has He said, and will He not do? Or has He spoken, and will He not make it good?
Numbers 23:19 NKJV

The LORD will cover you with His feathers. He will shelter you with His wings. His faithful promises are your armor and protection.
Psalm 91:4 NLT

"I'll call you back." "I will be there." "I'll do it right now." "I'll pray for you." Do you always keep your promises? Do people know they can rely on you? Reliability starts with the small things like being honest, even at the expense of yourself. It strengthens relationships and the confidence that people have in you. In a world where many things are uncertain, we know that God is reliable. He is always the same and never changes. Trust in Him and be reliable.

The God of Religion

...Saul was still breathing out murderous threats against the LORD's disciples. He went to the high priest and asked him for letters to the synagogues in Damascus, so that if he found any there who belonged to the Way, whether men or women, he might take them as prisoners to Jerusalem.
Acts 9:1-2 NIV

"But woe to you Pharisees! For you tithe mint and rue and every herb, and neglect justice and the love of God. These you ought to have done, without neglecting the others."
Luke 11:42 ESV

God, who made the world and everything in it, since He is LORD of heaven and earth, does not dwell in temples made with hands.
Acts 17:24 NKJV

For by grace you have been saved through faith. And this is not your own doing; it is the gift of God, not a result of works, so that no one may boast.
Ephesians 2:8-9 ESV

If you claim to be religious but don't control your tongue, you are fooling yourself, and your religion is worthless.
James 1:26 NLT

The difference between Christianity and other beliefs is that in other religions people must do everything in their power to come to God. With Christianity, God is reaching out to people. Be careful that the practice of religion never becomes more important than your relationship with God. Paul was an example of this, the persecutor who became the follower. Paul knew the God of religion, do you?

October

I will rejoice

IN THE LORD,

I will be

joyful

in

· GOD ·

MY SAVIOR.

Habakkuk 3:18

Remorse Is More Than Being Sorry

Wash me clean from my guilt. Purify me from my sin.
Psalm 51:2 NLT

For the honor of Your name, O LORD, forgive my many, many sins.
Psalm 25:11 NLT

My guilt has overwhelmed me like a burden too heavy to bear.
Psalm 38:4 NIV

Though we are overwhelmed by our sins, You forgive them all.
Psalm 65:3 NLT

Help us, God our Savior, for the glory of Your name; deliver us and forgive our sins for Your name's sake.
Psalm 79:9 NIV

You, God, know my folly; my guilt is not hidden from You.
Psalm 69:5 NIV

LORD, You are so good, so ready to forgive, so full of unfailing love for all who ask for Your help.
Psalm 86:5 NLT

If we confess our sins, He is faithful and just to forgive us our sins and to cleanse us from all unrighteousness.
1 John 1:9 NKJV

Therefore confess your sins to each other and pray for each other so that you may be healed.
James 5:16 NIV

Remorse is something that starts in your heart when, through the Spirit, you come to realize and recognize sin and evil. This realization leads to confession to God and those you have wronged. If you ever have the opportunity to stand before a remorseful person, forgive them, which will save you from a bitter soul. Forgive and forget, and if it's not possible to forget, forgive and remember with grace, as much as God has forgiven you.

Connect with God

Don't copy the behavior and customs of this world, but let God transform you into a new person by changing the way you think. Then you will learn to know God's will for you, which is good and pleasing and perfect.
Romans 12:2 NLT

You were taught, with regard to your former way of life, to put off your old self, which is being corrupted by its deceitful desires; to be made new in the attitude of your minds; and to put on the new self, created to be like God in true righteousness and holiness.
Ephesians 4:22-24 NIV

If anyone is in Christ, the new creation has come: The old has gone, the new is here!
2 Corinthians 5:17 NIV

We do not lose heart. Though our outer self is wasting away, our inner self is being renewed day by day. For this light momentary affliction is preparing for us an eternal weight of glory beyond all comparison, as we look not to the things that are seen but to the things that are unseen. For the things that are seen are transient, but the things that are unseen are eternal.
2 Corinthians 4:16-18 ESV

Most women love new things in their closets and in their homes. Spring is synonymous with cleaning the house, unpacking the cupboards, and making room for new things. Maybe it would be good if you unpacked and cleaned out your spiritual closet today. Do not let other people clutter your closets with their unnecessary baggage. Give the Holy Spirit the opportunity to renew your mind, to give new hope, to do some new priority planning for you, and to give your relationships new breath and life.

A Call to Real Surrender

If we confess our sins, He is faithful and just to forgive us our sins and to cleanse us from all unrighteousness.
1 John 1:9 NKJV

Repent, then, and turn to God, so that your sins may be wiped out, that times of refreshing may come from the LORD, and that He may send the Messiah, who has been appointed for you—even Jesus.
Acts 3:19-20 NIV

The LORD is not slow to fulfill His promise as some count slowness, but is patient toward you, not wishing that any should perish, but that all should reach repentance.
2 Peter 3:9 ESV

"Repent of your sins and turn to God, for the Kingdom of Heaven is near."
Matthew 3:2 NLT

Jesus answered them, "Healthy people don't need a doctor—sick people do. I have come to call not those who think they are righteous, but those who know they are sinners and need to repent."
Luke 5:31-32 NLT

"Go back to what you heard and believed at first; hold to it firmly. Repent and turn to Me again. If you don't wake up, I will come to you suddenly, as unexpected as a thief."
Revelation 3:3 NLT

Repent! Is this a cry of distress to unbelievers only, or also to those who belong to God? Repentance means to renew your mind or literally to turn around. You may have already experienced conversion from unbelief to faith. After believing, there is the daily conversion in faith where your thoughts are renewed, and you run away from wrong things—a daily turn from sin towards the image of Christ. Move from darkness to light, in your mind, your heart, and your deeds.

Building Your Faith on His Reputation

Never let loyalty and kindness leave you! Tie them around your neck as a reminder. Write them deep within your heart. Then you will find favor with both God and people, and you will earn a good reputation.
Proverbs 3:3-4 NLT

He who walks with integrity walks securely, but he who perverts his ways will become known.
Proverbs 10:9 NKJV

The wise are known for their understanding, and pleasant words are persuasive.
Proverbs 16:21 NLT

Even a child makes himself known by his acts, by whether his conduct is pure and upright. Proverbs 20:11 ESV

Choose a good reputation over great riches; being held in high esteem is better than silver or gold.
Proverbs 22:1 NLT

The LORD is known by His acts of justice; the wicked are ensnared by the work of their hands. Psalm 9:16 NIV

A good reputation is more valuable than costly perfume. And the day you die is better than the day you are born.
Ecclesiastes 7:1 NLT

Warren Buffet said, "It takes twenty years to build a reputation and five minutes to ruin it. If you think about that, you'll do things differently." Will you really do things differently though? Have you become a slave to your reputation—someone who constantly wears a mask? Or is the way you talk and act a true reflection of who you are? Do you know who Christ says you are? Take your mask off, see your heart and face, and live to the glory of God through your reputation.

Rescued by God

I trust in Your unfailing love. I will rejoice because You have rescued me.

Psalm 13:5 NLT

He reached down from heaven and rescued me; He drew me out of deep waters. He rescued me from my powerful enemies, from those who hated me and were too strong for me. He led me to a place of safety; He rescued me because He delights in me.

Psalm 18:16-17, 19 NLT

My whole being will exclaim, "Who is like You, LORD? You rescue the poor from those too strong for them, the poor and needy from those who rob them."

Psalm 35:10 NIV

The LORD says, "I will rescue those who love Me. I will protect those who trust in My name."

Psalm 91:14 NLT

The LORD hears His people when they call to Him for help. He rescues them from all their troubles.

Psalm 34:17 NLT

The LORD rescues the godly; He is their fortress in times of trouble.

Psalm 37:39 NLT

The LORD will rescue His servants; no one who takes refuge in Him will be condemned.

Psalm 34:22 NIV

I remember one time when a puppy fell into a dark, muddy hole. He barked, howled, and struggled so much that he just sank deeper and deeper into the hole. Eventually we had to lie on our stomachs to pull the puppy out of the mud. Sometimes sin and bad habits are like a muddy pit causing us to sink deeper into the mud. But God has seen our struggles, and His Son, Jesus, was sent to this world to rescue us out of the deep pit.

Resentment Is Poisonous

"When you stand praying, if you hold anything against anyone, forgive them, so that your Father in heaven may forgive you your sins."
Mark 11:25 NIV

Get rid of all bitterness, rage, anger, harsh words, and slander, as well as all types of evil behavior.
Ephesians 4:31 NLT

See to it that no one fails to obtain the grace of God; that no "root of bitterness" springs up and causes trouble, and by it many become defiled.
Hebrews 12:15 ESV

Resentment kills a fool, and envy slays the simple.
Job 5:2 NIV

He did not retaliate when He was insulted, nor threaten revenge when He suffered. He left His case in the hands of God, who always judges fairly.
1 Peter 2:23 NLT

A stone is heavy…but the resentment caused by a fool is even heavier.
Proverbs 7:23 NLT

"Judge not, and you shall not be judged. Condemn not, and you shall not be condemned. Forgive, and you will be forgiven."
Luke 6:37 NKJV

How much bitterness and anger do you harbor against people? How many hours do you spend thinking about the past and creating more bitterness? What you are actually doing is allowing the same people to have more control over your life. Resentment has devastating consequences for you. It's like releasing poison into your body. Resentment makes you blind to new possibilities. Forgive and let it go. You will be the first to benefit from it.

Respect Others

Glory, honor and peace for everyone who does good.
Romans 2:10 NIV

Show proper respect to everyone, love the family of believers, fear God.
1 Peter 2:17 NIV

Give to everyone what you owe them: If you owe taxes, pay taxes; if revenue, then revenue; if respect, then respect; if honor, then honor.
Romans 13:7 NIV

"All those who exalt themselves will be humbled, and those who humble themselves will be exalted."
Luke 14:11 NIV

Each one of you must love his wife as he loves himself, and the wife must respect her husband.
Ephesians 5:33 NIV

He will bless those who fear the LORD—small and great alike.
Psalm 115:13 NIV

Honor your father and your mother, so that you may live long in the land the LORD your God is giving you.
Exodus 20:12 NIV

Respect must be earned! Does this mean that you can decide whom you want to treat with respect and to which extent you want to do it? Is this not the reason why society is in such a mess? Respect is honoring the image of God in every person, even though they haven't earned it. Respect is truly listening and loving others. Have respect for your husband, children, family, friends, and even your enemies.

An Accountable Life

If you see your neighbor's ox or sheep or goat wandering away, don't ignore your responsibility. Take it back to its owner.
Deuteronomy 22:1 NLT

If your gift is to encourage others, be encouraging. If it is giving, give generously. If God has given you leadership ability, take the responsibility seriously. And if you have a gift for showing kindness to others, do it gladly.
Romans 12:8 NLT

Brothers and sisters, each person, as responsible to God, should remain in the situation they were in when God called them.
1 Corinthians 7:24 NIV

If anyone sins and does what is forbidden in any of the LORD's commands, even though they do not know it, they are guilty and will be held responsible.
Leviticus 5:17 NIV

"Your responsibility is to obey the terms of the covenant. You and all your descendants have this continual responsibility."
Genesis 17:9 NLT

"If you are faithful in little things, you will be faithful in large ones. But if you are dishonest in little things, you won't be honest with greater responsibilities."
Luke 16:10 NLT

We often hear about the many rights that people have. As stewards, the Lord gave us privileges to enjoy, but He also gave us responsibilities to fulfill. You are fortunate to have Bibles in different languages, but you have the responsibility to read and live it. You have a responsibility towards His creation, your family, your church, the people who cross your path, and your destiny. Don't just rely on your rights; be responsible.

Rest Is Necessary

The LORD replied, "My Presence will go with you, and I will give you rest."
Exodus 33:14 NIV

Instead, I have calmed and quieted myself, like a weaned child who no longer cries for its mother's milk. Yes, like a weaned child is my soul within me.
Psalm 131:2 NLT

"Come to Me, all who labor and are heavy laden, and I will give you rest."
Matthew 11:28 ESV

In peace I will lie down and sleep, for You alone, O LORD, will keep me safe.
Psalm 4:8 NLT

"Six days you shall work, but on the seventh day you shall rest; in plowing time and in harvest you shall rest."
Exodus 34:21 NKJV

My soul finds rest in God; my salvation comes from Him.
Psalm 62:1 NIV

"Take My yoke upon you. Let Me teach you, because I am humble and gentle at heart, and you will find rest for your souls."
Matthew 11:29 NLT

Having hope will give you courage. You will be protected and will rest in safety.
Job 11:18 NLT

With all the demands of being a woman, you may feel guilty about resting, but it is a command from God. You need to rest. Rest from your work to recharge and refuel. Rest with family to strengthen your relationships. Spiritual rest, quiet time with God where you can cry out or simply enjoy His blessings, is also important. You have to create time each day for physical, mental, and emotional rest.

Godly Restoration

In His kindness God called you to share in His eternal glory by means of Christ Jesus. So after you have suffered a little while, He will restore, support, and strengthen you, and He will place you on a firm foundation.
1 Peter 5:10 NLT

He restores my soul; He leads me in the paths of righteousness for His name's sake.
Psalm 23:3 NKJV

Though You have made me see troubles, many and bitter, You will restore my life again; from the depths of the earth You will again bring me up.
Psalm 71:20 NIV

"I will refresh the weary and satisfy the faint."
Jeremiah 31:25 NIV

Aim for restoration, comfort one another, agree with one another, live in peace; and the God of love and peace will be with you.
2 Corinthians 13:11 ESV

Restore to me the joy of Your salvation and grant me a willing spirit, to sustain me.
Psalm 51:12 NIV

Those who wait on the LORD shall renew their strength; they shall mount up with wings like eagles, they shall run and not be weary, they shall walk and not faint.
Isaiah 40:31 NKJV

Has it been a difficult year so far? Do you feel everything is collapsing—your finances, relationships, your whole life? Do not despair! God can bring restoration. He is the one who restores and heals. He restores your life and your priorities. He restores your marriage into a relationship that seeks His will. With His unconditional love, patience, and grace, He restores your relationship with Him. Will you allow Him to restore you?

The Resurrection of Jesus

With great power the apostles continued to testify to the resurrection of the Lord Jesus. And God's grace was so powerfully at work in them all.
Acts 4:33 NIV

I want to know Christ, yes, to know the power of His resurrection and participation in His sufferings, becoming like Him in His death.
Philippians 3:10 NLT

Praise be to the God and Father of our LORD Jesus Christ! In His great mercy He has given us new birth into a living hope through the resurrection of Jesus Christ from the dead.
1 Peter 1:3 NIV

Jesus said to her, "I am the resurrection and the life. He who believes in Me, though he may die, he shall live."
John 11:25 NKJV

He is not here, He has risen, just as He said. Come and see the place where He lay.
Matthew 28:6 NIV

Since we believe that Jesus died and was raised to life again, we also believe that when Jesus returns, God will bring back with Him the believers who have died.
1 Thessalonians 4:14 NLT

A few women were heading to Jesus' grave, thinking this was just another Sunday. But God had other plans; that Sunday would be remembered forever. He chose women to be the first bearers of the Good News on Resurrection Sunday. Death had been conquered; Jesus had risen! He broke down the doors of death, and He holds the key for everyone who wants to enter. He forgives your debt, and His resurrection power is promised and poured out on Pentecost. His resurrection changes grief and misery into comfort, hope, and glory.

Reverence for God

Reverence for the LORD is pure, lasting forever. The laws of the LORD are true; each one is fair.
Psalm 19:9 NLT

Stand up in the presence of the aged, show respect for the elderly and revere your God. I am the LORD.
Leviticus 19:32 NIV

Oh, worship the LORD in the beauty of holiness! Tremble before Him, all the earth.
Psalm 96:9 NKJV

A deep sense of awe came over them all, and the apostles performed many miraculous signs and wonders.
Acts 2:43 NLT

He said to them, "When you pray, say: 'Father, hallowed be Your name. Your kingdom come.'"
Luke 11:2 ESV

Therefore, my beloved, as you have always obeyed, so now, not only as in my presence but much more in my absence, work out your own salvation with fear and trembling.
Philippians 2:12 ESV

Whoever fears the LORD has a secure fortress, and for their children it will be a refuge. The fear of the LORD is a fountain of life, turning a person from the snares of death.
Proverbs 14:26-27 NIV

To have reverence for God means having a holy fear of the Lord. This fear is a respect for the God who commands galaxies, controls the air in our lungs, and has numbered our days to the second. Our reverence is also in response to God's love and how much He cares about us. It is the realization of what it cost God to make us His children. It is to take off your shoes and cover your face when you come before Him, for He is great.

A Life God Rewards

"When those hired at five o'clock were paid, each received a full day's wage. When those hired first came to get their pay...they, too, were paid a day's wage. When they received their pay, they protested...He answered, 'Friend, I haven't been unfair! Didn't you agree to work all day for the usual wage? Should you be jealous because I am kind to others?' So those who are last now will be first then, and those who are first will be last."
Matthew 20:9-11, 13-16 NLT

As for you, be strong and do not give up, for your work will be rewarded.
2 Chronicles 15:7 NIV

From the fruit of their lips people are filled with good things, and the work of their hands brings them reward.
Proverbs 12:14 NIV

Remember that the Lord will reward each one of us for the good we do.
Ephesians 6:8 NLT

"Rejoice and be glad, for your reward is great in heaven."
Matthew 5:12 ESV

Blessed are all who fear the LORD, who walk in obedience to Him. You will eat the fruit of your labor; blessings and prosperity will be yours.
Psalm 128:1-2 NIV

God and man's idea of reward differs completely. It is clear that God's reward for those who have worked longer is the same as for those who started working later. Eternal life is your reward. Your biggest reward is that you will always be in His presence. Heaven is not about us or who we will see—whether the streets are paved with gold or if there is an extra reward waiting for us—it's about God, His glory, and His presence.

The Riches of God

"Whoever can be trusted with very little can also be trusted with much, and whoever is dishonest with very little will also be dishonest with much. So if you have not been trustworthy in handling worldly wealth, who will trust you with true riches?"
Luke 16:10-11 NIV

Honor the LORD with your wealth and with the firstfruits of all your produce; then your barns will be filled with plenty, and your vats will be bursting with wine.
Proverbs 3:9-10 ESV

True humility and fear of the LORD lead to riches, honor, and long life.
Proverbs 22:4 NLT

The trustworthy person will get a rich reward, but a person who wants quick riches will get into trouble.
Proverbs 28:20 NLT

Be careful that no one entices you by riches; do not let a large bribe turn you aside.
Job 36:18 NIV

Yet true godliness with contentment is itself great wealth.
1 Timothy 6:6 NLT

I will be fully satisfied as with the richest of foods; with singing lips my mouth will praise You.
Psalm 63:5 NIV

If you could choose wealth today, would you choose material wealth, spiritual wealth, wealthy relationships, wisdom, or happiness? The Bible does not condemn riches. But God does speak up about greed and materialism. People whose lives revolve around money will never be satisfied. However, stewards who share their possessions discover an indescribable joy. The richest woman among her friends is the one who gets the most done with what she has and is satisfied.

Faith and Righteousness

Since we know that Christ is righteous, we also know that all who do what is right are God's children.
1 John 2:29 NLT

Your righteousness is like the mighty mountains, Your justice like the ocean depths.
Psalm 36:6 NLT

Therefore, since we have been made right in God's sight by faith, we have peace with God because of what Jesus Christ our Lord has done for us. Because of our faith, Christ has brought us into this place of undeserved privilege where we now stand, and we confidently and joyfully look forward to sharing God's glory.
Romans 5:1-2 NLT

No human being might boast in the presence of God. And because of Him you are in Christ Jesus, who became to us wisdom from God, righteousness and sanctification and redemption, so that, as it is written, "Let the one who boasts, boast in the Lord."
1 Corinthians 1:29-31 ESV

The LORD of Heaven's Armies will be exalted by His justice. The holiness of God will be displayed by His righteousness.
Isaiah 5:16 NLT

God made Him who had no sin to be sin for us, so that in Him we might become the righteousness of God.
2 Corinthians 5:21 NIV

Righteousness has to do with real relationships. Jesus came so that we can stand in right relationship with God. Realize that righteousness and grace are partners, and with gratitude set yourself aside for Him. Obey His commands and live out His Word. Righteousness is important in our relationship with the community and it is intensely important for social justice to prevail.

Sacrifices for God's Glory!

"Greater love has no one than this: to lay down one's life for one's friends."
John 15:13 NIV

Live a life filled with love, following the example of Christ. He loved us and offered Himself as a sacrifice for us, a pleasing aroma to God.
Ephesians 5:2 NLT

"Leave your sacrifice there at the altar. Go and be reconciled to that person. Then come and offer your sacrifice to God."
Matthew 5:24 NLT

To do righteousness and justice is more acceptable to the LORD than sacrifice.
Proverbs 21:3 ESV

"Go and learn what this means: 'I desire mercy and not sacrifice.' For I did not come to call the righteous, but sinners, to repentance."
Matthew 9:13 NKJV

"For whoever wants to save their life will lose it, but whoever loses their life for Me will save it."
Luke 9:24 NIV

Let my prayer be set before You as incense, the lifting up of my hands as the evening sacrifice.
Psalm 141:2 NKJV

Love! What does love, as God intended it in the Word and Jesus came to demonstrate, look like? It is different from red rose petals, champagne, and romantic candles. This love is self-sacrificing; it is to give without receiving back. He has called you to His service. This service is more than the romance of discipleship, wherein lies sacrifice, hard work, and time. Sacrifice your time, energy, and resources today so that God can win His church and get the glory.

The Salvation of God

The LORD takes pleasure in His people; He will beautify the humble with salvation.

Psalm 149:4 NKJV

Oh, sing to the LORD a new song! Sing to the LORD, all the earth. Sing to the LORD, bless His name; proclaim the good news of His salvation from day to day. Declare His glory among the nations, His wonders among all peoples.

Psalm 96:1-3 NKJV

It is good that one should wait quietly for the salvation of the LORD.

Lamentations 3:26 ESV

I delight greatly in the LORD; my soul rejoices in my God. For He has clothed me with garments of salvation and arrayed me in a robe of His righteousness, as a bridegroom adorns his head like a priest, and as a bride adorns herself with her jewels. For as the soil makes the sprout come up and a garden causes seeds to grow, so the Sovereign LORD will make righteousness and praise spring up before all nations.

Isaiah 61:10-11 NIV

There is salvation in no one else! God has given no other name under heaven by which we must be saved.

Acts 4:12 NLT

The five letter word that determined your future and cost the life of God's Son—saved! Not because you obey the law, go to church every Sunday, or because you live a holy life, but because Jesus came to save you by grace through His death on the cross. Through His Spirit, you become aware of your sin, you confessed it, and you repented. You become aware of how necessary His salvation is for you. Make this your own salvation by faith today.

Devoted to God

May God Himself, the God of peace, sanctify you through and through. May your whole spirit, soul and body be kept blameless at the coming of our Lord Jesus Christ.

1 Thessalonians 5:23 NIV

"Sanctify them by Your truth. Your word is truth. As You sent Me into the world, I also have sent them into the world. And for their sakes I sanctify Myself, that they also may be sanctified by the truth."

John 17:17-19 NKJV

It is God's will that you should be sanctified.

1 Thessalonians 4:3 NIV

For by a single offering He has perfected for all time those who are being sanctified.

Hebrews 10:14 ESV

Because of Him you are in Christ Jesus, who became to us wisdom from God, righteousness and sanctification and redemption, so that, as it is written, "Let the one who boasts, boast in the Lord."

1 Corinthians 1:30-31 ESV

God's will was for us to be made holy by the sacrifice of the body of Jesus Christ, once for all time.

Hebrews 10:10 NLT

Sanctification is the process of becoming holy. This is a lifelong process that starts right after salvation, where you allow the Holy Spirit to renew you and to gradually develop you into His own image. Sanctification happens in every aspect of your life—your thoughts, finances, and relationships. You are set apart by the Spirit of God, and as the bride you are ready to meet your groom.

He Satisfies Our Needs

Satisfy us in the morning with Your unfailing love, that we may sing for joy and be glad all our days.
Psalm 90:14 NIV

Let them give thanks to the LORD for His unfailing love and His wonderful deeds for mankind, for He satisfies the thirsty and fills the hungry with good things.
Psalm 107:8-9 NIV

Keep your lives free from the love of money and be content with what you have, because God has said, "Never will I leave you; never will I forsake you."
Hebrews 13:5 NIV

You open Your hand and satisfy the desires of every living thing.
Psalm 145:16 NIV

Godliness with contentment is great gain. For we brought nothing into the world, and we can take nothing out of it.
1 Timothy 6:6-7 NIV

Command those who are rich in this present world not to be arrogant nor to put their hope in wealth, which is so uncertain, but to put their hope in God, who richly provides us with everything for our enjoyment.
1 Timothy 6:17 NIV

What are your needs, and how quickly do you need them to be satisfied before unhappiness and dissatisfaction sets in? According to the world, satisfaction requires possessions, money, prestige, and status. However, your hunger is satisfied with bread, your thirst with water, and your basic spiritual needs are satisfied by Christ. When God created you, there was a space created in you that only He can satisfy. You'll long for fulfillment and satisfaction in things until you find it in Him.

Our True Savior

Praise the LORD; praise God our Savior! For each day He carries us in His arms. Our God is a God who saves! The Sovereign LORD rescues us from death.

Psalm 68:19-20 NLT

Believe in the Lord Jesus, and you will be saved—you and your household.

Acts 16:31 NIV

The sun will be turned to darkness and the moon to blood before the coming of the great and glorious day of the Lord. And everyone who calls on the name of the Lord will be saved.

Acts 2:20-21 NIV

"Truly, truly, I say to you, whoever hears My word and believes Him who sent Me has eternal life. He does not come into judgment, but has passed from death to life."

John 5:24 ESV

"I am the gate; whoever enters through Me will be saved. They will come in and go out, and find pasture. The thief comes only to steal and kill and destroy; I have come that they may have life, and have it to the full. I am the good shepherd. The good shepherd lays down His life for the sheep."

John 10:9-11 NIV

Who is Jesus to you? Is He really your Savior and Redeemer? Through the years God's children have learned that He will deliver them from the power of people like Pharaoh, that He saves them from natural disasters like He did with Noah, that He will save them from a giant like He saved David, and that He will save them from the storm on the boat. Do you need saving? What are you waiting for; get it from Him. He's already holding your salvation in His hand.

Seasons Come and Go

Seeing in the distance a fig tree in leaf, He went to find out if it had any fruit. When He reached it, He found nothing but leaves, because it was not the season for figs.
Mark 11:13 NIV

They are like wild waves of the sea, churning up the foam of their shameful deeds. They are like wandering stars, doomed forever to blackest darkness.
Jude 1:13 NLT

Then God said, "Let there be lights in the firmament of the heavens to divide the day from the night; and let them be for signs and seasons, and for days and years."
Genesis 1:14 NKJV

Be patient, therefore, brothers, until the coming of the Lord. See how the farmer waits for the precious fruit of the earth, being patient about it, until it receives the early and the late rains. You also, be patient. Establish your hearts, for the coming of the Lord is at hand.
James 5:7-8 ESV

For everything there is a season, a time for every activity under heaven. A time to plant and a time to harvest. A time to cry and a time to laugh. A time to grieve and a time to dance. A time to keep and a time to throw away. A time for war and a time for peace.
Ecclesiastes 3:1-8 NLT

Like clockwork, the seasons change. Sometimes it can feel like a season doesn't want to pass, and at other times we want to hit "pause" to remain in the season we are. Winter is ruthless and overwhelming, leaving us feeling fragile. When the cold winds cut through you like a knife, crave the warmth of His presence. In every season He brings the balance. Heat in winter, refreshment in the summer, buds of new life in spring, and a palette of colors in a dull autumn moment.

The Joy of Second Chances

If anyone is in Christ, the new creation has come: The old has gone, the new is here!
2 Corinthians 5:17 NIV

Put on the new self, which is being renewed in knowledge after the image of its creator.
Colossians 3:10 ESV

Don't copy the behavior and customs of this world, but let God transform you into a new person by changing the way you think. Then you will learn to know God's will for you, which is good and pleasing and perfect.
Romans 12:2 NLT

Give yourselves completely to God, for you were dead, but now you have new life. So use your whole body as an instrument to do what is right for the glory of God. Sin is no longer your master, for you no longer live under the requirements of the law. Instead, you live under the freedom of God's grace.
Romans 6:13-14 NLT

Now go and tell His disciples, including Peter, that Jesus is going ahead of you to Galilee. You will see Him there, just as He told you before He died.
Mark 16:7 NLT

The night is nearly over; the day is almost here. So let us put aside the deeds of darkness and put on the armor of light.
Romans 13:12 NIV

Do you long for a second chance today, one filled with forgiveness? Peter also made many mistakes in his life. After the promise that he would never deny Jesus, fear came over him, and he denied Jesus three times before he heard the rooster crow. But we serve a God of second chances, and after Jesus' resurrection, Peter in particular was offered a second chance in being an apostle. God is ready to give you a second chance too.

The Second Coming

"I will not leave you as orphans; I will come to you. Before long, the world will not see Me anymore, but you will see Me. Because I live, you also will live. On that day you will realize that I am in My Father, and you are in Me, and I am in you."
John 14:18-20 NIV

Behold, He is coming with clouds, and every eye will see Him, even they who pierced Him. And all the tribes of the earth will mourn because of Him. Even so, Amen. "I am the Alpha and the Omega, the Beginning and the End," says the Lord, "who is and who was and who is to come, the Almighty."
Revelation 1:7-9 NKJV

The day of the Lord will come as unexpectedly as a thief. Then the heavens will pass away with a terrible noise, and the very elements themselves will disappear in fire, and the earth and everything on it will be found to deserve judgment.
2 Peter 3:10 NLT

While they looked steadfastly toward heaven as He went up, behold, two men stood by them in white apparel, who also said, "Men of Galilee, why do you stand gazing up into heaven? This same Jesus, who was taken up from you into heaven, will so come in like manner as you saw Him go into heaven."
Acts 1:10-11 NKJV

Live for today but plan for tomorrow and your retirement. That's how most of us live—save money and get ready to die to be with Him forever. But how often do you really think of the second coming of Jesus? Do you really think it will happen in your lifetime? Do you still have the expectation that Jesus will come on the clouds to fetch you? It's amazing that we will see Him face-to-face. It's amazing that we will be able to praise Him together with angels. Maranatha! Come, Lord Jesus!

True Security

"I will put My dwelling place among you. I will walk among you and be your God, and you will be My people."
Leviticus 26:11-12 NIV

"I am with you always, even to the end of the age."
Matthew 28:20 NKJV

The LORD is near to all who call on Him, to all who call on Him in truth.
Psalm 145:18 ESV

Let the beloved of the LORD rest secure in Him, for He shields him all day long.
Deuteronomy 33:12 NIV

Those who trust in the LORD are like Mount Zion, which cannot be moved, but abides forever.
Psalm 125:1 NKJV

The LORD is my rock and my fortress and my deliverer, my God, my rock, in whom I take refuge, my shield, and the horn of my salvation, my stronghold.
Psalm 18:2 ESV

"Though the mountains be shaken and the hills be removed, yet My unfailing love for you will not be shaken nor My covenant of peace be removed," says the LORD.
Isaiah 54:10 NIV

Your goodness and unfailing love will pursue me all the days of my life, and I will live in the house of the LORD forever.
Psalm 23:6 NLT

Our security is mostly found in money and our paycheck at the end of the month. You trust your job security, and it makes you calm, because you know that you can pay all the bills, buy some bread, and put away a little something extra for an emergency. This makes you feel calm because you feel secure. We need to learn to trust in God, who always provides. Know that the God who gives more than enough for today, is your only Security.

Where Is God?

Let the hearts of those who seek the LORD rejoice! Seek the LORD and His strength; seek His presence continually! Remember the wondrous works that He has done, His miracles and the judgments He uttered. He is the LORD our God; His judgments are in all the earth.
1 Chronicles 16:10-12, 14 ESV

Let all those who seek You rejoice and be glad in You; let such as love Your salvation say continually, "The LORD be magnified!"
Psalm 40:16 NKJV

I love those who love me, and those who seek me diligently will find me.
Proverbs 8:17 NKJV

Those who know Your name will put their trust in You; for You, LORD, have not forsaken those who seek You.
Psalm 9:10 NKJV

Seek the LORD your God, and you will find Him if you seek Him with all your heart and with all your soul.
Deuteronomy 4:29 NKJV

The lions may grow weak and hungry, but those who seek the LORD lack no good thing.
Psalm 34:10 NIV

The LORD is with you while you are with Him. If you seek Him, He will be found by you, but if you forsake Him, He will forsake you.
2 Chronicles 15:2 ESV

Where is God? In a world with Christian radio stations, TV programs, movies, books, churches, and disciples, the question remains: Where is God? Sometimes you will find Him in the noise of a spectacular thunder storm, but sometimes He is in the soft whisper of the wind. The fact is, He is here—He was here yesterday and will be with you tomorrow.

Self-Control and the Power of Christ

Buy the truth, and do not sell it, also wisdom and instruction and understanding.
Proverbs 23:23 NKJV

Like a city whose walls are broken through is a person who lacks self-control.
Proverbs 25:28 NIV

A gentle answer turns away wrath, but a harsh word stirs up anger.
Proverbs 15:1 NIV

Guard your heart above all else, for it determines the course of your life.
Proverbs 4:23 NLT

God has not given us a spirit of fear and timidity, but of power, love and self-discipline.
2 Timothy 1:7 NLT

Make every effort to add to your faith goodness; and to goodness, knowledge; and to knowledge, self-control; and to self-control, perseverance; and to perseverance, godliness; and to godliness, mutual affection; and to mutual affection, love. For if you possess these qualities in increasing measure, they will keep you from being ineffective and unproductive in your knowledge of our Lord Jesus Christ.
2 Peter 1:5-8 NIV

An athlete is not crowned unless he competes according to the rules.
2 Timothy 2:5 ESV

To make the right choice, when other choices seem so much easier, is to live with restraint and to believe that the right way holds a future with God. God has given you the ability to manage yourself. You can choose whether to surrender to your anger, cravings, mood, and addictions that are disastrous for you and others around you. The Holy Spirit, however, gives you back your self-control, so forgive yourself and live a life of self-control in the future.

Me, Myself, and I

Turn my heart toward Your statutes and not toward selfish gain.
Psalm 119:36 NIV

An unfriendly person pursues selfish ends and against all sound judgment starts quarrels.
Proverbs 18:1 NIV

Don't be selfish; don't try to impress others. Be humble, thinking of others as better than yourselves. Don't look out only for your own interests, but take an interest in others, too.
Philippians 2:3-4 NLT

For where you have envy and selfish ambition, there you find disorder and every evil practice.
James 3:16 NIV

For jealousy and selfishness are not God's kind of wisdom. Such things are earthly, unspiritual, and demonic.
James 3:15 NLT

If you harbor bitter envy and selfish ambition in your hearts, do not boast about it or deny the truth.
James 3:14 NIV

Don't be concerned for your own good but for the good of others.
1 Corinthians 10:24 NLT

"Whoever wants to be My disciple must deny themselves and take up their cross daily and follow Me."
Luke 9:23 NIV

Me, myself, and I. It is often the subject of people's conversations. Do you know someone like this who manipulates, feels sorry for themselves, and is often discontent with what they have? Is this person perhaps you? Selfishness makes you blind to the needs of the world, and it makes you deaf to the voice of God. Selfishness is like a disease that can consume you. But you can be healed when you crucify yourself and focus on the risen Lord.

See Your Worth through God's Eyes

For You formed my inward parts; You covered me in my mother's womb. I will praise You, for I am fearfully and wonderfully made; marvelous are Your works, and that my soul knows very well.
Psalm 139:13-14 NKJV

"Do not look at his appearance or at his physical stature, because I have refused him. For the LORD does not see as man sees; for man looks at the outward appearance, but the LORD looks at the heart."
1 Samuel 16:7 NKJV

You have made him to have dominion over the works of Your hands; You have put all things under his feet.
Psalm 8:6 NKJV

God created human beings in His own image. In the image of God He created them; male and female He created them.
Genesis 1:27 NLT

The LORD your God is in your midst, a mighty one who will save; He will rejoice over you with gladness; He will quiet you by His love; He will exult over you with loud singing.
Zephaniah 3:17 ESV

You are altogether beautiful, my darling; there is no flaw in you.
Song of Songs 4:7 NIV

Your self-worth is not determined by whether you're smart, beautiful, or successful. It is determined by the awareness of who you are in Christ and how He sees you. God knows you're special. He dreamed about you, planned you, and created you. He knows the sum of the hair on your head, and He sees the tears on your cheeks. He has so many plans for you. See yourself through God's eyes, and you may discover what He already knows. You are a masterpiece whom He loves very much.

God's Heart Touches Yours

We who are strong must be considerate of those who are sensitive about things like this. We must not just please ourselves.
Romans 15:1 NLT

We know that we all have knowledge. Knowledge puffs up, but love edifies.
1 Corinthians 8:1 NKJV

Finally, all of you, be likeminded, be sympathetic, love one another, be compassionate and humble. Do not repay evil with evil or insult with insult. On the contrary, repay evil with blessing, because to this you were called so that you may inherit a blessing.
1 Peter 3:8-9 NIV

Be kind and compassionate to one another, forgiving each other, just as in Christ God forgave you.
Ephesians 4:32 NIV

Be of the same mind toward one another. Do not set your mind on high things, but associate with the humble. Do not be wise in your own opinion.
Romans 12:16 NKJV

Put on then, as God's chosen ones, holy and beloved, compassionate hearts, kindness, humility, meekness, and patience.
Colossians 3:12 ESV

When Jesus looks at people, He sees what lies behind the obvious and visible things. He sees the hurt, the disappointment, the fears, and the failures. May you see those around you in a different way today, with a heart that is shaped by the Holy Spirit, showing empathy as only God's children can. May you realize today that behind each person's defenses, a story is locked up.

Excellent Christian Service

"Anyone who wants to be first must be the very last, and the servant of all."
Mark 9:35 NIV

"You call Me 'Teacher' and 'Lord,' and rightly so, for that is what I am. Now that I, your Lord and Teacher, have washed your feet, you also should wash one another's feet."
John 13:13-14 NIV

"I tell you the truth, no servant is greater than his master, nor is a messenger greater than the one who sent him. Now that you know these things, you will be blessed if you do them."
John 13:16-17 NIV

"When you give to the needy, do not let your left hand know what your right hand is doing, so that your giving may be in secret. Then your Father, who sees what is done in secret, will reward you."
Matthew 6:3-4 NIV

"Give, and you will receive. Your gift will return to you in full—pressed down, shaken together to make room for more, running over, and poured into your lap. The amount you give will determine the amount you get back."
Luke 6:38 NLT

Most women like to be pampered and served once in a while—unlike at home where they're usually the servant of all. We want to be leaders. We want to sit in front, yet Jesus calls us to sit at the back and to give away the best places for others to enjoy. Jesus calls you to serve God and people. Perhaps servanthood is difficult because you don't see it as part of your testimony, but rather as being beneath you. Decide to serve with joy.

Shelter from the Storm

He who dwells in the shelter of the Most High will rest in the shadow of the Almighty.
Psalm 91:1 NIV

He will deliver you from the snare of the fowler and from the deadly pestilence. He will cover you with His pinions, and under His wings you will find refuge.
Psalm 91:3-4 ESV

You have been a shelter for me, a strong tower from the enemy. I will abide in Your tabernacle forever; I will trust in the shelter of Your wings.
Psalm 61:3-4 NKJV

Every word of God proves true; He is a shield to those who take refuge in Him.
Proverbs 30:5 ESV

Be my rock of safety where I can always hide. Give the order to save me, for You are my rock and my fortress.
Psalm 71:3 NLT

My God is my rock, in whom I find protection. He is my shield, the power that saves me, and my place of safety. He is my refuge, my savior, the one who saves me from violence.
2 Samuel 22:3 NLT

You have been a strength to the poor, a strength to the needy in his distress, a refuge from the storm, a shade from the heat; for the blast of the terrible ones is as a storm against the wall.
Isaiah 25:4 NKJV

In the middle of a storm, people will frantically run around trying to find safety, shelter, and protection from danger. In life, there are dangers that seem like massive storms, and we tend to wonder how we will survive. Read God's Word, meditate on it, pray, and thank Him that the waves become relatively smaller compared to the great God under whose wings you can find shelter and comfort.

November

Give all your
worries
and cares to

God,

— for —

He cares

about you.

1 Peter 5:7

God Heals His Children

The LORD sustains them on their sickbed and restores them from their bed of illness.
Psalm 41:3 NIV

My health may fail, and my spirit may grow weak, but God remains the strength of my heart; He is mine forever.
Psalm 73:26 NLT

"I am the LORD who heals you."
Exodus 15:26 NLT

Bless the LORD, O my soul, and forget not all His benefits, who forgives all your iniquity, who heals all your diseases.
Psalm 103:2-3 ESV

Are any of you sick? You should call for the elders of the church to come and pray over you…a prayer offered in faith will heal the sick, and the Lord will make you well.
James 5:14-15 NLT

LORD my God, I cried to You for help, and You restored my health.
Psalm 30:2 NLT

Heal me, O LORD, and I shall be healed; save me, and I shall be saved, for You are my praise.
Jeremiah 17:14 ESV

But He was wounded for our transgressions, He was bruised for our iniquities; the chastisement for our peace was upon Him, and by His stripes we are healed.
Isaiah 53:5 NKJV

What if I pray for healing, truly believe that it will come to pass, and then it doesn't happen? Is my faith weak? Did God want to punish me? Did I pray wrong? No! People die of diseases. But what about God's promises to heal? Disease is often associated with struggles within yourself, struggles with God, faith, and illness. The promise of healing is not only physical, but also spiritual. Sometimes eternal life is more victorious than physical life. Relax, God is in control!

A Sin-Torn World

Therefore, there is now no condemnation for those who are in Christ Jesus.
Romans 8:1 NIV

Sin shall not have dominion over you, for you are not under law but under grace.
Romans 6:14 NIV

To Him who loves us and has freed us from our sins by His blood, to Him be glory and power for ever and ever!
Revelation 1:5-6 NIV

If we confess our sins, He is faithful and just and will forgive us our sins and purify us from all unrighteousness.
1 John 1:9 NIV

He gave His life to free us from every kind of sin, to cleanse us, and to make us His very own people, totally committed to doing good deeds. **Titus 2:14 NLT**

"Come now, let us settle the matter," says the LORD. "Though your sins are like scarlet, they shall be as white as snow; though they are red as crimson, they shall be like wool."
Isaiah 1:18 NIV

So whoever knows the right thing to do and fails to do it, for him it is sin. **James 4:17 ESV**

Whoever commits sin also commits lawlessness, and sin is lawlessness.
1 John 3:4 NKJV

Sin is like a jellyfish. Jellyfish don't look harmful. In fact, they look quite attractive and nice to touch. But they're deadly. If you touch them, they might feel nice and soft, but soon thereafter you will feel numb, light headed, and confused. Sin works the same way. Initially it looks good and attractive, but then you cannot escape its paralyzing claws. Jesus came to save you from sin, and His grace is the loving arms that keep you safe.

Speak Life

Let your conversation be always full of grace, seasoned with salt, so that you may know how to answer everyone.
Colossians 4:6 NIV

"It's not what goes into your mouth that defiles you; you are defiled by the words that come out of your mouth."
Matthew 15:11 NLT

Let no corrupting talk come out of your mouths, but only such as is good for building up, as fits the occasion, that it may give grace to those who hear.
Ephesians 4:29 ESV

A gentle answer turns away wrath, but a harsh word stirs up anger.
Proverbs 15:1 NIV

A wholesome tongue is a tree of life, but perverseness in it breaks the spirit.
Proverbs 15:4 NKJV

Gracious words are a honeycomb, sweet to the soul and healing to the bones.
Proverbs 16:24 NIV

Let no corrupting talk come out of your mouths, but only such as is good for building up, as fits the occasion, that it may give grace to those who hear.
Ephesians 4:29 ESV

Sin is not ended by multiplying words, but the prudent hold their tongues.
Proverbs 10:19 NIV

Studies estimate that women speak 13,000 words more than men per day. If these statistics are correct in your case, what power and impact do your words have in your relationships and at work? The tongue is a very powerful weapon used by some women to speak evil, gossip, humiliate, and hurt. Your words can give life, heal, and build hope. Use your words to honor God and to speak life.

Grow Spiritually

Now may He who supplies seed to the sower, and bread for food, supply and multiply the seed you have sown and increase the fruits of your righteousness, while you are enriched in everything for all liberality, which causes thanksgiving through us to God.
2 Corinthians 9:10-11 ESV

Grow up in all things into Him who is the head—Christ—from whom the whole body, joined and knit together by what every joint supplies, according to the effective working by which every part does its share, causes growth of the body for the edifying of itself in love.
Ephesians 4:15-16 NKJV

So put away all malice and all deceit and hypocrisy and envy and all slander. Like newborn infants, long for the pure spiritual milk, that by it you may grow up into salvation.
1 Peter 2:1-2 ESV

For this reason we also, since the day we heard it, do not cease to pray for you, and to ask that you may be filled with the knowledge of His will in all wisdom and spiritual understanding; that you may walk worthy of the LORD, fully pleasing Him, being fruitful in every good work and increasing in the knowledge of God.
Colossians 1:9-10 NKJV

There is no quick three-step plan for growing spiritually. Spiritual growth requires discipline, time, and commitment. It requires you to read the Word systematically, meditate on it, and to accompany a congregation in worship and in prayer. Sometimes at the end of the year when the pace increases and we become busier, it is our time together with God that is neglected. Seek God's presence today through prayer, His Word, and community with His people.

Armed for Battle

For though we live in the world, we do not wage war as the world does. The weapons we fight with are not the weapons of the world. On the contrary, they have divine power to demolish strongholds.
2 Corinthians 10:3-4 NIV

We do not wrestle against flesh and blood, but against the rulers, against the authorities, against the cosmic powers over this present darkness, against the spiritual forces of evil in the heavenly places.
Ephesians 6:12 ESV

Submit yourselves therefore to God. Resist the devil, and he will flee from you.
James 4:7 ESV

Therefore, put on every piece of God's armor so you will be able to resist the enemy in the time of evil. Then after the battle you will still be standing firm.
Ephesians 6:13 NLT

Stand firm then, with the belt of truth buckled around your waist, with the breastplate of righteousness in place, and with your feet fitted with the readiness that comes from the gospel of peace. In addition to all this, take up the shield of faith, with which you can extinguish all the flaming arrows of the evil one.
Ephesians 6:14-16 NIV

Your great battle is against Satan, the deceiver, impostor, and prosecutor. He wants to rob you of your peace and hope through the seeds of fear, despair, and lies. Jesus has already overcome sin, and you are part of this victory. For this war you must wear the armor of God every day, 24 hours a day, and never take it off. When you tell a lie, you lose your belt, but through confession you can clothe yourself again. Are you fully dressed? The victory awaits you.

Your Status in Christ

"Let us make man in our image, after our likeness. And let them have dominion over the fish of the sea and over the birds of the heavens and over the livestock and over all the earth and over every creeping thing that creeps on the earth." So God created man in His own image, in the image of God He created him; male and female He created them.
Genesis 1:26-27 ESV

He made Himself nothing by taking the very nature of a servant, being made in human likeness.
Philippians 2:7 NIV

"So the last will be first, and the first will be last."
Matthew 20:16 NIV

I know how to live on almost nothing or with everything. I have learned the secret of living in every situation, whether it is with a full stomach or empty, with plenty or little. For I can do everything through Christ, who gives me strength.
Philippians 4:12-13 NLT

Hasn't God chosen the poor in this world to be rich in faith? Aren't they the ones who will inherit the Kingdom He promised to those who love Him? But you dishonor the poor!
James 2:5-6 NLT

"I have come that they may have life, and that they may have it more abundantly."
John 10:10 NKJV

Your status can be posted everywhere on social media. I'm sure you've read the funniest things on people's statuses, especially what they have to say about themselves. What is your status today? Do you realize that you are an ambassador of God, His representative on earth? In my distress and my abundance, I am more than a conqueror. I'm rich because I am an heir of the Kingdom of God. I'm in a relationship with Jesus, who delivered me from my deathly existence to a full life!

Christian Stewardship

This is how one should regard us, as servants of Christ and stewards of the mysteries of God.
1 Corinthians 4:1 ESV

Moreover it is required in stewards that one be found faithful.
1 Corinthians 4:2 NKJV

For an overseer, as God's steward, must be above reproach.
Titus 1:7 ESV

Since therefore Christ suffered in the flesh, arm yourselves with the same way of thinking, for whoever has suffered in the flesh has ceased from sin, so as to live for the rest of the time in the flesh no longer for human passions but for the will of God.
1 Peter 4:1-2 ESV

If you are a thief, quit stealing. Instead, use your hands for good hard work, and then give generously to others in need.
Ephesians 4:28 NLT

Each of you should use whatever gift you have received to serve others, as faithful stewards of God's grace in its various forms.
1 Peter 4:10 NIV

Bring the whole tithe into the storehouse, that there may be food in My house. Test Me in this," says the LORD Almighty, "and see if I will not throw open the floodgates of heaven and pour out so much blessing that there will not be room enough to store it."
Malachi 3:10 NIV

When we think of stewardship, we immediately think of money and how we manage it, but your body, health, time, and relationships belong to God. Everything you own today belongs to Him—you are simply the manager. Good stewardship means that a person uses everything she is and has to reveal God's will on earth. God's blessing to you is that you may bless others.

Be Strong in the Lord

Ah, LORD GOD! It is You who have made the heavens and the earth by Your great power and by Your outstretched arm! Nothing is too hard for You.
Jeremiah 32:17 ESV

Now to Him who is able to do immeasurably more than all we ask or imagine, according to His power that is at work within us, to Him be glory in the church and in Christ Jesus throughout all generations, for ever and ever!
Ephesians 3:20-21 NIV

"My grace is sufficient for you, for My strength is made perfect in weakness."
2 Corinthians 12:9 NKJV

Great is our LORD, and abundant in power.
Psalm 147:5 ESV

Yours, O LORD, is the greatness, the power and the glory, the victory and the majesty; for all that is in heaven and in earth is Yours; Yours is the kingdom, O LORD, and You are exalted as head over all.
1 Chronicles 29:11 NKJV

Honor and majesty are before Him; strength and gladness are in His place.
1 Chronicles 16:27 NKJV

"So do not fear, for I am with you; do not be dismayed, for I am your God."
Isaiah 41:10 NIV

How big and strong is God? The whole universe came into being through His words. If we take all the power of the universe and the power of nature as we see and experience things and put it together, it will be noticeably smaller compared to His greatness and power. He doesn't get tired or become weary. Have your perceptions, thoughts, life experiences, and struggles restricted God to someone who can fit in your reference frame and life? Be still in His creation and praise God today for who He is.

Dealing with Stress God's Way

When anxiety was great within me, Your consolation brought me joy.
Psalm 94:19 NKJV

As pressure and stress bear down on me, I find joy in Your commands.
Psalm 119:143 NLT

When people live to be very old, let them rejoice in every day of life. But let them also remember there will be many dark days. Young people, it's wonderful to be young! Enjoy every minute of it. But remember that you must give an account to God for everything you do. So refuse to worry, and keep your body healthy.
Ecclesiastes 11:8-10 NLT

So what do people get in this life for all their hard work and anxiety? Their days of labor are filled with pain and grief; even at night their minds cannot rest. It is all meaningless. So I decided there is nothing better than to enjoy food and drink and to find satisfaction in work. Then I realized that these pleasures are from the hand of God. For who can eat or enjoy anything apart from Him?
Ecclesiastes 2:22-25 NLT

Give all your worries and cares to God, for He cares about you.
1 Peter 5:7 NLT

I want you to be free from anxieties.
1 Corinthians 7:32 ESV

Stress and worry are like poison, polluting the mind and destroying your whole body. But we know it's not easy to have no stress, because whatever crisis that brings about stress will not just disappear. God invites you to give all your worries to Him. He will carry it for you and sort it out, because He has the power and authority to do so. In return for your stress, He gives you peace that surpasses all understanding.

He Makes Us Strong

Be strong in the Lord and in His mighty power.
Ephesians 6:10 NIV

I can do all things through Christ who strengthens me.
Philippians 4:13 NKJV

In Your strength I can crush an army; with my God I can scale any wall.
Psalm 18:29 NLT

God is my strength and power, and He makes my way perfect. He makes my feet like the feet of deer, and sets me on my high places.
2 Samuel 22:33-34 NKJV

The LORD is my strength and my song; He has given me victory.
Psalm 118:14 NLT

My health may fail, and my spirit may grow weak, but God remains the strength of my heart; He is mine forever.
Psalm 73:26 NLT

But they who wait for the LORD shall renew their strength; they shall mount up with wings like eagles; they shall run and not be weary; they shall walk and not faint.
Isaiah 40:31 ESV

Be strong and take heart, all you who hope in the LORD.
Psalm 34:21 NIV

When you reach the end of your strength, and the mountain is still steep, you realize your strength doesn't come from hours at gym or energy drinks, but your strength is in the Lord. Remember Peter? When he reached the end of his strength, standing around the fire; he called out, "I don't know Him!" Peter received new strength in the resurrection of Christ. Through the Spirit he preached, and 3,000 people came to know the Lord. Your strength comes from Him.

The Stubborn Christian

Rebellion is as sinful as witch-craft, and stubbornness as bad as worshiping idols.
1 Samuel 15:23 NLT

Don't be stubborn and rebellious as Pharaoh and the Egyptians were. By the time God was finished with them, they were eager to let Israel go.
1 Samuel 6:6 NLT

Blessed are those who fear to do wrong, but the stubborn are headed for serious trouble.
Proverbs 28:14 NLT

Therefore, change your hearts and stop being stubborn.
Deuteronomy 10:16 NLT

Whoever stubbornly refuses to accept criticism will suddenly be destroyed beyond recovery.
Proverbs 29:1 NLT

Do not be stubborn, as they were, but submit yourselves to the LORD.
2 Chronicles 30:8 NLT

They are darkened in their understanding and separated from the life of God because of the ignorance that is in them due to the hardening of their hearts.
Ephesians 4:18 NIV

If your mind is made up about something, it's hard to let go or change it. It creates a safe world where the outcome is predictable, your indulgence is answered, and you're in control. A stubborn heart and mind make relationships complicated. Stubbornness is not new. Early in the Word, we read of the Pharaoh's stubbornness that cost the life of his eldest son. Today, the consequences of stubbornness can still be devastating to you. Therefore, let God renew your mind.

Submitting to God's Purpose

Submit yourselves, then, to God. Resist the devil, and he will flee from you.
James 4:7 NIV

Serve the LORD with fear, and rejoice with trembling.
Psalm 2:11 ESV

Likewise, you who are younger, be subject to the elders. Clothe yourselves, all of you, with humility toward one another, for "God opposes the proud but gives grace to the humble."
1 Peter 5:5 ESV

The mind governed by the flesh is hostile to God; it does not submit to God's law, nor can it do so.
Romans 8:7 NIV

Submit to one another out of reverence for Christ.
Ephesians 5:21 NIV

"May Your Kingdom come soon. May Your will be done on earth, as it is in heaven."
Matthew 6:10 NLT

Trust in the LORD with all your heart; do not depend on your own understanding. Seek His will in all you do, and He will show you which path to take.
Proverbs 3:5-6 NLT

I delight to do Your will, O my God, and Your law is within my heart.
Psalm 40:8 NKJV

The word "submissive" holds very negative connotations in our society. This often brings tension into marriages and has become a manipulation tool for people. But to submit means to serve, and it starts in our relationship with God. Jesus is a great example of someone who did not cling to His status, but who came to serve. Submission is to be on your knees while others stand on your shoulders to see farther and better.

The Door to Success

You will succeed in whatever you choose to do, and light will shine on the road ahead of you.
Job 22:28 NLT

Take delight in the LORD, and He will give you the desires of your heart.
Psalm 37:4 NIV

Jesus said, "With man this is impossible, but with God all things are possible."
Matthew 19:26 NIV

Remember the LORD your God, for it is He who gives you power to get wealth, that He may confirm His covenant that He swore to your fathers, as it is this day.
Deuteronomy 8:18 ESV

All glory to God, who is able, through His mighty power at work within us, to accomplish infinitely more than we might ask or think.
Ephesians 3:20 NLT

You, LORD, have made me glad through Your work; I will triumph in the works of Your hands.
Psalm 92:4 NKJV

"For I know the thoughts that I think toward you," says the LORD, "thoughts of peace and not of evil, to give you a future and a hope."
Jeremiah 29:11 NKJV

The world is obsessed with success based on achievements—failure generates fear. Half stories are told, and pictures accompany our successes with pride, while failures are put away. Success is persevering and getting back up when you fail. It is sharing the beautiful flower as well as the seed that had to break for this flower to grow. It sounds strange, but the broken seed, the failure, is part of your success story. Tell the whole story.

Dealing with Suffering

God is our refuge and strength, always ready to help in times of trouble.
Psalm 46:1 NLT

Those who suffer according to God's will should commit themselves to their faithful Creator and continue to do good.
1 Peter 4:19 NIV

For in that He Himself has suffered, being tempted, He is able to aid those who are tempted.
Hebrews 2:18 NKJV

I consider that the sufferings of this present time are not worth comparing with the glory that is to be revealed to us.
Romans 8:18 ESV

We rejoice in our sufferings, knowing that suffering produces endurance, and endurance produces character, and character produces hope, and hope does not put us to shame, because God's love has been poured into our hearts through the Holy Spirit who has been given to us.
Romans 5:3-5 ESV

The more we suffer for Christ, the more God will shower us with His comfort through Christ.
2 Corinthians 1:5 NLT

After you have suffered a little while, the God of all grace will Himself restore you.
1 Peter 5:10 ESV

We live in a broken world where suffering is part of life. Job's suffering was accompanied by emotions: he tore his clothes, cut his hair, put ashes on his head, and lay on the ground in agony. You also have emotions and tears that release chemicals in your brain so you feel better. Sometimes we get answers to our questions and other times only peace that surpasses all understanding—knowledge that He knows, even when you don't and cannot understand.

Sufficiency in God

Not that we are sufficient of ourselves to think of anything as being from ourselves, but our sufficiency is from God, who also made us sufficient as ministers of the new covenant, not of the letter but of the Spirit; for the letter kills, but the Spirit gives life.
2 Corinthians 3:5-6 NKJV

"My grace is sufficient for you, for My power is made perfect in weakness." Therefore I will boast all the more gladly about my weaknesses, so that Christ's power may rest on me.
2 Corinthians 12:9 NIV

I can do all things through Him who strengthens me.
Philippians 4:13 ESV

God is able to make all grace abound toward you, that you, always having all sufficiency in all things, may have an abundance for every good work.
2 Corinthians 9:8 NKJV

"I am the vine; you are the branches. If you remain in Me and I in you, you will bear much fruit; apart from Me you can do nothing."
John 15:5 NIV

"The Spirit alone gives eternal life. Human effort accomplishes nothing. And the very words I have spoken to you are spirit and life."
John 6:63 NLT

When is enough really enough? When is your personal time, your time together with people you love, and your time with God really enough? When is your satisfaction enough? When Paul went through a difficult time, God gave him the assurance that His grace was enough. God said, "My grace is sufficient for you." The Lord says that He will give you exactly what you need, and today it is grace! His grace is sufficient.

His Help and Support

They confronted me in the day of my disaster, but the LORD was my support.
Psalm 18:18 NIV

When Moses' hands grew tired. Aaron and Hur held his hands up—one on one side, one on the other—so that his hands remained steady till sunset.
Exodus 17:12 NIV

You have given me the shield of Your salvation, and Your right hand supported me, and Your gentleness made me great.
Psalm 18:35 ESV

Bear one another's burdens.
Galatians 6:2 ESV

When I said, "My foot is slipping," Your unfailing love, LORD, supported me.
Psalm 94:18 NIV

If I go up to heaven, You are there; if I go down to the grave, You are there. If I ride the wings of the morning, if I dwell by the farthest oceans, even there Your hand will guide me, and Your strength will support me.
Psalm 139:8-10 NLT

"I have been a constant example of how you can help those in need by working hard. You should remember the words of the Lord Jesus: 'It is more blessed to give than to receive.'"
Acts 20:35 NLT

Your greatest supporter is God. Although there are institutions, support groups, and structures, God calls His children to support others in need. Identify the need and then look at your ability to provide support. Maybe it's spiritual support: a prayer, reading from the Word, or being a mentor. Maybe it's emotional support: to hold someone's hand or to help someone who's crying. Physically: to cook food for a family or drive their children to school. Pray that God will help you to support others.

Pay Your Taxes

Pay your taxes...For government workers need to be paid.
Romans 13:6 NLT

Give to everyone what you owe them: Pay your taxes and government fees to those who collect them, and give respect and honor to those who are in authority.
Romans 13:7 NLT

Let everyone be subject to the governing authorities, for there is no authority except that which God has established. The authorities that exist have been established by God.
Romans 13:1 NIV

Tell us, therefore, what do You think? Is it lawful to pay taxes to Caesar, or not?" But Jesus perceived their wickedness, and said, "Why do you test Me, you hypocrites? Show Me the tax money." So they brought Him a denarius. And He said to them, "Whose image and inscription is this?" They said to Him, "Caesar's." And He said to them, "Render therefore to Caesar the things that are Caesar's, and to God the things that are God's."
Matthew 22:17-21 NKJV

Whoever resists the authorities resists what God has appointed, and those who resist will incur judgment.
Romans 13:2 ESV

It is interesting that people want to brag about their riches, but to the revenue service, they want to prove how poor they are. To pay taxes or not is a question dating back to the days of Jesus. Jesus said that taxes belong to the emperor/government, but your life belongs to God. Pay your taxes with honesty and integrity, even if it costs you. Make sure you stand with a pure heart before God.

Teach Others

In everything set them an example by doing what is good. In your teaching show integrity, seriousness and soundness of speech.
Titus 2:7-8 NIV

Train up a child in the way he should go; even when he is old he will not depart from it.
Proverbs 22:6 ESV

"These commandments that I give you today are to be on your hearts. Impress them on your children. Talk about them when you sit at home and when you walk along the road, when you lie down and when you get up."
Deuteronomy 6:6-7 NIV

All your children shall be taught by the LORD, and great shall be the peace of your children.
Isaiah 54:13 NKJV

These older women must train the younger women to love their husbands and their children.
Titus 2:4 NLT

Instruct the wise and they will be wiser still; teach the righteous and they will add to their learning.
Proverbs 9:9 NIV

All Scripture is breathed out by God and profitable for teaching, for reproof, for correction, and for training in righteousness.
2 Timothy 3:16 ESV

As a woman and mother, you have a vital role to play in educating other women and children. The best way to teach is by example and to do it in love. I once heard a story of a mother who, each time one of her prayers was answered, placed a stone on a heap behind their house. When she died the stones were higher than the roof. Teach your children how to read the Bible, to pray, to trust, to keep believing, and to love deeply.

Work as a Team

Two are better than one, because they have a good reward for their labor. For if they fall, one will lift up his companion. But woe to him who is alone when he falls, for he has no one to help him up. Again, if two lie down together, they will keep warm; but how can one be warm alone? Though one may be overpowered by another, two can withstand him. And a threefold cord is not quickly broken.
Ecclesiastes 4:9-12 NKJV

Let each of you look out not only for his own interests, but also for the interests of others.
Philippians 2:4 NKJV

As iron sharpens iron, so one person sharpens another.
Proverbs 27:17 NIV

I appeal to you, brothers and sisters, in the name of our Lord Jesus Christ, that all of you agree with one another in what you say and that there be no divisions among you, but that you be perfectly united in mind and thought.
1 Corinthians 1:10 NIV

Let us consider one another in order to stir up love and good works, not forsaking the assembling of ourselves together, as is the manner of some, but exhorting one another, and so much the more as you see the Day approaching.
Hebrews 10:24-25 NKJV

People who have learned to work together in a team accomplish much more than people who do everything alone. When you are part of a loving and respectful team who share a single dream and goal, the rewards and the victory are great. Get yourself a team of women that will help to make life easier. Booker T. Washington said, "If you want to lift yourself up, lift up someone else."

A Bad Temper

A fool is quick-tempered, but a wise person stays calm when insulted.
Proverbs 12:16 NLT

A quick-tempered person does foolish things, and the one who devises evil schemes is hated.
Proverbs 14:17 NIV

A hot-tempered man stirs up strife, but he who is slow to anger quiets contention.
Proverbs 15:18 ESV

The one who has knowledge uses words with restraint, and whoever has understanding is even-tempered.
Proverbs 17:27 NIV

A gentle answer deflects anger, but harsh words make tempers flare.
Proverbs 15:1 NLT

Sensible people control their temper; they earn respect by overlooking wrongs.
Proverbs 19:11 NLT

Whoever is slow to anger is better than the mighty, and he who rules his spirit than he who takes a city.
Proverbs 16:32 ESV

My dear brothers and sisters, take note of this: everyone should be quick to listen, slow to speak and slow to become angry, because human anger does not produce the righteousness that God desires.
James 1:19-20 NIV

When you're battling to control your temper, you might blame other people and their actions all the time. Get control over your emotions. It starts when you acknowledge that you alone are responsible for them. No one can cause you to lose your temper, unless you give permission. Try to find out what situations are more likely to cause you to lose your temper, and try to avoid them. Take a moment and think about it before you respond in any way.

Overcoming Temptation

No temptation has overtaken you that is not common to man. God is faithful, and He will not let you be tempted beyond your ability, but with the temptation He will also provide the way of escape, that you may be able to endure it.
1 Corinthians 10:13 ESV

Then Jesus was led by the Spirit into the wilderness to be tempted there by the devil.
Matthew 4:1 NLT

Because He Himself suffered when He was tempted, He is able to help those who are being tempted.
Hebrews 2:18 NIV

In His kindness God called you to share in His eternal glory by means of Christ Jesus. So after you have suffered a little while, He will restore, support, and strengthen you, and He will place you on a firm foundation. All power to Him forever!
1 Peter 5:10-11 NLT

Let no one say when he is tempted, "I am tempted by God"; for God cannot be tempted by evil, nor does He Himself tempt anyone. But each one is tempted when he is drawn away by his own desires and enticed.
James 1:13-14 NKJV

Satan enjoys enticing believers. He even tried to tempt Jesus. The only difference is Jesus did not sin and could resist the temptation because He knew the Bible and His Father intimately. The truth can be subtly distorted and sound like great insight and knowledge. Theft is mitigated to borrowing something. Lust is mitigated to love. One theologian said that money, sex, and power are the three biggest temptations causing people's demise. By knowing God and His Word, you will be able to say no to temptation.

The Testing of Your Faith

Be truly glad. There is wonderful joy ahead, even though you must endure many trials for a little while. These trials will show that your faith is genuine. It is being tested as fire tests and purifies gold—though your faith is far more precious than mere gold. So when your faith remains strong through many trials, it will bring you much praise and glory and honor on the day when Jesus Christ is revealed to the whole world.
1 Peter 1:6-7 NLT

"Behold, I have refined you, but not as silver; I have tested you in the furnace of affliction."
Isaiah 48:10 NKJV

Consider it pure joy, my brothers and sisters, whenever you face trials of many kinds, because you know that the testing of your faith produces perseverance. Let perseverance finish its work so that you may be mature and complete, not lacking anything.
James 1:2-4 NIV

People may be pure in their own eyes, but the LORD examines their motives.
Proverbs 16:2 NLT

"In this world you will have trouble. But take heart! I have overcome the world."
John 16:33 NIV

There is a difference between temptations and trials. God doesn't lead you into temptation, because temptation leads to sin and God doesn't want you to sin. Affliction causes suffering and sometimes incomprehensible pain. These trials are tests of faith that allow us to grow spiritually and strengthen our faith in Him. It is during trials that we know God will never leave us, He will assist us, and carry us. He does, however, want you to be obedient to Him and His Word.

Thank God Always

Give thanks to the LORD and proclaim His greatness. Let the whole world know what He has done.
Psalm 105:1 NLT

Thanks be to God, who in Christ always leads us in triumphal procession, and through us spreads the fragrance of the knowledge of Him everywhere.
2 Corinthians 2:14 ESV

Thanks be to God for His indescribable gift!
2 Corinthians 9:15 NKJV

Enter His gates with thanksgiving and His courts with praise; give thanks to Him and praise His name.
Psalm 100:4 NIV

Thank God! He gives us victory over sin and death through our Lord Jesus Christ.
1 Corinthians 15:57 NLT

Sing and make music from your heart to the Lord, always giving thanks to God the Father for everything, in the name of our Lord Jesus Christ.
Ephesians 5:19-20 NIV

Be thankful in all circumstances, for this is God's will for you who belong to Christ Jesus.
1 Thessalonians 5:18 NLT

All parents want their children to have good manners, like saying please and thank you. The greater of these two "magic" words is thank you. The most important appreciation we can show is to God. Show gratitude that you may know Him—gratitude for human relationships that bring fulfillment, a warm bed, food to eat, and being able to read the Word without persecution. Write everything down that you are grateful for, and thank God for it today.

Godly Thinking

Fix your thoughts on what is true, and honorable, and right, and pure, and lovely, and admirable. Think about things that are excellent and worthy of praise. Keep putting into practice all you learned and received from me—everything you heard from me and saw me doing. Then the God of peace will be with you.
Philippians 4:8-9 NLT

Therefore gird up the loins of your mind, be sober, and rest your hope fully upon the grace that is to be brought to you at the revelation of Jesus Christ.
1 Peter 1:13 NKJV

Do not conform to the pattern of this world, but be transformed by the renewing of your mind. Then you will be able to test and approve what God's will is—His good, pleasing and perfect will.
Romans 12:2 NIV

"It is what comes from inside that defiles you. For from within, out of a person's heart, come evil thoughts, sexual immorality, theft, murder, adultery, greed, wickedness, deceit, lustful desires, envy, slander, pride, and foolishness."
Mark 7:20-22 NLT

If your mind had to be presented as a film for others to watch, would you be proud, or would you be mortified? What you think becomes your words, your words become your actions, your actions become your habits and your habits become your character. Therefore, be very careful of what's going on in your mind. Your daily thoughts will become your life. Thoughts also play a big role in your emotional world. May you allow God to renew this powerful tool.

Buying More Time!

To everything there is a season, a time for every purpose under heaven.
Ecclesiastes 3:1 NKJV

Come now, you who say, "To-day or tomorrow we will go into such and such a town and spend a year there and trade and make a profit"—yet you do not know what tomorrow will bring. What is your life? For you are a mist that appears for a little time and then vanishes.
James 4:13-15 ESV

"As long as it is day, we must do the works of Him who sent Me. Night is coming, when no one can work."
John 9:4 NIV

O LORD, You have made my life no longer than the width of my hand. My entire lifetime is just a moment to You; at best, each of us is but a breath. We are merely moving shadows, and all our busy rushing ends in nothing. We heap up wealth, not knowing who will spend it.
Psalm 39:5-6 NLT

See then that you walk circumspectly, not as fools but as wise, redeeming the time, because the days are evil. Therefore do not be unwise, but understand what the will of the Lord is.
Ephesians 5:16-17 NKJV

Teach us to realize the brevity of life, so that we may grow in wisdom.
Psalm 90:12 NLT

Every morning God deposits 86,400 seconds into your life. Your watch doesn't have to be your worst enemy. Learn to manage your time, or you will become a slave of your daily planner and others' expectations. Instead of running out of time, run your time. Live for today. Put your best dress on, put your "special occasion" necklace on, spray your best perfume, set the table with your best cutlery, and drink from your crystal glasses, because today is an opportunity. It is God's gift to you.

His Timing Is Perfect

This vision is for a future time. It describes the end, and it will be fulfilled. If it seems slow in coming, wait patiently, for it will surely take place. It will not be delayed.
Habakkuk 2:3 NLT

When the fullness of the time had come, God sent forth His Son, born of a woman, born under the law, to redeem those who were under the law, that we might receive the adoption as sons.
Galatians 4:4-5 NKJV

My times are in Your hands; deliver me from the hands of my enemies, from those who pursue me.
Psalm 31:15 NIV

The Lord is not slow in keeping His promise, as some understand slowness. Instead He is patient with you, not wanting anyone to perish, but everyone to come to repentance.
2 Peter 3:9 NIV

When we were utterly helpless, Christ came at just the right time and died for us sinners.
Romans 5:6 NLT

Then Jesus said to them, "My time has not yet come, but your time is always ready."
John 7:6 NKJV

God is always on time. Actually, His timing is just perfect—although we often disagree. Martha and Mary also disagreed. Their brother Lazarus died and Jesus was not there; they were convinced that it was too late. But Jesus appeared at the exact time God planned for Him to be there and a miracle happened—Lazarus rose from the dead. God's timing may be different to your timing, but He knows what's in store for you. His watch is set to His perfect time.

Tithe in Gratitude

Honor the LORD with your wealth and with the firstfruits of all your produce; then your barns will be filled with plenty, and your vats will be bursting with wine.
Proverbs 3:9-10 ESV

"Woe to you, scribes and Pharisees, hypocrites! For you tithe mint and dill and cumin, and have neglected the weightier matters of the law: justice and mercy and faithfulness. These you ought to have done, without neglecting the others."
Matthew 23:23 ESV

Blessed are those who are generous, because they feed the poor.
Proverbs 22:9 NLT

"Bring all the tithes into the storehouse, that there may be food in My house, and try Me now in this," says the LORD of hosts, "If I will not open for you the windows of heaven and pour out for you such blessing that there will not be room enough to receive it."
Malachi 3:10 NKJV

Remember this—a farmer who plants only a few seeds will get a small crop. But the one who plants generously will get a generous crop. You must each decide in your heart how much to give. And don't give reluctantly or in response to pressure. "For God loves a person who gives cheerfully."
2 Corinthians 9:6-7 NLT

There is a saying, "A good Jew gives his tithe, a true Christian gives his everything!" In the Old Testament your first tithe was given to thank God for His care and to show that you trust Him for the rest of the harvest or accrual. The New Testament adds a new dimension. Now you don't give because it is a law, but because you love Him, are grateful to Him, and realize everything already belongs to Him. God asks more than your tithe; He asks everything.

Godly Traditions

Jesus replied: And why do you break the command of God for the sake of your tradition?
Matthew 15:3 NIV

I was advancing in Judaism beyond many of my own age among my people and was extremely zealous for the traditions of my fathers. But when God, who set me apart from my mother's womb and called me by His grace, was pleased to reveal His Son in me so that I might preach Him among the Gentiles, my immediate response was not to consult any human being.
Galatians 1:14-16 NIV

"You leave the commandment of God and hold to the tradition of men."
Mark 7:8 ESV

See to it that no one takes you captive through hollow and deceptive philosophy, which depends on human tradition and the elemental spiritual forces of this world rather than on Christ.
Colossians 2:8 ESV

They teach customs which are not lawful for us, being Romans, to receive or observe.
Acts 16:21 NKJV

"But you say it is all right for people to say to their parents, 'Sorry, I can't help you. For I have vowed to give to God what I would have given to you.'"
Matthew 15:5 NLT

Traditions and customs are passed down from one generation to the next. Sometimes you don't even know why you do it, but it's tradition and makes you socially acceptable. Traditions can be in conflict with the Bible. Then we must have the courage to adhere—to choose the Word and be led by the Spirit—and choose in favor of the Word, against tradition. An example is that of slavery that was accepted in some traditions, but the Word is against it and the tradition was overcome.

A Place of Tranquility

The mind governed by the Spirit is life and peace.
Romans 8:6 NIV

The work of righteousness will be peace, and the effect of righteousness, quietness and assurance forever.
Isaiah 32:17 NKJV

You should clothe yourselves instead with the beauty that comes from within, the unfading beauty of a gentle and quiet spirit, which is so precious to God.
1 Peter 3:4 NLT

Aspire to live quietly, and to mind your own affairs.
1 Thessalonians 4:11 ESV

I urge you...to pray for...all who are in authority so that we can live peaceful and quiet lives marked by godliness and dignity.
1 Timothy 2:1-2 NLT

Those who live in the shelter of the Most High will find rest in the shadow of the Almighty.
Psalm 91:1 NLT

Therefore, since we have been justified by faith, we have peace with God through our Lord Jesus Christ.
Romans 5:1 ESV

Let the peace of Christ rule in your hearts, since as members of one body you were called to peace.
Colossians 3:5 NIV

Life is a mad rush. We crave tranquility and serenity on life's journey. Take the initiative for quieter meals around the table, routines before bedtime, and heartfelt conversations in the car. Sometimes we take a moment to be still, but during this time there is so much that needs to happen that we end up going to bed with more "noise" than tranquility. When we do take the time to just be still before the Lord, we will experience peace that cannot be described in words.

The Brevity of Time

Be very careful, then, how you live—not as unwise but as wise, making the most of every opportunity, because the days are evil. Therefore do not be foolish, but understand what the Lord's will is.
Ephesians 5:15-17 NIV

So teach us to number our days that we may get a heart of wisdom.
Psalm 90:12 ESV

Our days may come to seventy years, or eighty, if our strength endures; yet the best of them are but trouble and sorrow, for they quickly pass, and we fly away.
Psalm 90:10 NIV

Since his days are determined, and the number of his months is with You, and You have appointed his limits that he cannot pass, look away from him and leave him alone, that he may enjoy, like a hired hand, his day. For there is hope for a tree, if it be cut down, that it will sprout again, and that its shoots will not cease.
Job 14:5-7 ESV

My child, listen to me and do as I say, and you will have a long, good life.
Proverbs 4:10 NLT

God created everything for its own time. The change of seasons, night to day—that's the way God created it. For everything that is happening in the world, there is a time. Although time is transient, everything fits into the great masterpiece of God. Within God's eternal plan, not a second is accidental or unintentional. What do you do with your time? You can redeem your time and make the most of every opportunity or let time slip through your fingers. Choose wisely today.

December

"Be
still,
— and —
know that
I am
God."

Psalm 46:10

Godly Treasures

If you cry out for discernment, if you seek her as silver, and search for her as for hidden treasures; then you will understand the fear of the LORD, and find the knowledge of God.
Proverbs 2:4-5 NKJV

"Sell your possessions and give to those in need. This will store up treasure for you in heaven! And the purses of heaven never get old or develop holes. Your treasure will be safe; no thief can steal it and no moth can destroy it."
Luke 12:33 NLT

Jesus said, "Where your treasure is, there your heart will be also."
Matthew 6:21 NIV

In that day He will be your sure foundation, providing a rich store of salvation, wisdom, and knowledge. The fear of the LORD will be your treasure.
Isaiah 33:6 NLT

Be encouraged and knit together by strong ties of love. I want them to have complete confidence that they understand God's mysterious plan, which is Christ Himself.
Colossians 2:2 NLT

In Him lie hidden all the treasures of wisdom and knowledge.
Colossians 2:3 NLT

What treasures do you have? Over the years it might have evolved from dolls to jewelry and possessions to expensive vacations. The greatest treasure on earth is Jesus Christ. For Jesus, possessions are not important, but relationships and people are vital. Therefore He asks that what is valuable and precious to Him will become your treasure too. To comfort and support people should be more important than yet another piece of jewelry or clothing in the closet.

Trials Help Us Grow

Blessed is the one who perseveres under trial because, having stood the test, that person will receive the crown of life.

James 1:12 NIV

Consider it pure joy, my brothers and sisters, whenever you face trials of many kinds, because you know that the testing of your faith develops perseverance. Let perseverance finish its work so that you may be mature and complete, not lacking anything.

James 1:2-4 NIV

Share each other's burdens, and in this way obey the law of Christ.

Galatians 6:2 NLT

Beloved, do not think it strange concerning the fiery trial which is to try you, as though some strange thing happened to you; but rejoice to the extent that you partake of Christ's sufferings, that when His glory is revealed, you may also be glad with exceeding joy.

1 Peter 4:12-13 NKJV

The Lord knows how to rescue godly people from their trials.

2 Peter 2:9 NLT

The LORD hears His people when they call to Him for help. He rescues them from all their troubles.

Psalm 34:17 NLT

Suffering and trials are not foreign to us. However, your trials may be handled in different ways. You may experience self-pity and feel very negative, be angry with God because He allowed it, or you may want to run from your problems by shutting down. You can trust and know that your help will come from Him. Trials are a training camp where we become stronger and can spiritually grow into maturity. Hold on to Him who has already overcome every trial.

The Holy Trinity

There are different kinds of gifts, but the same Spirit distributes them. There are different kinds of service, but the same Lord. There are different kinds of working, but in all of them and in everyone it is the same God at work.

1 Corinthians 12:4-6 NIV

God the Father knew you and chose you long ago, and His Spirit has made you holy. As a result, you have obeyed Him and have been cleansed by the blood of Jesus Christ.

1 Peter 1:2 NLT

In Christ all the fullness of the Deity lives in bodily form.

Colossians 2:9 NIV

By building yourselves up in your most holy faith and praying in the Holy Spirit, keep yourselves in God's love as you wait for the mercy of our Lord Jesus Christ to bring you to eternal life.

Jude 1:20-21 NIV

For there are three that bear witness in heaven: the Father, the Word, and the Holy Spirit; and these three are one.

1 John 5:7-8 NKJV

The grace of the Lord Jesus Christ and the love of God and the fellowship of the Holy Spirit be with you all.

2 Corinthians 13:14 ESV

Do you believe in this one God who is three persons—Father, Son and Holy Spirit? Perhaps it is difficult for you to understand this mystery. It is difficult for our finite minds to understand the mysteries of an infinite God. However, we are witnesses of the work of the Trinity. The Father who accepted you as His own daughter, the Son whose blood gives you victory, and the Spirit who is your guide.

Victory in God

When the righteous triumph, there is great elation; but when the wicked rise to power, people go into hiding.
Proverbs 28:12 NIV

He has delivered me from every trouble, and my eye has looked in triumph on my enemies.
Psalm 54:7 ESV

The LORD shall go forth like a mighty man; He shall stir up His zeal like a man of war. He shall cry out, yes, shout aloud; He shall prevail against His enemies.
Isaiah 42:13 NKJV

It was not by their sword that they won the land, nor did their arm bring them victory; it was Your right hand, Your arm, and the light of Your face, for You loved them.
Psalm 44:3 NIV

Through God we will do valiantly, for it is He who shall tread down our enemies.
Psalm 60:12 NKJV

Thanks be to God who always leads us in triumph in Christ, and through us diffuses the fragrance of His knowledge in every place.
2 Corinthians 2:14 NKJV

All of us would love to win, but we know that there can only be one winner. Two opponents cannot win at the same time. Jesus already conquered evil, and through the Holy Spirit we share in His victory. You have to choose where you are and who your opponent is; otherwise you will destroy yourself by wanting to shift sides. The time is now to conquer your enemies, your past, and your fears. Do this through the guidance of the Spirit.

Learn to Trust Him

Blessed is the man who makes the LORD his trust, who does not turn to the proud, to those who go astray after a lie!
Psalm 40:4 ESV

I pray that God, the source of hope, will fill you completely with joy and peace because you trust in Him. Then you will overflow with confident hope through the power of the Holy Spirit.
Romans 15:13 NLT

In repentance and rest is your salvation, in quietness and trust is your strength.
Isaiah 30:15 NIV

Let me hear of Your unfailing love each morning, for I am trusting You. Show me where to walk, for I give myself to You.
Psalm 143:8 NLT

"If God so clothes the grass of the field, which today is, and to-morrow is thrown into the oven, will He not much more clothe you, O you of little faith?"
Matthew 6:30 NKJV

I will put my trust in Him.
Hebrews 2:13 NIV

Blessed is the one who trusts in the LORD, whose confidence is in Him.
Jeremiah 17:7 NIV

Trust is proven certainty based on past experiences. The experience of those who have trusted God confirm that it was worth it. His care may seem strange and incomprehensible. Think about the manna and quails. When looking back it is truly a miracle, a sign of love and care. The Israelite community was complaining because His care looked different. Sometimes you might feel that God's care is strange and insufficient. Stay confident and trust Him. His care is always for your good.

Speak the Truth

"You will know the truth, and the truth will set you free."
John 8:32 NLT

Lead me in Your truth and teach me, for You are the God of my salvation; On You I wait all the day.
Psalm 25:5 NKJV

The LORD delights in those who tell the truth.
Proverbs 12:22 NLT

Jesus said, "I am the way, the truth, and the life."
John 14:6 ESV

The LORD shall cover you with His feathers, and under His wings you shall take refuge; His truth shall be your shield and buckler.
Psalm 91:4 NIV

"When the Spirit of truth comes, He will guide you into all truth."
John 16:13 ESV

Lead me by Your truth and teach me, for You are the God who saves me. All day long I put my hope in You.
Psalm 25:5 NLT

The LORD is near to all who call upon Him, to all who call upon Him in truth.
Psalm 145:18 NIV

A little white lie is not as bad as the blatant lies of others! How many times has a white lie saved you from landing in trouble? But white lies are untruths. Lies made their appearance in the garden of Eden and brought separation between God and man. Jesus is the Way and the Truth and the Life. This means the truth is not head knowledge, but resides in a person. Do you have a relationship with Jesus? Do you live in the truth that will set you free for all eternity?

Godly Understanding

May the Lord give you understanding in all things.
2 Timothy 2:7 NKJV

The unfolding of Your words gives light; it imparts understanding to the simple.
Psalm 119:130 ESV

Your hands made me and formed me; give me understanding to learn Your commands. May those who fear You rejoice when they see me, for I have put my hope in Your word.
Psalm 119:73-74 NIV

Whoever is patient has great understanding, but one who is quick-tempered displays folly.
Proverbs 14:29 NIV

Tune your ears to wisdom, and concentrate on understanding. Cry out for insight, and ask for understanding. Search for them as you would for silver; seek them like hidden treasures. Then you will understand what it means to fear the LORD, and you will gain knowledge of God.
Proverbs 2:2-5 NLT

Blessed are those who find wisdom, those who gain understanding, for she is more profitable than silver and yields better returns than gold.
Proverbs 3:13-14 NIV

There is a big difference between knowing something and understanding it. Peter knew this as he walked alongside Jesus, sat by His feet to learn, and heard that He was going to die. Yet Peter didn't understand. That's why he drew a sword and slashed off the right ear of Malchus, because he did not understand that Jesus was about to give up His life for all people. So many times we know the words, but do we truly understand what we read? One day we will know and understand everything fully in heaven.

Perfectly Unique

We are God's masterpiece. He has created us anew in Christ Jesus, so we can do the good things He planned for us long ago.
Ephesians 2:10 NLT

"Are not two sparrows sold for a copper coin? And not one of them falls to the ground apart from your Father's will. But the very hairs of your head are all numbered. Do not fear therefore; you are of more value than many sparrows."
Matthew 10:29-31 NKJV

The LORD says, "Before I formed you in the womb I knew you, before you were born I set you apart."
Jeremiah 1:5 NIV

My frame was not hidden from You, when I was being made in secret, intricately woven in the depths of the earth. Your eyes saw my unformed substance; in Your book were written, every one of them, the days that were formed for me, when as yet there was none of them.
Psalm 139:16 ESV

You made all the delicate, inner parts of my body and knit me together in my mother's womb. Thank You for making me so wonderfully complex! Your workmanship is marvelous—how well I know it.
Psalm 139:13-14 NLT

You are unique. Among billions of people, there is no one exactly like you. You have a unique fingerprint, tongue pattern, and smell. Before you were born, God knew what you would look like and He knew your personality, because He dreamed about you. He planned everything and for your specific purpose He weaved you together and smiled, saying, "This is good. Don't desire to be someone else. You are unique, the Potter made you for a special purpose."

The Unity of God

I appeal to you, dear brothers and sisters, by the authority of our Lord Jesus Christ, to live in harmony with each other. Let there be no divisions in the church. Rather, be of one mind, united in thought and purpose.
1 Corinthians 1:10 NLT

May the God of endurance and encouragement grant you to live in such harmony with one another, in accord with Christ Jesus.
Romans 15:5 ESV

Fulfill my joy by being like-minded, having the same love, being of one accord, of one mind.
Philippians 2:2 NKJV

Let your conduct be worthy of the gospel of Christ, so that whether I come and see you or am absent, I may hear of your affairs, that you stand fast in one spirit, with one mind striving together for the faith of the gospel.
Philippians 1:27 NKJV

Be completely humble and gentle; be patient, bearing with one another in love. Make every effort to keep the unity of the Spirit through the bond of peace.
Ephesians 4:2-3 NIV

All of you, have unity of mind, sympathy, brotherly love, a tender heart, and a humble mind.
1 Peter 3:8 ESV

Unity within your marriage, family, church, work, cultures, and races—is it really possible? It is possible, but not easy. Unity doesn't mean similarity. An orchestra is a good example of unity. Each instrument is uniquely played. When these instruments play the same piece of music in unity with each other, everything is in harmony. You are a unique instrument playing in unity with other instruments to make godly music in the world.

A Sincere Heart

May integrity and uprightness protect me, because my hope, Lord, is in You.
Psalm 25:21 NIV

He who walks with integrity walks securely, but he who perverts his ways will become known.
Proverbs 10:9 NKJV

The word of the Lord is upright, and all His work is done in faithfulness.
Psalm 33:4 ESV

Light shines on the righteous and joy on the upright in heart. Rejoice in the Lord, you who are righteous, and praise His holy name.
Psalm 97:11-12 NIV

The integrity of the upright will guide them, but the perversity of the unfaithful will destroy them.
Proverbs 11:3 NKJV

For the Lord is righteous; He loves righteous deeds; the upright shall behold His face.
Psalm 11:7 ESV

The wisdom that comes from heaven is first of all pure; then peace-loving, considerate, submissive, full of mercy and good fruit, impartial and sincere.
James 3:17 NIV

Have you ever come across a woman who is very friendly to your face, but as soon as you turn your back, she spreads rumors about you? God expects us to live sincere lives. He expects us to always be the same person who shares genuine love and puts others first. If you want to say something about someone, do it during your prayer time where you can place the person at God's feet.

Let Go of Grudges

Do not take revenge, my dear friends, but leave room for God's wrath, for it is written: "It is Mine to avenge; I will repay," says the Lord.
Romans 12:19 NIV

"You have heard the law that says the punishment must match the injury: 'An eye for an eye, and a tooth for a tooth.' But I say, do not resist an evil person! If someone slaps you on the right cheek, offer the other cheek also."
Matthew 5:38-39 NLT

He did not retaliate when He was insulted, nor threaten revenge when He suffered. He left His case in the hands of God, who always judges fairly.
1 Peter 2:23 NLT

"You shall not take vengeance, nor bear any grudge against the children of your people, but you shall love your neighbor as yourself: I am the LORD."
Leviticus 19:18 NKJV

Make sure that nobody pays back wrong for wrong, but always strive to do what is good for each other and for everyone else.
1 Thessalonians 5:15 NIV

"Vengeance is Mine, and recompense; their foot shall slip in due time; for the day of their calamity is at hand, and the things to come hasten upon them."
Deuteronomy 32:35 NKJV

In biblical times, it was almost normal to take revenge. The problem with vengeance is it is a downward spiral. Your hurt and anger come to the fore if you have not dealt with it properly. Vengeance is where unforgiveness becomes the seed for more revenge. Jesus taught us to turn the other cheek and that we shouldn't repay evil with evil. A woman who can do this has a godly character.

Victory over Death

Thanks be to God! He gives us the victory through our Lord Jesus Christ.
1 Corinthians 15:57 NIV

The LORD your God is the one who goes with you to fight for you against your enemies to give you victory.
Deuteronomy 20:4 NIV

The horse is made ready for the day of battle, but the victory belongs to the LORD.
Proverbs 21:31 ESV

The LORD gives victory to His anointed. He answers him from His heavenly sanctuary with the victorious power of His right hand.
Psalm 20:6 NIV

I put no trust in my bow, my sword does not bring me victory; but You give us victory over our enemies, You put our adversaries to shame.
Psalm 44:6-7 NIV

Victory comes from You, O LORD. May You bless Your people.
Psalm 3:8 NLT

Some nations boast of their chariots and horses, but we boast in the name of the LORD our God. Those nations will fall down and collapse, but we will rise up and stand firm.
Psalm 20:7 NLT

We all sit glued to our TVs when our country's top athletes are participating in the Olympic Games. Or we all watch when our favorite team makes it to the finals. You sit in anticipation as if you are the one playing, because the athlete or the rugby team is winning on your behalf too. In the same way joy should grow in you because you have achieved victory through Jesus' crucifixion. You won't win your battles on your own, but through Jesus, redemptive power is given. The power that resurrected Him is also available to you.

Godly Virtues

Supplement your faith with virtue, and virtue with knowledge, and knowledge with self-control, and self-control with steadfastness, and steadfastness with godliness, and godliness with brotherly affection, and brotherly affection with love. For if these qualities are yours and are increasing, they keep you from being ineffective or unfruitful in the knowledge of our Lord Jesus Christ.
2 Peter 1:5-8 ESV

If there is any virtue and if there is anything praiseworthy—meditate on these things.
Philippians 4:8 NKJV

Therefore, as God's chosen people, holy and dearly loved, clothe yourselves with compassion, kindness, humility, gentleness and patience. Bear with each other and forgive one another if any of you has a grievance against someone. Forgive as the Lord forgave you. And over all these virtues put on love, which binds them all together in perfect unity.
Colossians 3:14 NIV

Who can find a virtuous wife? For her worth is far above rubies.
Proverbs 31:10 NLT

Has anyone ever praised you for your beautiful virtues as it is done in Proverbs 31? What do your behavior and actions look like? Do they reflect excellence and above all a relationship with God? In God's world your virtues matter so much more than outward beauty; it is more precious than rubies. Sympathy, kindness, humility, and tolerance are virtues that will make you a true inspiration to everyone around you.

Keep Your Word

From You comes the theme of my praise in the great assembly; before those who fear You I will fulfill my vows.
Psalm 22:25 NIV

Make thankfulness your sacrifice to God, and keep the vows you made to the Most High.
Psalm 50:14 NKJV

I will ever sing in praise of Your name and fulfill my vows day after day.
Psalm 61:8 NIV

What mighty praise, O God, belongs to You in Zion. We will fulfill our vows to You, for You answer our prayers.
Psalm 65:1-2 NLT

I will pay my vows to the LORD in the presence of all His people.
Psalm 116:14 ESV

It is a trap to dedicate something rashly and only later to consider one's vows.
Proverbs 20:25 NIV

The LORD always keeps His promises; He is gracious in all He does.
Psalm 145:13 NLT

Not one of all the LORD's good promises to Israel failed; every one was fulfilled.
Joshua 21:45 NIV

God's way is perfect. All the LORD's promises prove true. He is a shield to all who look to Him for protection.
Psalm 18:30 NLT

God keeps His promises. As you become more and more like Jesus, your word and your life should reflect honesty. Your "yes" must be your "yes" and your "no" should remain "no." People will often make a pledge and give the impression that they will stick to their promise, while they're actually planning an escape route. Jesus said we should always keep our word.

Waiting on God

Wait on the LORD, and keep His way, and He shall exalt you to inherit the land.
Psalm 37:34 NKJV

I waited patiently for the LORD; He inclined to me and heard my cry.
Psalm 40:1 ESV

Wait for the LORD; be strong, and let your heart take courage; wait for the LORD!
Psalm 27:14 ESV

We wait in hope for the LORD; He is our help and our shield. In Him our hearts rejoice, for we trust in His holy name. May Your unfailing love be with us, LORD, even as we put our hope in You.
Psalm 33:20-22 NIV

My soul, wait silently for God alone, for my expectation is from Him. He only is my rock and my salvation; He is my defense; I shall not be moved.
Psalm 62:5-6 NKJV

Be still in the presence of the LORD, and wait patiently for Him to act. Don't worry about evil people who prosper or fret about their wicked schemes. Stop being angry! Turn from your rage! Do not lose your temper—it only leads to harm. For the wicked will be destroyed, but those who trust in the LORD will possess the land.
Psalm 37:7-9 NLT

We live in an instant world of quick-fixes where everything happens quickly and immediately. People have even started doing instant quiet times. Reading the Bible and praying quickly while you wait in the car or between TV programs. We have forgotten how to wait. We get impatient with God because He is too slow. Because you don't want to wait, you make your own plans and excuses as to why God's promises haven't come true. Wait on Him, and trust His perfect timing.

God's Final Warning

The LORD is at the head of the column. He leads them with a shout. This is His mighty army, and they follow His orders. The day of the LORD is an awesome, terrible thing. Who can possibly survive? That is why the LORD says, "Turn to Me now, while there is time. Give Me your hearts."
Joel 2:11-12 NLT

The Lord is not slow to fulfill His promise as some count slowness, but is patient toward you, not wishing that any should perish, but that all should reach repentance.
2 Peter 3:9 ESV

"Now learn a lesson from the fig tree. When its branches bud and its leaves begin to sprout, you know that summer is near. In the same way, when you see all these things taking place, you can know that His return is very near, right at the door... However, no one knows the day or hour when these things will happen, not even the angels in heaven or the Son Himself. Only the Father knows. And since you don't know when that time will come, be on guard! Stay alert!"
Mark 13:28-29, 32-33 NLT

Evangelism movements ask, "If you die tonight, are you going to heaven or hell?" It's as if death is a greater reality than the second coming of Christ. Do you really believe that Jesus will return on the clouds, or does it sound too much like a fairy tale? How will everyone see Him at once? Will everyone be taken together on the clouds? We don't have all the answers, but we have the promise that He will return and we will see God and experience the fullness of the ultimate victory.

Our Weaknesses and God's Power

He said to me, "My grace is sufficient for you, for My strength is made perfect in weakness." Therefore most gladly I will rather boast in my infirmities, that the power of Christ may rest upon me. Therefore I take pleasure in infirmities, in reproaches, in needs, in persecutions, in distresses, for Christ's sake. For when I am weak, then I am strong.
2 Corinthians 12:9-10 NKJV

Although He was crucified in weakness, He now lives by the power of God. We, too, are weak, just as Christ was, but when we deal with you we will be alive with Him and will have God's power.
2 Corinthians 13:4 NLT

Likewise the Spirit also helps in our weaknesses. For we do not know what we should pray for as we ought, but the Spirit Himself makes intercession for us with groanings which cannot be uttered.
Romans 8:26 NKJV

We do not have a High Priest who is unable to empathize with our weaknesses, but we have one who has been tempted in every way, just as we are—yet He did not sin.
Hebrews 4:15 NIV

He remembered us in our weakness. His faithful love endures forever.
Psalm 136:23 NLT

Do you feel like throwing in the towel because you're not succeeding? It is precisely because of your weakness that God's love and truth meet you where you're at. Think about a seed that is covered under the ground. It doesn't matter if the ground is heavy; the small seed will push upward from under the ground. Keep going, push through, and this small seed will eventually turn into a beautiful flower garden.

Money, Greed, and God

Give freely and become more wealthy.
Proverbs 11:24 NLT

Keep your life free from love of money, and be content with what you have.
Hebrews 13:5 ESV

My God will meet all your needs according to the riches of His glory in Christ Jesus.
Philippians 4:19 NIV

It is a good thing to receive wealth from God and the good health to enjoy it. To enjoy your work and accept your lot in life—that is indeed a gift from God.
Ecclesiastes 5:19 NLT

"Again I tell you, it is easier for a camel to go through the eye of a needle than for someone who is rich to enter the kingdom of God."
Matthew 19:24 NIV

Teach those who are rich in this world not to be proud and not to trust in their money, which is, so unreliable. Their trust should be in God, who richly gives us all we need for our enjoyment.
1 Timothy 6:17 NLT

"Beware! Guard against every kind of greed. Life is not measured by how much you own."
Luke 12:15 NLT

The Bible sounds rather negative about wealth. "It is easier for a camel to go through the eye of a needle" sounds quite impossible. If you trust in your wealth for security, fulfillment, and a sense of self-worth, it will be impossible for you to enter eternal life. But through faith in Jesus, the debt of your sins is paid, and money ceases to be your functional god. Rich people should be able to leave behind their belongings, bow down before God, the Giver of their wealth, and use what they've received in service of the Kingdom.

The Will of God

Be thankful in all circumstances, for this is God's will for you who belong to Christ Jesus.
1 Thessalonians 5:18 NLT

Do not be conformed to this world, but be transformed by the renewal of your mind, that by testing you may discern what is the will of God, what is good and acceptable and perfect.
Romans 12:2 ESV

God's will is for you to be holy, so stay away from all sexual sin. Then each of you will control his own body and live in holiness and honor.
1 Thessalonians 4:3-4 NLT

For this is the will of God, that by doing good you should put to silence the ignorance of foolish people.
1 Peter 2:15 ESV

"What do you think? If a man has a hundred sheep, and one of them has gone astray, does he not leave the ninety-nine on the mountains and go in search of the one that went astray? And if he finds it, truly, I say to you, he rejoices over it more than over the ninety-nine that never went astray. So it is not the will of My Father who is in heaven that one of these little ones should perish."
Matthew 8:11-14 ESV

Sometimes God's will is clear, like on love and forgiveness. Sometimes it is more complicated, like your occupation and where you should stay. God's Word gives clear guidance about His will. In prayer we can seek Him until we experience the peace of His will within us. Sometimes we get that peace through the opinion of a Christian friend, but living according to God's will is a way of life with Christ. A life lived according to His will is a life lived in a close relationship with Jesus.

Winning God's Way

Thanks be to God! He gives us the victory through our LORD Jesus Christ.
1 Corinthians 15:57 NIV

The LORD your God is the one who goes with you to fight for you against your enemies to give you victory.
Deuteronomy 20:4 NIV

The LORD gives victory to His anointed. He answers him from His heavenly sanctuary with the victorious power of His right hand.
Psalm 20:6 NIV

Victory comes from You, O LORD. May You bless Your people.
Psalm 3:8 NLT

In all these things we are more than conquerors through Him who loved us.
Romans 8:37 NIV

I am overwhelmed with joy in the LORD my God! For He has dressed me with the clothing of salvation and draped me in a robe of righteousness.
Isaiah 61:10 NIV

I press on toward the goal to win the prize for which God has called me.
Philippians 3:14 NIV

"Stand firm, and you will win life."
Luke 21:19 NIV

I've never heard of anyone who trains hard because they want to lose. You don't step onto the field with the intention of losing. You don't plan to lose a game of chess. You want to win—it's a natural desire of any human being. You are wearing the victor's crown and are already victorious, because of Jesus' sacrifice for you. Don't plan to lose while wearing the winner's crown—run to win.

The Wisdom of God

Do not forsake wisdom, and she will protect you; love her, and she will watch over you.
Proverbs 4:6 NIV

The wisdom that comes from heaven is first of all pure; then peace-loving, considerate, submissive, full of mercy and good fruit, impartial and sincere.
James 3:17 NIV

If you need wisdom, ask our generous God, and He will give it to you. He will not rebuke you for asking.
James 1:5 NLT

Wisdom will multiply your days and add years to your life.
Proverbs 9:11 NLT

By wisdom a house is built, and by understanding it is established; by knowledge the rooms are filled with all precious and pleasant riches.
Proverbs 24:3-4 ESV

Wisdom will enter your heart, and knowledge will fill you with joy. Wise choices will watch over you. Understanding will keep you safe. Wisdom will save you from evil people, from those whose words are twisted.
Proverbs 2:10-12 NLT

The law of the LORD is perfect, refreshing the soul. The statutes of the LORD are trustworthy, making wise the simple.
Psalm 19:7 NIV

Knowledge is to be aware of information. Wisdom is knowing how to apply the information. To know about Communion is, for example, to be able to give all the meanings and definitions thereof, but wisdom is to know that Jesus is present in everything. Wisdom is knowing there is something more to Communion than just eating bread and drinking wine. Is your faith only head knowledge, or do you live wisely from your heart?

Witnessing Without Fear

Jesus came and said to them, "All authority in heaven and on earth has been given to Me. Go therefore and make disciples of all nations, baptizing them in the name of the Father and of the Son and of the Holy Spirit, teaching them to observe all that I have commanded you. And behold, I am with you always, to the end of the age."

Matthew 28:18-20 ESV

In your hearts revere Christ as Lord. Always be prepared to give an answer to everyone who asks you to give the reason for the hope that you have. But do this with gentleness and respect.

1 Peter 3:15 NIV

"You are My witnesses, O Israel!" says the LORD. "You have been chosen to know Me, believe in Me, and understand that I alone am God."

Isaiah 43:10 NLT

I am not ashamed of the gospel, because it is the power of God that brings salvation to everyone who believes: first to the Jew, then to the Gentile.

Romans 1:16 NIV

"You will receive power when the Holy Spirit comes on you; and you will be My witnesses in Jerusalem, and in all Judea and Samaria, and to the ends of the earth."

Acts 1:8 NIV

Jesus calls you to be a witness. Perhaps you, like many other women, have made excuses: "I don't know the Bible well enough, and I don't really have time." To be a witness you must become still before God. Revel in His greatness, and find your strength in Him—then you can go out and talk to others about what you have experienced from God. It starts at your home, at work, among friends, and family.

Changing Lives through the Word

For the word of God is alive and active. Sharper than any double-edged sword, it penetrates even to dividing soul and spirit, joints and marrow; it judges the thoughts and attitudes of the heart.
Hebrews 4:12 NIV

All Scripture is inspired by God and is useful to teach us what is true and to make us realize what is wrong in our lives. It corrects us when we are wrong and teaches us to do what is right.
2 Timothy 3:16 NLT

"Heaven and earth will pass away, but My words will not pass away."
Matthew 24:35 ESV

Study this Book of Instruction continually. Meditate on it day and night so you will be sure to obey everything written in it. Only then will you prosper and succeed in all you do.
Joshua 1:8 NLT

Those who obey God's Word truly show how completely they love Him. That is how we know we are living in Him.
1 John 2:5 NLT

But be doers of the word, and not hearers only, deceiving yourselves.
James 1:22 NKJV

The Bible is more than just a best-selling book. It is a book that has touched the lives of people for centuries. Maybe it's because the Bible is not just words on paper; it's words that come to life through the illumination of the Spirit. The Author of the Bible lives in you, so you can understand every word of it. Saint Augustine said, "The Bible is shallow enough for a child not to drown, yet deep enough for an elephant to swim."

The Words of God

In the same way, the tongue is a small thing that makes grand speeches. But a tiny spark can set a great forest on fire.
James 3:5 NLT

A word fitly spoken is like apples of gold in a setting of silver.
Proverbs 25:11 ESV

Before a word is on my tongue You know it completely, O LORD.
Psalm 139:4 NIV

Gracious words are a honeycomb, sweet to the soul and healing to the bones.
Proverbs 16:24 NIV

The words of the godly are a life-giving fountain; the words of the wicked conceal violent intentions.
Proverbs 10:11 NLT

"You must give an account on judgment day for every idle word you speak. The words you say will either acquit you or condemn you."
Matthew 12:36-37 NLT

Receive…instruction from His mouth, and lay up His words in your heart.
Job 22:22 NKJV

When Your words came, I ate them; they were my joy and my heart's delight.
Jeremiah 15:16 NIV

Words are very powerful. They have the power to do good, but also to cause a lot of damage. Therefore, words must be used responsibly. God gave you the amazing ability to use your words to give comfort and hope—to inspire people and share your testimony of how He works in your life. This same ability helps you to pray with words, be able to read God's words, and use words to praise and worship Him. What are you doing with your words today?

Work Hard

Whatever you do, do it heartily, as to the Lord and not to men.
Colossians 3:23 ESV

"Be strong, all you people of the land," declares the LORD, "and work. For I am with you," declares the LORD Almighty.
Haggai 2:4 ESV

The LORD your God will bless you in all your harvest and in all the work of your hands, and your joy will be complete.
Deuteronomy 16:15 NIV

Anyone who enters God's rest also rests from their works, just as God did from His.
Hebrews 4:10 NIV

The one who plants and the one who waters work together with the same purpose. And both will be rewarded for their own hard work.
1 Corinthians 3:8 NLT

God is not unjust to forget your work and labor of love which you have shown toward His name, in that you have ministered to the saints, and do minister.
Hebrews 6:10 NKJV

Good planning and hard work lead to prosperity.
Proverbs 21:5 NLT

All hard work brings a profit, but mere talk leads only to poverty.
Proverbs 14:23 NIV

To be employed in today's economic climate is a wonderful privilege. To be healthy enough to do the work is an even greater gift. However, you must find a balance between your work, getting enough rest, and spending time with people you love. Are you dreaming of working full time for the Lord? Your workplace might be a good starting point for you to spread the Word. God has been waiting for you to realize that this is part of your destiny.

His Wonderful World

Do not love the world or the things in the world. If anyone loves the world, the love of the Father is not in him. For all that is in the world—the desires of the flesh and the desires of the eyes and pride of life—is not from the Father but is from the world. And the world is passing away along with its desires, but whoever does the will of God abides forever.
1 John 2:15-17 ESV

Do you not know that friendship with the world is enmity with God? Whoever therefore wants to be a friend of the world makes himself an enemy of God.
James 4:4 NKJV

We are instructed to turn from godless living and sinful pleasures. We should live in this evil world with wisdom, righteousness, and devotion to God.
Titus 2:12 NLT

"Do not store up for yourselves treasures on earth, where moths and vermin destroy, and where thieves break in and steal. But store up for yourselves treasures in heaven."
Matthew 6:19-20 NIV

"If you were of the world, the world would love you as its own; but because you are not of the world, but I chose you out of the world."
John 15:19 ESV

Do you realize that you are a citizen of God's Kingdom, and therefore you cannot be conformed to this world? A worldly lifestyle is that of pride, sin, and selfishness. Your words, actions, reactions, and dealings, however, must demonstrate that you are a stranger to this world. Proclaim His Word wherever you go without adjusting it to suit your needs. Jesus said friendship with God means enmity with the world.

Don't Worry. Be Happy!

Worry weighs a person down; an encouraging word cheers a person up.
Proverbs 12:25 NLT

Don't worry about anything; instead, pray about everything. Tell God what you need, and thank Him for all He has done.
Philippians 4:6 NLT

"Don't worry about tomorrow, for tomorrow will bring its own worries."
Matthew 6:34 NLT

"Fear not, for I am with you; Be not dismayed, for I am your God. I will strengthen you, yes, I will help you, I will uphold you with My righteous right hand.'"
Isaiah 41:10 NKJV

Don't worry about the wicked or envy those who do wrong. For like grass, they soon fade away. Like spring flowers, they soon wither.
Psalm 37:1-2 NLT

"Therefore I tell you, do not be anxious about your life, what you will eat or what you will drink. Look at the birds of the air: they neither sow nor reap nor gather into barns, and yet your heavenly Father feeds them. Are you not of more value than they?"
Matthew 6:25-26 ESV

"Let not your heart be troubled; you believe in God, believe also in Me."
John 14:1 NKJV

All of us have experienced worry so intense that it felt like our lives were hanging by a mere thread. Usually most of the things we worry about don't happen, but unfortunately worry becomes a bad habit that steals our joy. Do you believe that Christ is fully in control, that He has all the power in heaven and on earth, and is present in the church? Trust Him to take care of you. Give your worries to Him, and count your blessings.

A Life of Worship

Come, let us worship and bow down. Let us kneel before the LORD our maker, for He is our God. We are the people He watches over, the flock under His care.

Psalm 95:6-7 NLT

"The hour is coming, and now is, when the true worshipers will worship the Father in spirit and truth; for the Father is seeking such to worship Him. God is Spirit, and those who worship Him must worship in spirit and truth."

John 4:23-24 NKJV

Let us go to the sanctuary of the LORD; let us worship at the footstool of His throne.

Psalm 132:7 NLT

Exalt the LORD our God, and worship at His holy mountain in Jerusalem, for the LORD our God is holy!

Psalm 99:9 NLT

Give to the LORD glory and strength. Give to the LORD the glory due His name; bring an offering, and come before Him. Oh, worship the LORD in the beauty of holiness! Tremble before Him, all the earth.

1 Chronicles 16:28-30 NKJV

Through Him then let us continually offer up a sacrifice of praise to God, that is, the fruit of lips that acknowledge His name.

Hebrews 13:15 ESV

During worship, music expresses the language of your heart. Calvin said that music is the funnel through which God's Word invades your heart. That's exactly what worship does. During worship we are carried away to the throne room where you serve God with your mind and lips, and you admire Him for His marvelous ways. It's one of the most intimate moments for His children. This is where you inhale God's love and salvation, and exhale His praise.

You Are Treasured

"Are not two sparrows sold for a penny? Yet not one of them will fall to the ground outside your Father's care. And even the very hairs of your head are all numbered. So don't be afraid; you are worth more than many sparrows."
Matthew 10:29-31 NIV

"God so loved the world that He gave His only begotten Son, that whoever believes in Him should not perish but have everlasting life."
John 3:16 NKJV

"See, I have engraved you on the palms of My hands; your walls are ever before Me."
Isaiah 49:16 NIV

"Look at the lilies and how they grow. They don't work or make their clothing, yet Solomon in all his glory was not dressed as beautifully as they are. And if God cares so wonderfully for flowers that are here today and thrown into the fire tomorrow, He will certainly care for you. Why do you have so little faith?"
Luke 12:27-28 NLT

"Since you were precious in My sight, you have been honored, and I have loved you."
Isaiah 43:4 NKJV

How precious are you? When Jesus came to this world, He made you acceptable, precious, and valuable. He came to buy you at a price, with His blood. His love letter of salvation is written for you. You were created in a miraculous way. You are worth more than your weight, the price of your clothes, the brand of your shoes, and your bank balance. You're worth more than you can ever imagine, because the Lord of heaven loves you.

The Wrath of God

God shows His anger from heaven against all sinful, wicked people who suppress the truth by their wickedness.
Romans 1:18 NLT

"Whoever believes in the Son has eternal life, but whoever rejects the Son will not see life, for God's wrath remains on them."
John 3:36 NIV

Riches do not profit in the day of wrath, but righteousness delivers from death.
Proverbs 11:4 ESV

It is a fearful thing to fall into the hands of the living God.
Hebrews 10:31 NKJV

"Don't be afraid of those who want to kill your body; they cannot touch your soul. Fear only God, who can destroy both soul and body in hell."
Matthew 10:28 NLT

Behold, the day of the LORD comes, cruel, with wrath and fierce anger, to make the land a desolation and to destroy its sinners from it.
Isaiah 13:9 ESV

Though I walk in the midst of trouble, You preserve my life; You stretch out Your hand against the wrath of my enemies, and Your right hand delivers me.
Psalm 138:7 ESV

We hear many sermons about God's grace and love, but the wrath of God is not such a popular topic in church services. God is like a diamond: When the light in which we move shifts, we discover and meet another characteristic of Him that was hidden. God's wrath is not only about punishing the wicked but also justly defending the weak.

Zeal for the King

Never be lacking in zeal, but keep your spiritual fervor, serving the Lord.
Romans 12:11 NIV

Do not let your heart envy sinners, but always be zealous for the fear of the LORD.
Proverbs 23:17 NIV

Now who is there to harm you if you are zealous for what is good? But even if you should suffer for righteousness' sake, you will be blessed.
1 Peter 3:13-14 ESV

"Those whom I love, I reprove and discipline, so be zealous and repent."
Revelation 3:19 ESV

He put on righteousness as a breastplate, and a helmet of salvation on His head; He put on the garments of vengeance for clothing, and was clad with zeal as a cloak.
Isaiah 59:17 NKJV

Since you are zealous for spiritual gifts, let it be for the edification of the church that you seek to excel.
1 Corinthians 14:12 NKJV

The LORD goes out like a mighty man, like a man of war He stirs up His zeal; He cries out, He shouts aloud, He shows Himself mighty against His foes.
Isaiah 42:13 ESV

Sometimes circumstances and experiences can affect women's efforts to be witnesses of God wherever they go. When you realize that your calling comes from God, you can rediscover new zeal and passion to witness for Him. In tough times live out your calling with the help of the Holy Spirit and your mediator, Jesus at the right hand of God. Live with zeal and enjoy the gifts you received from the Spirit, so the Kingdom may come quickly on earth.

Thematic Index

Norma Rossouw is a pastor with a passion for serving God and the ministry He called her to. Although she has fulfilled many leadership roles in the church, it is the leadership role of mother to her son G. J. that she holds closest to her heart. She is married to Gert and feels blessed to experience the peace of life on a farm every day.